Civic Engagement, Digital Networks, and Political Reform in Africa

Okoth Fred Mudhai

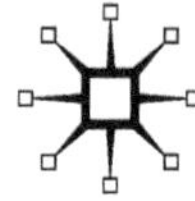

CIVIC ENGAGEMENT, DIGITAL NETWORKS, AND POLITICAL REFORM IN AFRICA

First published in 2013 by
PALGRAVE MACMILLAN®
in the United States—a division of St. Martin's Press LLC,
175 Fifth Avenue, New York, NY 10010.

Where this book is distributed in the UK, Europe and the rest of the world, this is by Palgrave Macmillan, a division of Macmillan Publishers Limited, registered in England, company number 785998, of Houndmills, Basingstoke, Hampshire RG21 6XS.

Palgrave Macmillan is the global academic imprint of the above companies and has companies and representatives throughout the world.

Palgrave® and Macmillan® are registered trademarks in the United States, the United Kingdom, Europe and other countries.

ISBN: 978–0–230–11792–1

Library of Congress Cataloging-in-Publication Data

Mudhai, Okoth Fred.
Civic engagement, digital networks, and political reform in Africa / by Okoth Fred Mudhai.
p. cm.—(Palgrave Macmillan series in international political communication)
ISBN 978–0–230–11792–1 (alk. paper)
1. Political participation—Technological innovations—Africa. 2. Information technology—Political aspects—Africa. 3. Communication in politics—Technological innovations—Africa. 4. Africa—Politics and government—21st century. I. Title. II. Series: Palgrave Macmillan series in international political communication.

JQ36.M84 2013
306.209609051—dc23 2012034528

A catalogue record of the book is available from the British Library.

Design by Newgen Imaging Systems (P) Ltd., Chennai, India.

First edition: January 2013

10 9 8 7 6 5 4 3 2 1

Transferred to Digital Printing in 2013

On a personal level, this book is dedicated to my valuable companion Flo, who from our undergraduate years put up with my very busy life (initially as a journalist and later as an academic), and to Ruth, Jean, Alex, and near-anagrammatic Fares-Fraser. All of you had to do without my expected presence (physical and mental) on many occasions—enduring my immersion in my work many a times.

More generally and fundamentally, this book is a tribute to all of Africa's genuine, selfless, brave, and dedicated on-the-ground civil society activists and reform advocates who have sacrificed their comforts, and—for some—even their lives, to fight for better conditions in-country and on the continent, as their loved ones endure intolerable hardships. To you and your families, take great pride in your contribution to the greater good in Africa—knowing change would hardly ever "happen," solely on benevolence of politicos, without your often extremely challenging "push" activities and actions.

Contents

Part IV A Tale of Two Countries—Kenya and Zambia

Part V Conclusion

Figures and Tables

Figures

Tables

Preface

When the journey leading to this book began in 2000, not much serious academic and general public attention was being paid to the link between digital information and communication technologies (ICTs) and political activities—especially in Africa. At a 2001 event hosted by the British High Commission in Nairobi, a Kenyan politician spoke to me and a senior UK diplomat rather dismissively but politely about any attempts to link ICTs and politics in the Kenyan [and African] context; yet before long in July 2002, in the run up to that year's general election, one presidential aspirant had a huge banner displaying his website above and across a major street leading into the capital city from the upmarket Westlands suburbs. "I love that website, the ideas...," was the comment about the politician's website by a member of one of Kenya's oldest online discussion forums, Mashada.[1] The fact that the website of this former member of parliament did not last long and that his presidential bid was short-lived, because he was up against much more dominant opponents (especially in consideration of ethnic factors) and despite his having proposed a popular but stillborn financial bill, shows the limits to the efficacy of any progressive politics that embrace ICTs without taking into account the local dynamics. All the same such early attempts at doing politics online encouraged me to refresh my interest in new ICT media and politics in Africa, especially in the online-digital activities of the civic-minded citizens.

My conversations with ordinary people in Tunis streets during the World Summit on the Information Society (WSIS), in November 2005, revealed a great deal of desire by the younger generation to express themselves freely, especially online, amidst a great deal of fear about heavy state surveillance of off-line and web activities. At that time, hardly anybody could predict that activists who were being arrested as web sites were being blocked during the WSIS event, held in an exclusive upmarket urban village, would slowly build up their networks and anger—leading to the ouster of erstwhile dominant President Zine El Abidine Ben Ali in the January 2011 uprising peak, and set the tone and trend for North Africa and the Middle East. Despite their fears, a number of youthful Tunisians I had informal chats with in Tunis told me that there were limits to how far and how long the regime could try to cut them off from each other and the rest of the world.

Such personal experiences and interactions whetted my initial appetite in the subject of this book, even though the cell phone networks had yet to penetrate most of Africa as widely as has happened in the last few years, and long before the popularity of social networking sites such as Facebook and Twitter. In the period leading to the publication of this book, I attended, was involved in, or followed a number of activities relating to this topic. Let me highlight a selection of these to depict the attitudes of organizers, and funders, on ICT-politics in relation to Africa (especially sub-Sahara). One category is the Africa promise or Africa potential stance by those who believe in the utility of a specific focus on ICT and politics in Africa, enough to be positively selective in paying attention to the sub-Sahara sphere of the continent. Examples in this category include two linked Africa–US collaborative events in Nigeria, "ICTs and Civil Society: Nigeria" in July 2009[2] and the follow-up "ICT and Civic Engagement in Nigeria: The 2011 Presidential Election and Beyond" in Abuja, July 2010.[3] Another example is the mid-June 2012 London conference, "ICTs, New Media and Social Change in Africa"—which had an open call.[4] The second category is a selective stance—like conventional news media—linked to publicity, paying more attention to the regions or areas exhibiting the greatest spectacles at a given time without declaring so in the conference title, brief, or theme. Focus for this category is on those geographical areas in the mainstream news discourse, and academic or related voices given platform are either those in the public domain or those well known in Western media theory realms, especially from the United Kingdom and the United States. In this category is the April 2012 London conference "Media Power and Revolution: Making the 21st Century"[5] at which there was no visible interest in a sub-Saharan Africa perspective (at least going by the intimation of a London-based academic), with North African happenings viewed *much more* in terms of the Arab or Middle East perspective than in relation to Africa. The third stance is that of a "global" promise or "global" potential that takes a non-selective or non-discriminative approach in relation to sub-Saharan Africa, focusing on areas in the news as well as regions off-news, and giving platform to voices as diverse as possible. Under this falls the October 2010 "New Media / Alternative Politics: Communication Technologies and Political Change in the Middle East and Africa" in Cambridge, UK[6] and the mid-year "Global Voices Citizen Media Summit 2012" in Nairobi, Kenya.[7] The foci, activities, and goals of each of such stances and events depend on the organizers, funders, and context—and they all emphasize the increasing engagement with the debates and practices relating to new ICT media in politics.

The biggest challenge is to study and analyze trends that could help in understanding of a buildup to what is ahead, rather than follow news in over-dwelling on what has happened already. Such an approach would have helped us listen more carefully to ordinary Tunisians in 2003 and foresee a buildup to the so-called Arab Spring rather than celebrate how spectacularly 'new' or revolutionary the phenomenon is several years later. In 2003, many analysts would have given strong arguments why such an uprising could not happen in Tunisia or Egypt. In 2012, a number of mostly different arguments have been given why an ICT-catalyzed uprising will for certain not happen in Zimbabwe, South Africa, Nigeria, and many other sub-Saharan African countries. Context is important. While we may be certain of a historical context, we cannot be sure of the ever-changing contemporary context—which is partly formed by new media technologies, whose political uses are often unforeseen by their inventors or policy-makers. This book takes the approach that anything is possible, and nothing can be ruled out—whatever happens depends on local, regional, and global contexts, in that order, rather than on information and communication technologies alone.

Acknowledgments

I am grateful to all those individuals, groups, institutions, and organizations that have supported through feedback/collegiality/funding, papers and presentations (at seminars, conferences, and workshops) as well as data collection and other research activities related to the content of this book over the past 12 years. Too many to name, but a few deserve mention.

At Coventry University, I am thankful to the following for my short sabbatical in early 2012 among other support: Andrew Noakes, associate senior lecturer in Journalism; Dr. Stefan Herbrechter, MA programmes manager; Gary Hall, professor of Media and Performance; Dr. Shaun Hides, Media Head of Department; professor Martyn Woolley, associate dean of Applied Research, School of Art and Design; professor Ian Marshall, deputy vice-chancellor (Academic). I am also grateful for the contributions of the African Studies Centre and Politics and International Studies research groups as well as the support of the founding director of Coventry's Centre for Media Arts and Performance research group, Karen Ross (professor of Media and Public Communication, University of Liverpool). I should not forget a number of my recent postgraduate students for their input.

In relation to The Nottingham Trent University, especially the International Relations (IR) unit I am thankful to: professor of IR, Stephen Chan, OBE (currently in the School of Oriental and African Studies, London); Dr. Chris Farrands; Dr. Roy Smith; professor Lloyd Pettiford; Dr. Jason Abbott (currently in the Department of Political Science, University of Louisville, USA).

With regard to facilitation of part-funding attendance at various conferences, I owe gratitude to: founder convenor of Highway Africa (HA) new media annual conference at South Africa's Rhodes University (RU), professor Guy Berger (currently director for Freedom of Expression and Media Development, UNESCO, Paris); HA director, Chris Kabwato; former SAB Miller-UNESCO Chair of Media and Democracy at RU, Fackson Banda (currently programme specialist, Media and Citizen Participation, UNESCO, Paris); University of Stellenbosch through professor Herman Wasserman (currently at Rhodes University, South Africa).

On my attendance at the insightful July 2010 symposium on 'ICT and Civic Engagement in Nigeria: The 2011 Presidential Election and Beyond', I wish to thank associate professor of International Affairs and Interactive Computing Dr. Michael L. Best (The Sam Nunn School of International Affairs, Georgia Institute of Technology, USA) and his team for the event co-organized by Georgia Tech, Harvard University's Berkman Centre for Internet and Society, the US National Democratic Institute, and Nigeria's Digital Bridge Institute, and sponsored by MacArthur Foundation.

My gratitude also goes to the Information Technology and International Cooperation Programme of the U.S. Social Science Research Council for their support through the Information Technology and Civil Society Network (2003–2005). It was an inspiring collaboration that resulted in a book on IT and global civil society (Dean, Anderson and Lovink 2006).

Thanks also go to the US-based International Studies Association, the British International Studies Association, the International Press Institute, and the Commonwealth Telecommunications Organization, among others, for supporting my attendance at their conferences in various locations around the world. I cannot forget the friendly and hospitable civic actors who granted me interviews and material—corporeally and virtually, most at very short notice—which inform the content of this book.

Without editorial assistants Sarah Nathan and Isabella Yeager as well as editor Farideh Koohi-Kamali together with production team of Kristy Lilas and Deepa John midwifing this project patiently and delicately, its delivery would have been much more traumatizing. They were tolerant and professional even with due dates breached. I am thankful to the anonymous reviewer for the very constructive appraisal of the proposal for this book and to series editor professor Philip Seib for being supportive. In varying ways, this book makes some connections with some of the others in the series (Seib, 2007; Crack, 2008; Ibelema, 2009).

For those supportive forces I have not mentioned, I extend my thanks to you all for your role. Of course all errors and infelicities remain my responsibility and your input does not imply endorsement of the content or views in this book.

Permission Acknowledgments

The author, series editor, and the publisher would like to acknowledge permission for use of the following materials:

- Main cover image: From South Africa September 17, 2011 Right 2 Know Campaign protests dubbed "March to Parliament!" – © Clare Louise Thomas (www.imageincubator.com).
- "How Africa Tweets" map [Figure 6.1] – © Portland Communications, London.
- Some of the content previously appeared in: Mudhai, O. F. (2004) Researching the Impact of ICTs as Change Catalysts in Africa, *Ecquid Novi* 25(2): 313–35. Copyright © Institute of Media Analysis in South Africa (IMASA), reprinted by permission of Taylor & Francis Ltd, www.tandfonline.com / www.informaworld.com on behalf of IMASA.
- Some of the content previously appeared in: Mudhai, O. F. (2006) Exploring the Potential for More Strategic Civil Society Use of Mobile Phones. In J. Dean, J. W. Anderson, and G. Lovink (eds.) *Reformatting Politics: Information Technology and Global Civil Society*, pp. 107–20. Copyright © Routledge, Taylor & Francis Group.

Abbreviations and Acronyms [Selected]

AU	African Union
ATM	Automated Teller Machine
BBC	British Broadcasting Corporation
BCE	Before Common Era, used in place of Before Christ (BC)
BFN	*Between Facts and Norms* (by Jurgen Habermas)
CBOs	Community Based Organizations
CE	Common Era, used in place of Anno Domino (AD)
CJA	Citizens Journalism in Africa
CMC	Computer Mediated Communication
CPJ	Committee to Protect Journalists
CSO(s)	Civil Society Organization(s)
DFID	The UK government Department for International Development
DSF	Digital Solidarity Fund
EC	European Community
ECA	United Nations Economic Commission for Africa
ESD	Electronic Service Delivery [especially in e-governance realms]
EU	European Union
FDI	Foreign Direct Investment
GII	Global Information Infrastructure
GCSOs	Global Civil Society Organisations
HTML	Hyper Text Mark Up Language (for WWW text or graphics)
ICT	Information and Communication Technology
IMF	International Monetary Fund
IR	International Relations
ISP	Internet Service Provider
IT	Information Technology
ITU	International Telecommunication Union

LAN	Local Area Network
LDCs	Least Developed Countries
MMD	Movement for Multiparty Democracy
MNC	Multinational Corporations
NIGD	Network Institute for Global Democratisation
NGO	Nongovernmental Organization
ODA	Official Development Assistance
OAU	Organisation of African Union
PC	Personal Computer
SNS	Social Networking Site
STPS	*Structural Transformation of the Public Sphere* (by Jurgen Habermas)
SSA	Sub-Saharan Africa
TDFs	Transnational Data Flows
TNCs	Transnational Corporations
TNCSOs	Transnational Civil Society Organizations
UNDP	United Nations Development Programme
URL	Uniform Resource Locator (or web address)
VOA	Voice of America
WSIS	World Summit on the Information Society
WTM	Watch Tower Movement
WTO	World Trade Organization
WWW	World Wide Web

PART I

Introduction

CHAPTER 1

General Introduction: Civic Challenge of Ruling Elite via New Digital Media in Africa

The revolts that overthrew long-time North African strongmen, Tunisia's Zine al-Abidine Ben Ali in January 2011, Egypt's Mubarak a month later, and Libya's Muammar Gaddafi in October the same year were popularly attributed to new media and civic activism—although these factors were only part of the variables. Two decades earlier, internal and external factors had led to political changes in a number of countries in sub-Saharan Africa (SSA). The central argument in this book is that the mainly urban-based civic networks, especially political civil society organizations (CSOs) that include nongovernmental organizations (NGOs) and some news media, in selected African countries, perceive information and communication technologies (ICTs) as presenting them with significant opportunities for achieving the goals of their struggle for improved national democracy in the context of global trends. Representatives of these non-state anti-incumbent actors view the world wide web (WWW) in general, and e-mail, cell phone applications that include short messaging service (SMS), social networking sites (SNS) and blogs, in particular, as tools that have not only enhanced their operational efficiency but also helped them overcome obstacles that the ruling elites often erect—using human, material, and ideological state machinery—to stifle any form of challenge to their incumbency. Increasingly, the new media enable the non-state actors to engage in cross-border communicational activities as a way of effecting reform within states—facilitating what David Held (1995: ix, 20) has described as webs of relations and networks that stretch across national borders. However, unlike some cosmopolitan approaches to democratic theory and practice, the approach here is to privilege local conditions and off-line factors concomitant with the use of rapidly diffusing new media technologies.

By providing an insight into perceptions on, and use of, new media by a category of sub-Saharan Africa's political actors who have not only been considered early ICT adopters and topmost users, but have also largely been accredited for the recent waves of democratization, the approach here is to eschew overly deterministic approaches that typically favor technological and conjectural slants to new media in the developing world or take the other extreme. The book presents a general overview of recent happenings and trends across Africa as well as takes a closer look at developments in Kenya and Zambia over a momentous epoch of two decades or so, from the early 1990s to 2012. Although methodologically the main focus is on the voting or election epoch, a time when civic actors in these countries and territories reach the height of their political hyperactivity, this pragmatic approach also provides avenues for analyzing ways in which ICTs could, and do, aid governance and activism in general outside of such periods.

Change Catalysis and Trend Amplification

It is the argument in this book that ICTs have not in themselves brought about socio-political transformations in the continent and in the specific countries examined, but that they have acted as change-catalysts and trend-amplifiers. It is for this reason that this approach takes into account the significance of the background and context within which ICTs are used by mainly urban political CSOs especially in the election epoch.

With the advent of pluralism in most African countries in the late 1980s and early 1990s came two distinct phenomena—the rise of a new type of urban CSOs, especially NGOs, and the emergence of new forms of communications media that could not be easily monitored or controlled by the ruling elite and their institutions of governance as well as instruments of oppression. This book probes the link between these two developments, using a holistic and contextual approach, taking into account the perspectives of the CSO actors—for instance whether they use the new media, why and how, and with what perceived impact. The question as to whether their efficiency, if any, has led to effectiveness—in the sense of influencing policies and actions of politicians—is complex and not easy to determine conclusively and therefore is not of primary concern here, but is explored for purposes of analysis.

To place the study firmly in its broader theoretical and contextual framework, the book examines major themes that run through most, if not all, attempts to explain the epochal movement from authoritarian and autocratic regimes towards some kind of democracy not only in Africa but also around the world in about the same time frame. One is the idea of the wave metaphor. There are two distinct but related aspects of this image–both of which the civic networks are associated with: one is democracy and the other the idea of an information society (or network society or post-industrial society, among others).[1] "Third wave democracy" is most prominently associated with Samuel Huntington (1991) who popularized it, but the concept has been taken up quite universally. For instance, the United Nations Development Programme (UNDP) (2002: 10) work on "deepening democracy in a fragmented world," alludes to the third wave in its "human development balance sheet" that juxtaposes "global progress" and "global fragmentation." The first item under "democracy and participation" on the "global progress side" is the fact that from 1980, an unprecedented number of countries took significant steps towards democracy, many of them replacing military rule with civilian governments, with more (nearly two-thirds) holding multiparty elections "than at any time in history"; yet just over half of the countries that progressed were fully democratic as many transitions to democracy stalled or the countries lapsed back into authoritarianism or conflict (ibid). Recent Freedom House / Puddington (2012: 29) figures indicate that whereas the proportion of electoral democracies jumped from 41 percent in 1989 to 57 percent in 1993, the figure has stabilized between 59 percent (1994, 2010) and 64 percent (2005, 2006) with an average trend of reduction in the five years to 2011, when the proportion was 60 percent. In a number of African countries such as Kenya, Zimbabwe, and Côte d'Ivoire elections in the five years to 2012 were marred by irregularities, violence, and bitter power tussles that ICT could not have helped.

This progress–retreat trend remains significant given the recent developments in a number of African countries even as recently as 2012. Both Kenya and Zambia were among the first countries in Africa to readopt multiparty politics in euphoric moments, the former in 1992 and the latter in 1991. In fact Zambia was seen as the shining star for other African people encumbered with the excesses of autocrats and military rulers. In this sense, both countries fell within the UNDP's "progress" bracket. However, this celebration was short-lived as opposition disunity handed Kenya's incumbent President, Daniel Arap Moi, victory with less than half the popular vote for another two terms of five years each. Once back in the driving seat, Moi did everything to show he was still in charge until the constitution compelled him to leave office in 2002, but not before he had tried to change the supreme law of the land to achieve his ambition of celebrating his silver jubilee as president. His political scheming ensured he left in charge his former Vice President Mwai Kibaki and old networks that did everything to hold on to power, culminating in the largely rigged 2007 presidential election that resulted in unprecedented "ethnic" violence. The Zambians on the other hand managed to throw the long-serving Kaunda out of power at the first multiparty elections, but it was not long before they were disillusioned by Chiluba's autocratic tendencies and started agitating for a "third republic." Although Chiluba failed in his attempts to hold on to power (trying to bar Kaunda from re-contesting and to change the constitution) and his successor the late Levy Mwanawasa got some credit for not protecting him from anti-corruption court cases, the domination by the Movement for Multiparty Democracy (MMD) for nearly two decades with only limited progress in expansion of civil liberties and strengthening of political opposition exhibits elements of a de jure single-party era. In other words, these two cases correspond closely to the UNDP's explanation of their movement to multipartyism followed by a relapse in some form—although in Zambia the 2011 defeat of MMD's Rupiah Banda by the Patriotic Front's Michael Sata offered some hope. Still, the undying nature of the old-guard networks remains a feature in a number of African countries—including in post-Mubarak Egypt's mid-2012 epochal election. Certain deep structural and socio-cultural factors stutter political reform in a manner that ICT and civic actors can hardly help.

The second juxtaposition that the UNDP makes relates to the proliferation of CSOs—NGOs in local and global realms. On the "progress" side, "in 2000 there were 37,000 registered international NGOs, one fifth more than in 1990," with many of them enjoying consultative status in the UN Economic and Social Council and the UN Department of Public Information. On the other hand, 51 countries had not ratified a Freedom of Association convention, 39 had not ratified a Collective Bargaining convention, and no NGO had consultative status with the UN Security Council. Although this book focuses on Africa, the UNDP juxtaposition illustrates the limits to which CSOs can go in their desire to participate in the governance or political process. This opening up of the public sphere and the existence of limitations to participation in such realms is addressed theoretically in this book, with the concept of power and influence used to examine cosmopolitan democracy as well as cyberdemocracy. It is the argument in this book that whereas civic networks such as CSOs—NGOs have gained some ground with regard to civil liberties and political rights, state forces still possess and are in control of apparatuses that make it difficult for the non-state actors—not to mention their own operational weaknesses—to surmount bottlenecks put in their way. A similar argument can be applied to the new media—the tools the civic networks use as part of their attempts and strategies to exercise their "soft power" in balance with the state's coercive potential, which takes us to the next UNDP juxtaposition.

The third juxtaposition is about the emergence of a free or partly free press in 125 countries, with 62 percent of the world population, accompanied by the doubling of daily newspapers in developing countries and the 16-fold increase in TVs being countered with 61 countries, with 38 percent of the population, without a free press with journalists still being tortured or killed. While recent Freedom House (2012) statistics indicate the proportion [out of 100 per cent total] of Free plus Partly-Free (F+PF) compared to Not-Free (NF) countries, that is F+PF:NF, jumped from 54:46 in 1972 and 61:39 in 1982 to 77:23 in 1991 and 79:21 in 1992, the figures dropped to 71:29 in 1993 before stabilizing to around 75:25 until 2011, when 35 percent of the global population lived in Not-Free countries that formed 24 percent of 195 countries. In Africa, the unsteady trends in freedom continued to play out as recently as in 2012 for instance with South Africa's secrecy bill, in spite of protests enhanced by ICTs. Whereas the UNDP does not mention new media at this point, this juxtaposition is applicable in the new media realms. Although part of this book touches on the liberating characteristics of the new media of the internet (www), e-mail and mobile cellular phones and others look at the use of these media as conventional ("old") media (for news) as well as to distribute conventional media content, there are also highlights and discussions in this book on the digital divide, the risks, and limitations of McLuhanesque new media capabilities. Both the "progress" and "risks" perspectives of new media are also covered in parts of the book which report respondents' views following fieldwork findings based on "efficiency" approach—the assumption that new media enhance the efficiency of civic actors in carrying out their routine functions that may or may not result in their exercise of "soft power."

Through the informational activities of the civic networks, ICTs are largely perceived to offer unprecedented plurality that challenges the hitherto excessive powers and influence of Africa's ruling elites.

Before the advent of ICTs, many African leaders tightly controlled information dissemination—allowing only the dominant political views to pass through. ICTs in general and the internet in particular are assumed to challenge state hegemony, especially in Africa–where "Africa's cell phone boom", going by a *Newsweek International* Africa edition cover story on how "the new [cell phone] technology is causing a revolution on the old continent" (Ashurst, 2001). The magazine had "changing Africa: let freedom ring" as second front-cover headline, with further explanations on "how Africans are unleashing the power of the mobile phone" (Ashurst, 2001). Some commentators have argued that Africa's cell phone boom is "sweeping up all levels of society" and that "no other technology, not even the internet, has changed lives and work in Africa as much as the mobile phone has" (White, 2003). Scholars (Ott and Smith, 2001; Ott and Rosser, 2000; Ott, 1998) have pointed out that in Africa the impact of the internet is, ironically, disproportionately greater than its overall spread. This fits within the general argument that the libertarian culture accorded by ICTs shifts the balance of power between states and citizens, especially in developing countries (Loader, 1997; Tsagarousianou et al., 1998; Wheeler, 1998; Hague and Loader, 1999; Ott and Smith, 2001; Ferdinand, 2000; Spitulnik, 2002). ICTs have been perceived as an impetus to the notion of the third wave of democratization (Hyslop, 1999; Huntington, 1991) as they somewhat reduce the influence of political middlemen (Grossman, 1995). While significant, some of these earlier literature were rather too celebratory.

Central to this book are related democracy theories, mostly revolving around the recently modified public sphere concept. Although writing on the public service model, Keane (1991: xii) refers to "representative structures of communication" that he considers "analogous to representative government"; in both cases irresponsibility can permanently threaten democratic societies.

> A revised public service model requires the development of a plurality of non-state and non-market media that function as permanent thorns in the side of state power, and serve as the primary means of communication for citizens living within a diverse and horizontally organised civil society. And emphasis is given to the democratic potential of the new microelectronic technologies...encouraging the perception of communication as complex flows of opinion through networks of public spheres. (Keane, 1991: xii)

Various recent surveys indicate that the average internet user in Africa belongs to an NGO or news media (as well as private firms and universities), apart from being young, male, well-educated, English-speaking and above-average earner, and that ICTs have "helped the proliferation and strengthening of NGOs and other private associations" (Franda, 2002: 18,19). Harrison (2002: 1–2) outlines a conceptualization of popular political struggle and demonstrates the enduring importance of struggle in any understanding of African politics–offering a different "angle" from that of repression, authoritarianism, and generalized decline. This way, he counters the images of passivity, helplessness, and incompetence as well as of violence and malice.

Also taken into consideration in this book are questions on the appropriateness of such actors or channels as CSOs and such media as ICTs for Africa. In an age of unprecedented worldwide prosperity, 40 percent of sub-Saharan Africa's population exists on less than US$1 per day, and one-third of its 54 recognized states are affected by conflict. The continent is said to be in a moment of peril and opportunity (Herbst and Mills, 2003; UNDP, 2002). From the perspective of peril, the effects of further weakening of already weak states whose inability to maintain security and provide basic social services are perceived as the main cause of dire conflict and poverty.

> The ability of African states to provide for their citizens has not, it would appear, improved with the spread of globalisation—in the form of increased capital and trade flows and debt reduction. In fact, African states have, on average, become increasingly marginalized from the world economy, with their share of global trade and capital falling during the 1990s from 7% and 6% respectively in 1950 to 2% and 1% in 2003. Africa's share of developing countries' global foreign direct investments reduced from around 30% in the 1980s to approximately 7% in 2003. (Herbst and Mills, 2003: 7)

While Africa's economic growth has been relatively higher than developed countries in the recent global downturn (UN, 2011), its share of world trade, despite rising slightly in recent years, remains low at just about three percent (Rugwabiza, 2012). Whereas recent figures of 2011 show a sharp increment in Africa's share of global official development assistance (ODA) and an even steeper rise in foreign direct investment (FDI),[2] a large percentage of the FDI inflow—about 75 per cent—is to oil-exporting countries, with the services sector led by the telecommunications industry having some significance (AEO, 2012). The possible impact of the recent uprisings would be caution by investors, making economic conditions worse before getting better. "A larger negative effect of North Africa on FDI to Africa is conceivable if investors interpret recent events in North Africa as a sign of increasing political instability across the continent" (AEO, 2012).

Other signs of peril for Africa are chronic problems: terrorism threats (especially in eastern Africa—Kenya in particular), armed conflict costing Africa US$18 billion a year (Ahmed, 2012), refugee crises, natural disasters, and diseases (HIV/Aids, malaria). Should these or ICTs and CSOs be Africa's priorities? For Herbst and Mills (2003), the future of Africa seems to lie squarely with the state and the benevolence of its leaders. Civil society and the media in general or new media in particular do not seem to have a role in the duo's analysis. Yet a number of African leaders have themselves been at the forefront promoting ICTs, saying it is no longer a matter of choosing between ICTs and other development goals—the two should go hand in hand. To tackle its problems, some African leaders want to de-emphasize the blame laid on colonial legacy and instead to focus on twenty-first-century solutions, like modern technology.

This is the point of view from which opportunity may be seen to be knocking, especially at a time when western leaders are keen on Africa's progress for greater global peace and prosperity, especially after 9/11. Africa is "important" to the world, with the US government in her post-9/11 strategy considering countries like Kenya, South Africa, and Nigeria her "key allies"[3]; so there is a great deal of interest in the continent's development towards such vague values as freedom, free enterprise, democracy, and economic progress. The success of the "partnerships" between western states and Africa depends on how genuine the westerners are, especially with regard to ICT projects. As part of this context, the book touches on such issues.

Conceptual and Methodological Clarifications

Africa in general, and SSA in particular, is not viewed here as one great homogeneous whole, as almost one country with one pattern and one inevitable destiny (Barton, 1979: ix). There needs to be more care and more subtlety in how scholars differentiate regions, states, and communities in discussions of the impact of ICTs in Africa, and this study attempts to do that. So conclusions drawn here may not necessarily be intended to provide generalized patterns that could be applied easily to the continent as a whole. The strengths and limitations of the scope of the book are taken into consideration as much as possible.

The focus on civic engagement here is mainly on political activities, especially those involving the use of new ICT media–that allow participation in the determination of collective destiny. Both formally registered groupings and loose informal networks and activities are taken into account.

> Civic engagement is a necessary step that needs to occur for countries to develop. Civic engagement enables local organizations and people to voice local opinions and promote activism among populations. In their 1993 Human Development Report, the UNDP emphasized civic engagement as "a process, not an event that closely involved people in the economic, social, cultural and political processes that affect their lives." As this description highlights, civic engagement is about people having a hand in shaping their own lives and circumstances. (Soll and Ali, 2012)

Civic actors examined include the urban-based "national" civil society, which typology by Jørgensen (1996: 47) indicates inclusion of international dimensions, bearing in mind this author's argument that a highly evolved civil society exists on all levels, including "middle-range" and grassroots, at once. Of course other than area-based categorization, there are issue-based categories too, for instance environmental, political, health, educational, and communications CSOs. Emphasis is on political civic actors or political aspects of civic activities—with a bias on operational communicational activities that allow their inclusion and participation in political and related policy processes and discourses.

Why Perception?

The point of entry into the CSO use of ICTs is in part a probe into what these actors themselves perceive about the impact of such usage. In her study of ICTs in Egypt, Deborah L. Wheeler relies on respondents' first-hand experiences (Cline-Cole and Powell, 2004: 8). This is in line with the assertion that "our beliefs about the internet and what its properties are can be opened up to enquiry just like . . . any other ethnographic topic" because "beliefs about the internet may have important consequences for the ways in which we relate to the technology and [to] one another through it" (Hine, 2001: 8). Hine (2001) uses some of the common theoretical projections of the internet's significance to emphasize the foreshadowed problems (key research areas/questions) for an ethnography of the internet use. How do the users of the internet understand its capacities? What significance does its use have for them? How do they understand its capabilities as a medium of communication and who do they perceive their audience to be?

By way of elaboration, it is important to note that because so many analyses of Africa have been done from the desktops of the west, a number of researchers are increasingly keen to get an insight into the views of Africans through their own voices. In noting that Malawian "churches have to *regard themselves* [my emphasis] as custodians of democratic values, champions of the constitution and spokespersons for the people," Ross (2004) relies on a survey of the statements issued by the churches and an analysis of heir role in the defeat of the third-term proposal. The author combines his analysis with the *perceptions* of the actors to assess their *effectiveness* and arrive at the judgment that "within civil society, the churches have proved to be the most effective agents in challenging the ruling elite" and that "the unity and unanimity with which they opposed the third-term bid is identified as the key to their effectiveness." In a similar vein, Potts and Mutambirwa (1997: 549), noting that "less attention has been paid in published academic and official literature to how the people of Zimbabwe assess the land resettlement program," examine resettled people's own "perception that redistribution of land is a moral issue." The subjects' "perceptions about the resettlement programme were gathered via semi-structured interviews" and the researchers "wanted the results to be as true a reflection of the people's 'voices' as possible" (Potts and Mutambirwa, 1997: 552).

Why Urban?

Focusing on CSOs inevitably leads to relatively more concentration on the urban environment—especially the capital cities, such as Nairobi, Lusaka, and Johannesburg. There are theoretical as well as practical-political reasons for this. "Does the city have a future in democracy?" After asking this question, Engin Isin (2000: blurb) goes ahead to identify the urban environment as "the bedrock of democracy and citizenship" or simply a "space" of democracy, one of those that "constitute themselves as political and social agents"—alongside other emergent non-state actors such as "the cyberspace of the internet and international organizations such as the IMF, UN, World Bank, the European Union and Greenpeace" which have gripped the attention of popular media and scholarship. Rather than create a nostalgic image of the city-state as it existed before the nation-state, contributors to the volume edited by Isin "articulate empirically founded but normative ideas about how the city must be rethought as a space of democracy" (Isin, 2000: blurb). While the focus of the book is global—and it arose out of a June 1998 Toronto symposium whose "substantive focus was liberal democracies in predominantly English-speaking states such as Canada, America, Great Britain, Australia and New Zealand" (Isin, 2000: ix)—it brings to theoretical focus issues of relevance to cities in general, including those in the developing world.

Whereas the bulk (on average 70%) of most African populations resides in rural areas and many a politician like Zimbabwe's Mugabe and former Kenyan President Moi would at the height of political tension go to any length—including orchestrating "land" and "ethnic" clashes in rural locations—to divert or focus attention, urban areas in general and capital cities in particular are normally the bedrock of political activism. Scholars such as Manuel Castells and Saskia Sassen have, in their work from 1970s to 1990s, drawn attention to recent strategic role of cities in societal change and technological innovation in a globally integrated environment despite spatially dispersed nature of activities (cited in Webster, 1995: 193, 194, 200, 201). Major cities function as "highly concentrated command posts" (Sassen, 1991: 3, cited in Webster, 1995: 200), and an increasing number of workforce of these [information] cities are informational employees (Castells, 1989: 184, cited in Webster, 1995: 201). The level of informatization may not be as high in Africa as it is in developed countries, but some African cities like Nairobi host groups, individuals, and firms that are much more technically conscious and globally in touch than many of their counterparts in New York or London. It is through this prism that we can view Cheikh Guèye's work on the intersection between urbanization and ICT use in Touba, Senegal's second largest city (1998, cited in Cline-Cole and Powell, 2004: 7).

The political role of cities was displayed at the Geneva 2003 World Summit on the Information Society (WSIS) when Geneva and Lyons symbolically asserted their "sovereignty" as they made initial contributions to the controversial Africa-originated Digital Solidarity Fund (DSF), an initiative their western states had refused to agree to.[4] Geneva mayor Christian Ferrazino and Lyon mayor Gerard Collomb accused states of only paying lip service to major issues affecting citizens. On the issue of ICTs comes some practical considerations that Paul Ansah (cited in Berger 1998: 602) puts into proper perspective:

> Whereas access to and availability of mass communication facilities are fairly even and widespread in the west, one notices glaring disparities

> in Africa. On the one hand, there is a relative abundance of mass media facilities in the urban areas, where the elite minorities live and where the situation is close to what obtains in the Western societies; on the other hand, there is a media scarcity in the rural areas, where the vast majority of the people live. This means that in terms of penetration and possible effects, the situation is not comparable to that of the West, and in the African situation it may be more accurate to examine issues at two different levels.

This obviously limits the impact of the modern mass media on the rural dwellers. However, Africa is unique enough for a two-step flow model of communication to work fairly well. The elite with media access constantly pass on, even through traditional face-to-face encounters, information of relevance and political significance to those who are poorer information-wise. This is because, for instance, an overwhelming number of Kenyan urban workers are still tightly tied to the rural peasant community. To them, the city is a temporary place to earn a wage, it is not home. Many city workers register and vote in rural areas in national parliamentary general elections. "Indeed, they are expected to be full members of the local church while in rural areas. These same workers are subject to the local chief's authority, and once one or any member of the family dies, the burial place is on the farm in a rural area. The city or town is a place to generate a cash income to buy a farm if one has none, or simply to sustain one's own family" (Nyangira, 1987: 23). At times nearly every weekend or fortnight, some city dwellers, including most members of parliament, leave their urban "houses" to spend time with families and folk in their rural "homes".

> In Kenya, towns were generally looked upon as the potential centers of development of a new social order that would provide a basis for a new kind of politics. Urban workers, it was felt, would form a political consciousness along the lines of common economic interests cutting across ethnic barriers. Instead the cities generally became centers of increased ethnic awareness, although personal contacts among men of different ethnic groups were often friendly. (Kaplan et al., 1976: 222)

In the Mau Mau freedom struggle era, "it was in Nairobi that politics acquired much of its violence; but it was in Nairobi's competitive ethnic political economy that divisions between Africans ensured that militant politics would be confined largely to the Kikuyu."[5] It is in Nairobi that establishment politics was most decisively overturned by militant action. When invited by the rural gentry to assist, urban militants overturned strategic premise of political mobilization, changing it from a weapon of political control to a lever for direct action (Lonsdale, 1986: 174–5). In recent years, both Lusaka and Nairobi as well as other African cities have been the seats of radical NGOs and alternative news media. This may be seen to negate the very focus on such CSOs, but as explained above there exist dynamics—albeit imperfect—on rural–urban networking, including through formal civic education programs by political NGOs.

The Nature of Inquiry

Taking into account the optimist–pessimist views on information society, this study takes a "dialectical" approach, cognizant of different kinds of informationality (or digitality), in different settings, with specific socio-cultural and political expressions (Castells, 2000a: 5, 13, 20–1; Van Audenhove et al, 1999). The epistemological and ontological premises of this study are that people studied construct their own reality and that human action is determined by various environmental conditions. The inquiry goes beyond the people's conceptions and everyday life, and looks at power relations too (see Gunter, 2000: 1–22; May, 1998: 38ff; Lindlof, 1995: 27ff). Taking cue from Miller and Slater (2000: 5), the study treats ICTs, mainly the internet, as "continuous with and embedded in other social spaces,...within mundane social structures and relations." It is largely about how specific civil societies form part of the forces that constitute global ICTs, but do so quite specifically as groups with particular physical space and goal commonality (see Miller and Slater, 2000: 5). It is for this reason that the internet is seen within a context as numerous new practices and technologies, used by diverse people, in diverse real-world locations—not as a monolithic "virtuality" or denaturalized placeless cyberspace "disembedded" and disconnected from offline reality (Miller and Slater, 2000: 1, 3 and 4). This conception departs from the focus on virtuality in internet discourse (Miller and Slater, 2000: 5).

Of particular relevance to this study are the works on mediation by Bruno Latour, which demonstrate how to avoid the pitfalls in the dualism of sociologism and technology, or more generally science and society (Miller and Slater, 2000: 8; Whitley, 1999). Latour would affirm the internet as an "actant," contrary to Castells' primary distinction between the Net and the Self which, treating the Net as a monolithic "reified" structure or "morphology," runs too close to technological determinism and replicates the sociological distinction between structure and agency (Miller and Slater, 2000: 8). Much as the internet media positions people as actors in more global stages, the networks or "spaces of flows" that transcend immediate location only place users in wider flows of cultural, political, and economic resources. It does not uproot users from their actual settings.

The emphasis here is given to the point of view of the civic actors—especially their reasons for using ICTs and their narration of how they use them—hence the other aspect of observation, of online activities of some of the groups under focus.

The primary focus, of the three types of "Internet politics" identified by Margolis and Resnick (2000: 8–21), is *political uses of the Net* (WWW and e-mail) as well as the mobile phone, by the civil society and media organizations. Margolis and Resnick (2000: 14) define *political uses of the Net* as the activities of ordinary citizens, political activists, organized interests, political parties, and governments to achieve political goals having little or nothing to do with the internet *per se*. It refers to employing the Net to influence political activities offline, an extension of political life off the Net. This concurs with the conception of the link between ICTs and politics as a phenomenon that has to be looked at within the context of organic (offline) politics. Inevitably, the book may touch on *politics that affects the Net*—the host of public policy issues and government actions—and to a lesser extent *politics within the internet* (intra-Net politics)—matters that can be settled without reference to political or legal entities outside the Net community itself. The central focus is however *political uses of the internet* by people acting on behalf or as part of civic networks and media organizations. This book probes claims that these "special interests, pressure groups, and non-partisan public interest groups have found the Net a cheap and fast way to communicate with their members and inform and plead their causes" (Margolis and Resnick, 2000: 14).

Consideration of Elections

In general, election time provides the ultimate conditions for democratic practice (Adar, 1999; Dunleavy and O'Leary, 1987: 26, 32). "Election time is the type of period of high excitement when it is perhaps right to inject into a political system something like the fluorescent tracers, used by doctors in medical diagnosis, to follow something like the primary channels of political communication" (Fagan, 1966: 34–5). For instance in Kenya just before and after independence, "the most important areas of political participation—attendance at rallies, voting, joining a party, paying party dues, working for a candidate, etc—were election-related while the others—following the news, talking politics, making contacts with higher placed persons—were to do with acquiring information and presenting views and demands to the elite" (Bienen, 1974: 14–15, citing M. H. Ross).

Consideration of Kenya and Zambia

Kenya and Zambia were chosen due to the commonality of historical and political experiences. Both countries share characteristics typical of most African states. Both are former colonies—specifically of Britain—that won independence around the same time, towards the mid-1960s. Both adopted single-party politics, *de facto* or *de jure*, on gaining self-rule and both embraced multipartyism around the same time in the early 1990s. In both, incumbents attempted to manipulate the constitution to extend their limited terms of office. The opposition parties have been divided and non-party urban civil society actors have been active in providing checks.

Conclusion

A number of core arguments are discernible in this book. First is the argument that democratization in a number of African countries, as illustrated in the cases of Kenya and Zambia among other selected countries, is not merely illusionary, and that the new digital media have played some role in the transfer of power and political activity from a narrow political elite. To that extent at least, it supports the widespread "democratisation through new media" thesis. At the same time, and second, the book takes a critical view of the naivety of many of the proponents of that argument, and points out that such naivety is sustained at least in large part by a tendency to overgeneralize. Through a combination of broad and detailed examination of recent developments, the book demonstrates that the process of both democratization and the deployment of the new digital media by civic organizations, especially CSOs–NGOs, is more complex and much more nuanced than the growing literature on the subject usually suggests. Third, the book is grounded in the fieldwork as well as virtual observations conducted during or after significant epochs over about a decade, including a number of visits to the case study countries plus interviews, communications, and interactions with many of the key players as well as some theorists in the field—taking into account the "dangers" of methodological proximity. Fourth, and finally, the book takes a critical look at theories and concepts such as the Habermassian notion of the public sphere and their relationships to the potential for degrees of genuine emancipatory democracy. Such concepts are helpful in explaining processes of socio-political change in Africa, but their limitations may also be helpful to explain why the process of democratization, though real, has been partial, and why the new digital media have only partially fulfilled the aspirations that their strongest proponents have held for them in the specific contexts studied here. To this extent, the findings reported and discussed in the book show that ICTs have, especially from the point of view of civic activists, enhanced efficiency and helped hasten democratic transition but only as trend-amplifiers rather than radical agents of change as trumpeted by those who priviledge ICTs platforms with expressions such as "Facebook Revolution" or and "Twitter Revolution".

PART II

The Setting

CHAPTER 2

Private–Public Sphere: Civic Engagement, New Media, and Democracy Theory

Introduction

This chapter takes a look at democracy—or democratic—theory, with a focus on two main related aspects. One is the civic networks perspective, which includes the civil society theory (Cohen and Arato, 1992: vii) that provides an insight into political activity outside of the realms of the state, and the social movements theory. The civil society theory does not put emphasis on political institutions – but its attempt to view political and economic societies distinctly from civic ones can be problematic. It is an approach in recognition of the fact that democratic structures and fairer laws cannot produce democracy without strong civil societies. Given the inevitable tendency of power to concentrate and control citizens, citizens cannot sustain involvement and influence without strong civic organizations (VeneKlasen, 1996: 239).

The other theory is recent modifications of Habermas' notion of the "public sphere" following the rapid erosion of hegemony of the early modern unified public by the development of various networked spaces of communication through the new information and communication technologies (ICTs)—taking into account the links between new media and democracy. The open arena for public debate may not be completely "protected" but the role of civic actors in balancing state power and defending individual liberty from state intrusion has, even if only to some extent, been enhanced by networked new media such as cell phones and their applications, e-mail, world wide web, and social networking sites (SNS) such as Facebook and Twitter.

Highlighting a twisted "refeudalization" of the public sphere concept, the chapter looks at the movement from unified to disintegrated public sphere, from the eighteenth-century coffee houses, salons, and table societies to the twenty-first-century cyber cafes and "hot spots," from rational ideal-type consensus-seeking reasoning by the bourgeoisies to ordinary exchanges by all sorts of, often antagonistic, Information Age interlocutors. The idea of a radically "deterritorialized" communication space is not wholly embraced here while recent thinking around the private sphere is incorporated.

Non-State Actors and Democracy Theory

The politics of protest is an elusive and poorly defined area of study, "sitting uncomfortably between revolutionary models of structural change and pluralist/functionalist conceptions of pressure group politics" (Camilleri and Falk, 1992: 199). Neither of these two stances adequately characterizes or explains what is now a global phenomenon. However we will focus on the ambiguous and contentious pluralism. Indeed, "there is no single, definitive statement of pluralism" (Baggott, 1995: 33). Nicholls (1974) looks at three traditions of pluralism concerned with the distribution of power and authority in democratic systems, and crucially with the role of the state, and the balance between state and society. To Grillo (1998: 6), "plural societies are conceived as democracies in which there exist groups and institutions mediating between state and individual." However, there are different views of pluralism, and we will cite two of them. In the British-English view, non-state actors serve to limit the autocratic tendencies of the sovereign authority by locating some power outside the central institutions; between the state and the individual are numerous associations and groups of various kinds—cultural, religious, economic, and civic, among others. These groups absorb much of the life of the individual, and have an existence that does not derive from the state (Nicholls, 1974: 1). The American version, also concerned with "countervailing powers," differs somewhat by emphasizing the role of groups external to the state as "interest groups," whose task it is to promote their particularistic view. The state as "umpire" (Nicholls, 1974: 22) arbitrates and balances. Plural societies are thus defined as "non-authoritarian, non-totalitarian democratic societies," in which different interests are recognized as legitimate, and in which mechanisms exist for promoting those interests. That is, pluralists are concerned with the existence and strength of what others would call the institutions of the "civil society," though they would not normally use that term, just as those who speak of civil society would not normally refer to "pluralism" (Grillo, 1998: 6). In most of postcolonial Africa, pluralism was suppressed until the early 1990s.

The early forerunner of pluralism in political science was known as "(interest) group theory," associated—especially in the 1950s United States—with Arthur Bentley, Robert Dahl, J. K. Galbraith, James Madison, Wright Mills, and David Truman (Berry, 1997: 1–11). It was Galbraith who described it as the "theory of countervailing power," and originator Bentley described a group as "the raw materials of political life" (Dunleavy and O'Leary, 1987: 16, 36). Madison (1751–1836) considered interest groups the core of civil society (Hajnal, 2002: 1, 13). It is in this context that Dahl introduced polyarchy, where non-leaders exercise a relatively high degree of control over leaders, amidst challenges from critics like Thedore Lowi[1] (cited in Jordan, 1993: 50). Baggott (1995: 32ff) identifies five political perspectives on the nature and extent of group participation in the political system, and a judgment about the consequences of their involvement. These are: pluralism, neo-pluralism, corporatism (stable and close relationships with government and specific groups have monopoly over representation in their specific area), the New Right (self-interested organizations that distort views of the public), and Marxism (cynical about the ability of pressure groups to challenge capitalist interests). There are various manifestations of these in Africa, but of concern here are the first two.

Pluralism in democracies has tended to focus on pressure groups with the following principles central to pluralist thinking: power should be dispersed throughout society, rather than narrowly concentrated; government should be based on public consent; government should share power with the people's chosen representatives; the public participation in decision-making should be encouraged; and diversity in society should be at least tolerated, if not encouraged (Baggott, 1995: 33). However, there exists a distinction between the old pluralism and the new pluralism, neo-pluralism, that emerged towards 1980s in the works of Dahl and others.

> Neo-pluralism is a more pessimistic perspective than the traditional pluralist standpoint. Although neo-pluralists accept the basic principles of traditional pluralism (indeed, many are former pluralists who have revised their ideas), they doubt that these are being upheld in practice. Compared with the pluralist standpoint, neo-pluralists are less optimistic about the democratic contribution of pressure groups. In particular they are less likely to accept that the balance of power between pressure groups mirrors the strength of support for them

> in society. They are also less likely to see pressure groups as autonomous, independent of government manipulation, and accept that the inequalities between groups are systematic and often damaging to democracy. (Baggott, 1995: 40)

All the same, few neo-pluralists have lost faith entirely in modern democracy; they still favor more participation of non-state actors in governance. Of particular interest is social pluralism, which not only rejects absolute, unified, and uncontrolled state power but also opposes the majoritarian tyranny of the institutional pluralism.

> The ways in which mass public controls its government and politicians have less to do with parliaments and constitutional constraints, and more to do with elections, party competition and interest group activity. The chief watchdog guarding the "public interest" against governments are not the law courts but the news media. (Dunleavy and O'Leary, 1987: 25)

It is in this context that we can view adoption of pluralist politics in Africa, albeit with imperfections. As we have seen, non-state actors in this context have moved from being "interest groups" to "pressure groups" (Baggott, 1995) and, more recently, "civil society." Those who have written on "groups" or "interest groups" include Loveday (1962), Fagan (1966), Bienen (1974), and Jordan (1993) but it is those who have overstretched the elasticity of the term, like Cammisa (1995) who refer to government and state agencies as interest groups, who have contributed to the abandonment of this concept. It is the "civil society," and related terms (Camilleri and Falk, 1992: 206), that has attracted the most number of writers to the extent that there is emerging a theory of civil society within (neo-)pluralism realms.

Civil society is defined as "a sphere of social interaction between economy and state...created through forms of self-constitution and self-mobilisation" (Cohen and Arato, 1992: ix).[2] However, civil society is not necessarily always opposed to the state and the economy, nor is it confined to the social sphere. Besides, antagonistic relations only exist when mediation fails. "The political role of civil society in turn is not directly related to the control or conquest of power but to the generation of influence through the life of democratic associations and unconstrained discussion in the cultural public sphere. Such a political role is inevitably diffuse and inefficient" (Cohen and Arato, 1992: x). This may be dependent on the nature of interactions or civil society organization (CSO) type (Jørgensen, 1996: 47).

On CSO power and influence, Jørgensen (1996) argues that the more favorable the political and legal conditions, the educational standard, *the access to means of communications* [my emphasis], among others, the stronger civil society will be able to grow (p. 47)—but there needs to be external and internal preconditions or enabling environments for CSOs to operate effectively (pp. 48–9).

The text italicized in Table 2.1 are the conditions that most concern us here, and which help highlight the "efficiency model" relating to better operations for CSOs in a bid to realize their objectives.

The seminal political socialization study by Almond and Verba (1963), relating civic culture to political attitudes and behavior, seems relevant to the politics of new and weak developing countries. To the duo, the heart of democracy has to do with citizen competence and participation (Bienen, 1974: 9), what many African CSOs strive to achieve through some of their projects. Karl Deutsch and his students analyzed processes of social mobilization and the creation of new patterns of social interaction and political participation.[3] He called attention to the expansion of politically relevant strata. In the case of Africa, this politically active layer is the urban elitist group from which CSOs derive their core staff.

Compared to the more formal political civil society theory, the related social movement theory takes a more informal sociocultural approach

Table 2.1 Pre-conditions for successful CSO operations

Pre-conditions for CSOs	*Enabling environment for CSOs*
*A functioning state apparatus and some measure of social stability within recognized national borders. *Democratic institutions and the rule of law. *Social and cultural homogeneity (or at least lack of open conflict between sections of society) and a sense of "cohesiveness" or willingness to cooperate with others. *Freedom to conduct economic activities and the existence of a business sector (and of a middle class). **Literacy and access to communications technology.* **Freedom of speech and organization.* People with organizational experience.	*They should be free to organize themselves. *Regulations for registration and incorporation should be as simple as possible, not least for small organizations. *They should be allowed to raise funds from the public and to receive funds from funding agencies abroad. *Government controls of CSOs' administration and accounts should be simple and politically neutral. *There should be tax concessions for CSOs doing work, which benefits the public.

Source: Compiled from explanations by Jørgensen (1996: 48–9).

without necessarily abandoning the political—through sub-theories such as resource mobilization, political opportunity-process, constructionism, and new social movement. ICT and the recent diffusion of protests in urban settings, especially the Occupy movement around the world, have revived interest in the social movement theory (Van de Donk et al., 2004; Carroll, 2006). While the TIMN (tribal to institutional to markets to networks) evolution approach by Ronfeldt (2009) is problematic especially if it is to be applied to Africa due to implied backwardness, his link of recent civic networks to John Keane's idea of "monitory democracy" (Ronfeldt, 2012b) makes sense in tying together the various related concepts. Ronfeldt (2012a) notes that Keane's core argument is about "increases in monitoring roles played by NGOs and other actors representing civil society" which, unlike "representative democracy... belonging to an age of nations, hierarchies, and limited connections," is "a new age of densely transnational, networked connections...its dynamics—latticed, inter-laced, and often non-linear, viral, and chaotic." I agree that monitory democracy and network theory work well, even though the proponents tend to be a bit too optimistic at times.

Habermasian Rationalist Public Sphere

> I cannot understand how anyone can make use of the frameworks of reference developed in the 18th and 19th centuries in order to understand the transformation into the post-traditional cosmopolitan world we live in today...Where most post-modern theorists are critical of grand narratives, general theory and humanity, I remain committed to all of these, but in a new sense. (Beck, 2000: 211 and 226)

The public sphere notion, linked to related thinking by Kant and Hegel among other earlier scholars,[4] continues to be relevant in analyzing such problems of democracy as moves to "colonize the lifeworld"—attempts that often engender the civil society. It has thrived despite, as well as because of, several critical responses (Holub, 1991; Calhoun, 1992; Roberts and Crossley, 2004; Crack, 2008). In his seminal *Structural Transformation of the Public Sphere* (STPS), Habermas' socio-political concept *Öffentlichkeit* or "public sphere,"[5] an arena of public interaction and debate, is often used to analyze problems of democracy—especially the emancipatory discursive-deliberative type, particularly as it relates to the civil society (Baynes, 1995; Chambers, 1995; Warren, 1995; White, 1995).[6]

Referring to Ernest Gellner's 1994 phrase, "no civil society, no democracy,"[7] Fukuyama (2001: 11), argues that the civil society subsists in a "protected sphere"—serving to balance the power of the state and to protect individual liberty from state interference—in liberal democracy. To Larry Diamond the civil society, "involves citizens acting collectively in a public sphere . . . (as) an intermediary entity, standing between the private sphere and the state."[8]

Habermas' account of the public sphere has two sides, one optimistic and the other pessimistic. On the brighter side, eighteenth-century Britain, France, and Germany boasted intellectual journals and periodicals, salons, and coffee houses that provided forums for rational-critical and literary debate among elites. However, in the late nineteenth century the franchise expanded with the growth of the popular press and increasing sophistication of government. Habermas feared that the commercializing of news mass media would lead to a homogenization of political information and a shift from "real" to "virtual" political debate (Norris, 2000: 25). With the degeneration of opinion formation emerged interest groups (corporations, trade unions, and political parties) bent on manipulating public opinion (Calhoun, 2002)—as the bourgeoisie and literary intellectuals had done. In other words, what Habermas calls the transformation of the public sphere involves a shift from publicity in the sense of openness to the modern sense of the term in journalism, advertising, and political communication—resulting in a "gap between the constitutional fiction of public opinion and the social-psychological dissolution of its concept" (Outhwaite, 1996: 7–8). Intertwined in Habermas' promising-worrying narrative is the question whether a people's lifeworld would be defined by the *influences* of reasoning and communication or by the *powers* of inherited tradition (culture), politics, and economics (wealth).[9] Hence for Habermas, the main issue is whether a citizenry could guide a state. Indeed in his focus mainly on political life he assumes the existence of a state to be influenced (Calhoun, 2002), and the demise or collapse of the bourgeoisie public sphere occurred because of the intervention of the state into private affairs and the penetration of society into the state (Holub, 1991: 6).

> The nation-state is what gives unity to Habermas' public sphere. Habermas doesn't thematize the place of the public sphere in securing particular national identities; nevertheless, he appeals to these identities in Structural Transformation as he highlights the German Tischgesellschaften, the English coffeehouses, and the French salons. Moreover, he describes the political activity of the public sphere as targeting the state. (Dean, 2002: 153)

Specifically, Habermas (1989: 5–14) describes the demise of representative publicness. After examining feudalism when the "public realm" existed merely as a *representation* rather than as a sphere of interaction and debate, he describes the emergent forms of trade and finance capitalism and the eventual pull towards the establishment of a civil society, underpinned by the ideology of "private" autonomy, that eventually subjected "publicness" to radical transformation (Goode, 1999: 11). Of course the earlier mercantilist era had significant implications for a newly emergent sense of "publicness." "The feudal powers, the Church, the prince, and the nobility, who were the carriers of representative publicness, disintegrated in a process of polarisation" (Habermas, 1989: 11) as the Reformation contributed to the "privatization" of religion, as public authority assumed more bureaucratic dimensions (including a greater demarcation of parliament and judiciary), and as the state budget was increasingly separated from the monarch's private holdings (Habermas, 1989: 11–12; Goode, 1999: 11). The people were still merely subjects, but "public" now signified an unprecedented depersonalized state authority (Habermas, 1989: 18) while the publicness and public significance of the noble and aristocratic courtly cultures began to diminish (Goode, 1999: 12). "Civil society came into existence as the corollary of a depersonalized state authority" (Habermas, 1989: 19). At this juncture, it is worth pointing out the comparison by Cohen and Arato (1992: xv, 177–341) of Habermas and his rediscovery in the mediation model of the bifurcation of the public with Hannah Arendt's notion and with Niklas Luhmann's idea of differentiation as well as with other modifiers – Carl Schmitt Reinhart and Michel Foucalt – of the Hegelian notion of civil society.[10] Habermas recaptures a richer set of mediations between civil society and state (compared to Schmitt) and re-emphasizes and revalorizes the normative claims of the public sphere (Cohen and Arato, 1992: 211).

Dean (2002) argues that the aspirational quality of publicity features strongly in Habermas' work but takes issue with its configuration within a depoliticized—a legitimized rather than an inciting—use of universality.

> From STPS to *Between Facts and Norms* (BFN),[11] Habermas has argued for the ultimately universal character of the public. Unlike in the accounts of the "public" by earlier critical theorists like Marx and Mercuse, Habermas' emphasis on the public sphere shifts critical theory's attention away from the agents to the sites of political change (or, more precisely, to the spaces that agents produce in the course of

> their communicative engagements). What the concept of the public sphere does is find within society and the state, within the norms of the bourgeoisie, the potential for, minimally, the democratic legitimation of the late-capitalist state and, maximally, the possibility of universal emancipation through the rule of law. (Dean, 2002: 152–3)

In other words, Dean (153) is concerned that Habermas replaces revolutionary energy with democratic procedure and political will with democratic will-formation. Habermas' focus on legitimation is ultimately depoliticizing as it posits in advance a unified community, withdrawing the revolutionary energy long associated with claims to universality (171). Though she does not explicitly mention it, Dean seems to favor Arendt (1998) who, writing slightly earlier than Habermas in 1958, emphasizes the broader process of creating social institutions and also the moments of creation of states in acts of founding and revolutions.[12] Dean further points out that the universal claim for the public sphere, which Kapoor (2002: 476–81) faults as noted earlier for being too Western-oriented, appears in a somewhat different—although still depoliticized—version in Habermas' theory of communicative action. Here, Habermas emphasizes the fundamental inclusivity of the public sphere, the primacy of reason (rational argumentation), and the ultimately legitimizing role the public plays. The aspirational and universalizing dimensions of the public that Habermas systematically reconstructs have a historical context in the nation-state, a *national* public (Dean, 2002: 153).

Habermas acknowledges the process of globalization but is, understandably, careful not to abandon his earlier focus on the state as a crucial element of identity formation.

> In BFN, Habermas continues to highlight the universality of democratic norms even as he acknowledges the historical link between popular sovereignty and "the nation". In fact, at the same time that he appeals to the possibility of "the phenomenon of a world public sphere" which is today "becoming political reality for the first time in a cosmopolitan matrix of (global) communication,"[13] he grants a certain priority to the nation. He admits that "up to the present the political public sphere has been fragmented into national units." So again, as in STPS, Habermas' appeal to a cosmopolitan public sphere remains bounded by the priority of the nation. (Dean, 2002: 154)

Part of the problem could be Habermas' attempt to modify his earlier thoughts without appearing to have changed his mind—especially from "a normatively obtuse, monolithic, administrative state" to "a differentiated state" with a multiplicity of "public spheres" emerging across civil society and other formal political institutions (White, 1995: 13). On his part, Goode (1999: 5) seems to prefer "public spheres" more localized and specific than the state, as opposed to what he terms a "globalizing approach pursued by Habermas." He argues that Habermas' emphasis on commonality (measuring politics against a yardstick of rationality) situates differential modes of political participation within a pre-constructed binary framework that underplays the distinctiveness, the unclassifiable aspects of specific, localized practices. This is of interest given Dean's argument for a more non-territorial approach. It is worth noting that territoriality lends states power to control apparatuses such as the media.

> Unlike his "poststructuralist" adversary Michel Foucault who argues, in Power/Knowledge: Selected Interviews and Other Writings 1972–1977, that "power" should not always be conceptualised as a negative force working "only through the mode of censorship, exclusion and repression", Habermas focuses on the negative conception—the dynamics that serve to limit and obstruct the fullest possible interplay of information and argument in the public sphere. (Goode, 1999: 4)

For Habermas the public sphere is constituted by moral-practical discourse,[14] which is rational-critical interaction free from domination—oriented to resolving political problems (White, 1995: 6; Dahlberg, 2001). In contrast to other concepts in communication studies (like cultural imperialism or media hegemony) the concept of public sphere is posited as a positive one, a mode of communication seen by many to be a desirable and attainable state of affairs. It is an idealized communication venue or "theatre"[15] into which all people can freely enter (Schuler, 2000). The public sphere concept has over the years been used to analyze the role of traditional mass media—the press, radio, and TV—in relation to the state, particularly with regard to press freedom and public service broadcasting (Garnham, 1992; Price, 1995; Lacey, 1996; Goode, 1999; Barker and Burrows, 2002). In the view of Dean (2002), the theoretical ideal of the public sphere, based on the public's right to know, reduces real-world politics to the drama of the secret and its discovery. She asserts that democracy has become a spectacle, and that theories of the "public sphere" endanger democratic politics in the Information Age.

Several authors, as indicated earlier, have cast doubts on the public sphere ideal (Fraser, 1994). The concept has been critiqued actively or passively by contributors to the volume edited by Calhoun (1992), by Arendt (see Benhabib, 1992), by Latour (Whitley, 1999), by Dean (2002), by Mouffe (see Kapoor, 2002), among many others. Vitally, Kapoor (2002) questions the relevance for the developing world of Habermas-Mouffe "debate" over democratic theories. The fact that Habermas' point of reference is the eighteenth-century West, that he ignores thorny colonialism-imperialism issues and, albeit to a lesser extent, downplays the significance of economic conditions and the role of the state, means his theory "can be projected onto other parts of the world only up to a point" (Kapoor, 2002: 476–81). This calls for modifying rather than discarding his idea. The conditions and circumstances under which Habermas discussed the concept no longer prevail but this does not invalidate his idea of the public sphere—"a category typical of an epoch," a historical category that cannot be abstracted, transferred or "idealtypically generalised" (Habermas, 1989: xvii; Calhoun, 1992: 6).[16]

Goode (1999: 1) is more cautious: "As we remain focused on democratic ideals, we risk losing sight of the fact that the goalposts themselves have shifted. We are, says Habermas, no longer in pursuit of quite the same ideals as our 18th century forebears." As Garnham (1992: 360) puts it, criticism does not detract from the virtues of the central thrust of Habermas' approach;[17] the public sphere notion continues to be refined and developed.

In spite of public interest journalism and public service broadcasting (Dunleavy and O'Leary, 1987: 25; Goode, 1999; McNair, 2000: 1–41), the "old media" tends to be dominated by a few voices, flow is vertical, and commercialization has been heightened to the extent that the tenets of the libertarian or free press theory has been undermined (Innis, 1951; Bryan et al., 1998; McQuail, 2000: 143, 148), especially in Africa (Bourgault, 1995; Mudhai, 2002), so the public sphere concept has recently been re-directed to the relatively freer "new media" – especially the internet—even if not completely free from government. Indeed one of the basic problems that all concepts of digital democracy address is the dysfunctional role of space-biased (Innis, 1951) "old" mass media in the political process (Hagen, 2000).

Conceptualizing the New Public Sphere: With Private Dimensions

Berger (1998: 609) terms it "a transnational public space," Tambini (1999: 306) sees it as the new "third sphere," Calhoun (2002) calls it "international public sphere," Roman Gerodimos (2004) views it as "21st century public sphere," and other authors such as Crack (2008) refer to it as "transnational public sphere". Dean (2002) terms it a "world public sphere," citing later Habermas (1996), or "digital public sphere." It is perceived as a decentered yet integrated space-of-flows, operating in real time, existing alongside the spaces-of-places (Ruggie in Nye, 2004a: 84). In recent times, there has been a tremendous increase in literature arguing for modifications of the public sphere concept, for instance by Keane (2000: 76–7, 83–7) and by Sassi (2000: 92–4).

More recently, Papacharissi (2010: 131–2) argues that, "in contemporary democracies the citizen becomes politically emancipated via a private sphere of reflection, expression, and behavior. " It serves "the values of autonomy, control, and self-expression" (137). This "mode of civic engagement" (137) has "five new civic habits" (138ff): (1) the networked self and the culture of remote connectivity (without entering public spaces); (2) a new narcissism of blogging (organizing information according to one's own interest); (3) the rebirth of satire and subversion, for instance on Youtube (preference for the playful, non-mainstream, and the unexpected); (4) social media news aggregation and the plurality of collaborative filtering (personal selection and endorsement); (5) agonistic pluralism of online activism (connect and sustain subversive movements of a liquid and fleetingly collective nature). This "personal connections" (Baym, 2010) approach addresses one of the weaknesses of the Habermasian notion on the private–public distinction, which some deem to reflect domination viewpoints (Crack, 2008: 35).

In the new media environment, the early modern unified public sphere is regarded as obsolete, and its hegemony is rapidly being eroded by the development of a multiplicity of networked spaces of communication.

> The old dominance of state-structured and territorially bounded public life mediated by radio, television, newspapers and books is coming to an end...public life is today subject to "refeudelisation," not in the sense in which Habermas' *Strukturwandel der Offentlichkeit* used the term, but in the different sense of the development of a complex mosaic of differently sized, overlapping and interconnected public spheres.(Keane, 2000: 76)

In presenting "a revised political theory of the role of public spheres", Keane (2000: 77–83) distinguishes between micro- (sub-nation state), meso- (nation state level), and macro- (supranational or global) public spheres, identifying the internet as a key stimulant for their link. Emphasis is not on consensus (Keane, 2000: 85; Sassi, 2000: 92–4). Instead, Keane (1988, 1991 and 2000: 86) argues for a non-foundationalist understanding of democracy as a regime enabling plurality of individuals and groups in power disputes over who gets what, when, and how. Indeed even Habermas has recently, partly in response to feminist critics, conceded to the existence of fragmented and unorganized public spheres (Sassi, 2000: 93).

The emergence of public spheres—such as the internet—results in de-territorialization (Keane, 2000: 86–7; Van Dijk, 1999: 164–5). The processes of globalization, which include worldwide communication networks, challenge the configuration of the public sphere in terms of a national public given that "the nation can no longer provide the fantasy of unity necessary for the ideal of a public"; in fact "the nation was never unified, whole or coherent . . . national public, as Bentham makes clear, was split" (Dean, 2002: 156 and 159). To be fair, Habermas while discussing "Citizenship and National Identity" envisages "the phenomenon of a world [rather than a national] public sphere . . . becoming political reality for the first time in a cosmopolitan matrix of [networked] communication" (Habermas, 1996: 514; also see Dean, 2002: 156–7). The circulation of "information content and points of view uncoupled from the thick contexts of simple interactions" (Habermas, 1996: 361) promote democratic discourse. "Put somewhat differently, the digitisation of contemporary telecommunications doesn't simply enable the realization of the public sphere; it is the public sphere" (Dean, 2002: 157). In other words, Habermas has in his recent writings recognized the reconfiguration of the public sphere in terms of the new ICTs. However, Crack (2008: 41) notes that "he remains ambivalent about the democratic potential of ICTs" – warning that "they also promote the fragmentation of society."

Nye Jr. (2004a: 81) points out that from their advent about a century ago, the truly mass mediums of communications and broadcasting, though not the telephone, "tended to have a centralizing political effect." He elaborates that, "while information was more widespread, it was more centrally influenced even in democratic countries than in the age of the local press" (Nye, 2004a: 81). The centralized control of mass media has been particularly prevalent in developing regions like Africa (Bourgault, 1995). "Not only can the new media be harnessed to reverse the decline of public communication due to commercialization and bias, but they offer new possibilities to surpass all that was previously achieved using old media" (Bryan et al., 1998: 6).

This is because "the internet is more difficult for governments to control" (Nye, 2004a: 82). Supporters of civic networks readily voice the advantages of new media. "Many explicitly make reference to a broader Habermasian view of the new media as providing hope of a new arena of communication, a new public sphere that can replace the old one now crippled by commodification and fragmentation" (Bryan et al., 1998: 6–8). Of course there is the risk society perspective on the dangers of imperialism, digital divide, conflicts, and confusion with regard to ICTs (Ott, 1998; Beck, 2000; Slevin, 2000; Schiller, 1999; Hacker and Van Dijk, 2000: 220; Abbott, 2001a; Main, 2001; Norris, 2004). Despite Bill Gates' contention that the internet will create conditions for what he hails, in his 1995 book *The Road Ahead*, as a "friction-free capitalism," new ICTs are commerce-driven in what has been termed informational capitalism (Castells, 2000a) and cybercornucopia or *digital capitalism* (Schiller, 1999: xiii). Dean (2002: 157) finds it "astounding . . . that even as Habermas acknowledges—indeed fully supports—the digitisation of communication, he says nothing about the ruthless economic preconditions of this digitisation." The fact that the publics still count on states to invest in the global digital information infrastructure for global competitiveness shows that the revision or further expansion of the public sphere does not lead to absolute theoretical progress.

Keane acknowledges the fact that his "attempt to radically rethink the theory of the public sphere . . . opens up new bundles of complex questions with important implications for research in politics and communication" (Keane, 2000: 84). Indeed while my research on new media and democracy in Africa concurs with the idea of fragmented and complex public spheres blurring public–private distinction,[18] it slightly contradicts the Keanean conception of space by the very fact that here, as per Miller and Slater (2000: 5), we look at the use of ICTs in physical territorial spaces that are still occupied and claimed by state powers. Wherever they are in the world, networked people share citizenship, heritage, and concern for political issues in their specific states. This specificity is still in recognition of the fact that, as Sassi (2000: 95) notes, all kinds of combinations of issues and publics, local and global, are possible on the Net.

Granted, the discourse of nation-building, especially in postcolonial societies like Africa's, is no longer relevant but digital politics cannot be de-linked from flesh-and-blood organic politics if—as illustrated by the Chinese and Malaysian cases—political, social, cultural, physical, material, and even mental conditions are crucial factors (Hacker and Van Dijk, 2000: 218–19; Abbott, 2001a and

2001b). Henri Lefebvre may have predicted movement from a society in which space is seen as an "absolute" towards one in which there are ongoing "trials of space,"[19] but offline space—including that of the territorial nation state—has yet to be rendered irrelevant. In fact Van Dijk (1999: 165) points out that the exact ways in which new public spheres will be reconstructed cannot be anticipated yet. The ongoing reconstruction does not mean that the three conditions of the modern public sphere (territoriality, unitary, and public–private distinction) will disappear completely and all common ground for societies at large will dissolve.

> Public communication will be less tied to the parameters of time, place and territory than ever before. But this does not mean that the physical, social and mental make-up of the people engaged and the material environment of the resources used in this type of communication will no longer matter... Their relevance will even grow as the new media offer better chances to select and confront directly the different conditions, needs and opinions of their users. (Van Dijk, 1999: 165, 222)

This study is not about a transitory global civil society, an attenuated sense of global commonality of "a people lacking a past in common" (Tomlinson, 1994 in Sassi, 2000: 94, 102). It is about groups of individuals who, wherever they are in the world, share citizenship, heritage, and concern for political issues in their specific states. This specificity is still in recognition of the fact that, as Sassi (2000: 95) notes, all kinds of combinations of issues and publics, local and global, are possible on the Net. Noting that "we cannot make sense of localized practices and experiences without reference to wider social dynamics that cannot be apprehended empirically," Goode (1999: 5–6) writes:

> I would like to see studies of specific "public spheres" carried out in a more empirical and ethnographic vein as a necessary complement to the theoretical and, yes, globalising approach pursued by Habermas.

Of particular interest is the view by Hagen (2000: 55, 66) that political, cultural, economic, and social factors shape the forms and extents of political uses of ICTs which, rather than changing political system, are only trend amplifiers. This is linked to the argument by Rogers and Malhotra (2000)[20] that the role of actors and their interests has been decisive in the development of new technological applications. This is significant given that urban civil society has been credited most for the recent democratization efforts in developing regions like Africa (Hyslop, 1999) and surveys indicate NGOs are some of the largest users of ICTs particularly in Africa (Jensen, in Ott and Smith, 2001). Much as the internet "actant," as Bruno Latour would call it, positions people as actors in more global stages, the networks or "spaces of flows" that transcend immediate location only place users in wider flows of cultural, political, and economic resources; it does not uproot users from their actual settings (Miller and Slater, 2000: 8; Latour, 1991), or "spaces of places."

Public Sphere, New Media, and Democracy

The decline in voting support in established democracies in Europe and the United States is one widely noted feature of recent elections.[21] One might ask how far new media and new techniques of organizing elections can revive voting confidence in the electoral system. While this is a relevant question, which highlights the expectations put on e-democracy, it may seem less of an issue in an African context. But there is behind this idea an assumption that e-democracy can transform the public sphere, which is certainly relevant to an African context—and all the more if technological developments continue.

E-Democracy Theory and Practice

Tambini (1999: 310) has pointed out that e-democracy is not a new phenomenon in so far as Ben Barber had it in mind in the development of cable TV when envisaging "strong democracy" in 1984, while in 1972 Amitai Etziomi called for "electronic town halls" to provide for deliberation on local policy issues. Others have traced the concept much further back (Graham, 1999: 65–6). New means of communication and new avenues for the expression of political opinion shaped political behavior in the seventeenth and eighteenth centuries, beginning with the technological innovation of the printing press. Indeed, this helped to found the idea and practice of representative democracy (Graham, 1999: 66). More recently, at the level of democratic theory and practice, new technologies are altering the relationships between the governors and the governed and are raising new questions of campaign communication, public policy, and, perhaps most significantly, the nature of political competition (Meadow, 1993: 442–3). However, the specific political consequences of the new technologies are the subject of much controversy (Fagan, 1966: 149). Although we can agree that the presidential campaign in the age of national television is a phenomenon qualitatively different from the campaign of whistle-stop days, we can nevertheless argue at length on both empirical and normative grounds about why and in what ways the new differs from the old…to specify and evaluate the political consequences of the new technologies is by no means easy (Fagan, 1966: 150). The critical question is: *Who shall control the new instruments of communication, and for what purpose shall they be used?* Obviously this is neither a new question nor a new problem. But it assumes a special urgency and a new relevance in the twentieth century due to three factors. First, centralization: the pervasiveness and potentialities of the new mass media and our dependence on them for political information define a system in which a limited number of persons in key communication roles control vast power for the short-term (and ultimately the long-term) conduct of politics (Fagan, 1966: 150).

The second point, that of access, is related to the first. The scale, complexity, and increasing centralization of the new technology create a host of what might be called problems of access and diversification. No matter how serious or well founded one's "cause" may be, even in a political system that purports to encourage diversity in public communication, it is neither easy nor cheap to get a national hearing unless the organization or individual already enjoys special mass communication privileges or automatic access. Issues of resources and access are intertwined: money buys access; poverty or isolation denies it. And there is a further point, privacy. The most dramatic manifestation of the problem is seen in the surveillance of the electronic media: wire taps, long-range and miniature microphones and recording machines, and infrared gadgets and camera systems backed by computer systems for gathering, transmitting, cataloguing, storing, and retrieving astronomical amounts of information (Fagan, 1966: 152).

E-democracy is therefore not free of problems, and raises many of the issues that other forms of democratic openness do as well as some new ones. Tambini, in arguing for a "very broad notion of democracy and participation," points out that the new technologies have implications not only for information provision, voting, and polling, as well as party and community activism, but for the very formation and organization of political identities (Tambini, 1999: 306). We might therefore note that ICTs have a role, for good or ill, in the managerial use of new technologies, some of which might enhance real democratic potential, while others enhance the capacity for state or elite control. ICTs also have a considerable range of uses in political campaigning (Meadow, 1993: 453), including the shift from broad- to narrow-casting, focused political activity looking at key groups of marginal voters or ensuring that supporters come out to vote while opponents are encouraged to sit on their hands at home. One can ask whether new media make it more likely that there will be more information for voters, and what the quality of that information might be (Meadow, 1993: 457). The answers to these questions, though not certain, indicate that not all the consequences of the new technologies will be positive. In the United States, at the state level, the election for governor in Minnesota in 1998, which led to the victory of Jesse Ventura as Governor, was recorded as the first that could be attributed to superior campaigning based on the internet (Ferdinand, 2000b: 10–11).

Having said that, ICTs have not yet affected the practice of voting itself. Even the United States has yet to embrace internet voting. Attempts have been made in the United States to use the net or e-mail to improve voter-turnout, to reduce absentee voting, where ballots are mailed to voters before election, and "early voting," whereby voting machines are set up in shopping malls and other public places for up to three weeks before election day so that citizens may stop by at their convenience and cast their votes (Traugott, 2004). In this context, across the United States as a whole, more than one-fifth of the electorate cast their ballot before what was formerly known as "election day" (Traugott, 2004). In other countries, while experiments with e-democracy have been tried, no elections have been held based on net technologies. But the web does facilitate deliberation amongst the voter public. A great variety of equipment is becoming available to allow us to say, or write, more to one another in less time than ever before. (McLean, 1989: 1). Drawing on Alexis de Tocqueville, Klein (1999) focused on online forums as one way of using the internet to create and sustain citizen associations, during and outside election time. One radical approach links new technology to direct or "strong" democracy, where citizens get together in some form of virtual community or digital agora or plebiscites (Budge, 1996: 193; Barber, 1984 and 1998). Proponents of this perspective, Ferdinand (2000b: 6) notes, argue that "the need for representatives to make decisions in their name is no longer so great" especially in the West where representative democracy is in crisis. Thus ICTs could potentially change the triangular relationship between citizens, parties, and parliament, especially if all the parties have internet facilities. There are a number of other examples from countries such as Germany, the United Kingdom, and Sweden that show shifts in this configuration, which it is unnecessary to develop here (Berger, 1998; White, 1999.

See also: Grossman, 1995; Raab et al., 1996: 283; Bryan et al., 1998; Ott, 1998; Dahlberg, 2001; Jay G. Blumler and Stephen Coleman, 2001; Kahney, 2003; Clift, 2004; Norris, 2004).

In early discussions of "teledemocracy," it was often suggested that wide citizen use of ICTs was a way around the continuing frustrations of representative institutions and the political process. There are examples where citizens from the outside have established new online news sources (like Malaysikini.com), forums, and e-organized citizen campaigns (like the e-mail and text-messaging efforts supporting protests to force the resignation of Philippines President Estrada) that do have political agenda-setting power and ability to generate public opinion. They have potential, but successful efforts of a dramatic nature are extremely rare (Clift, 2004: 22). Nonetheless, it has been claimed that "The potential for public sphere online, where people become citizens online, is an area of increasing interest" (Clift, 2004: 33). Lincoln Dahlberg (2001), in his study already cited, explores Minnesota E-Democracy's facilitation of online forums (e-mail discussion lists) that meet many of Habermas' attributes required of the "public sphere." The Minnesota project has influenced online projects within the United States (with chapters in Iowa and Chicago among other areas) and globally (for instance in the United Kingdom and Nova Scotia) (Dahlberg, 2001). The Minnesota E-Democracy project focuses deliberations upon "real" political problems of those living within a particular geographically bounded political jurisdiction (Dahlberg, 2001). The key researcher concludes, "My research also found a number of areas where these exchanges tend to fall well short of the public sphere conception...the colonization of cyberspace by state and (increasingly) economic interests is limiting the extension and autonomy of online discourse." (Dahlberg, 2001).

The issue of e-governance rose to prominence when the World Wide Web emerged as a mass medium following the launch of the first graphical point-and-click browser (Mosaic in 1993), Netscape Navigator (in October 1994), and Microsoft Explorer (in August 1995) (Norris, 2004: 1). It marked changes, Pippa Norris suggested, that could be collectively seen as a shift from the Weberian bureaucratic state towards "networked governance" with power diffused to multiple agencies, including the non-profit sector (Norris, 2004: 2). However it is the governance or administrative functions of state systems rather than the participatory functions that e-governance has supported effectively (Norris, 2004: 3). This outcome might well be anticipated in both developed and developing societies. Thus the earlier optimism that the internet would transform the relationship between citizens and states has been tempered in more recent years by greater skepticism about the power of technology to alter bureaucratic government organizations, deep-rooted patterns of civic engagement, and the structure of the state (Norris, 2004: 17). Similarly, Raab et al. (1996) explore the emergence of an "information polity" in which the development of tools for use in an electronic democracy is intertwined with those involved in the electronic delivery of public services. To the extent that the new ICTs will open up the processes of administration to outside observers much more effectively than before, as Ferdinand (200b: 5) has also claimed, they may at least increase transparency. On balance, as Norris concludes in her assessment, the new ICTs have greater potential for deepening pluralist and representative democracy, by strengthening government transparency and by improving public satisfaction with the delivery of routine public services, more than by stimulating new forms of civic activism, even though no positive outcome is inevitable in this process (Norris, 2004: 19).

Countering E-Democracy: Does the Centre Hold?

Meyer (2002: 119–22) points out that objections can be raised against optimistic scenarios for democratic renewal via ICTs on four different planes: society and culture; mass culture; communication theory; and, socioeconomic conditions. The first and the last can be manifested through "digital divide." On the second issue, one challenge is the "widespread tendency for the older media to colonize the new ones" (hence the distribution by "old" media of news via the internet, as explored later), and another related one is the fact that "the net is literally swamped by overt or covert commercial entertainment." On the third level, "the internet tends to largely privatize the political public sphere, since individuals can only tap its potential in isolation" (Meyer, 2002: 121). These criticisms only rein in overdrawn expectations. They do not defuse the main argument, that the internet does in principle offer new possibilities for democratic communications. It is also true that the internet is unlikely to change the habits of most user-groups, but instead reinforce the tendencies they have already shown in their response to the more traditional public sphere (Meyer, 2002: 122–3).

> Alongside the optimistic arguments, there are also criticisms of the internet's possible role in deliberative democracy as well as its use for public discourse. Cass Sunstein suggests that citizens will self-select

> online exchanges and information that represent "extreme echoes of our own voices"...Despite these and other cautions, I see an online path towards higher levels of citizen engagement and deliveration. (Clift, 2004: 33).

Certainly, there has been widespread evidence of concern about the growth of internet extremism and the promotion of extreme agendas in Europe and elsewhere, but this potential has not evolved to a point where it affects democracy as a whole in any country the literature can identify.

Of course, the strength of the internet as a medium does not automatically translate into a strong democratic moment: reactionary elites can also use their access to the internet to strengthen themselves and consolidate anti-democratic trends. But the medium is there, it is growing, and if we resist the temptation to overrate the political power of the media in relation to developing democracy, it will have a significant impact (cf. Berger, 1998: 609).

Africa and the New Public Sphere Concept

Whereas African communications scholars (Ansah, 1994; Ndlela, 2007) question how applicable Western theories are in developing countries, Berger (1998: 605) asserts that "the role of a public sphere outside a single source of power seems to be something that transcends both North and South, and has value for all societies." While Europe and America worry about the freedom that the World Wide Web, the e-mail, and the cell phone has given to hacktivists and global civil society protesters (alongside cybercriminals and cyberterrorists), Asian countries, especially China, India, and South Korea, are investing huge resources on censorship technology to muffle the ICTs tide. In Africa, where anti-terrorism legislation and other strategies have been used to censor the internet,[22] the continent is changing, having "let freedom ring" as "Africans are unleashing the power" of new technology that "is causing a revolution" (Ashurst, 2001; White, 2003). For instance, in 2003 Nigerian consumers switched off their cell phones and denied network providers revenue to protest exorbitant airtime charges and poor road conditions (Mudhai, 2006). Of concern for researchers is how to discern myth from reality and, in doing so, whether to use old theories and methods.

There are those scholars who decry the absence of a coherent broad-based research approach due to the recentness of the new media, the complexity of development dynamics, and methodological challenges.[23] For others, the way out is not to jettison but to modify old theories and apply them to ICT research. "The new media need to be included in traditional communication research, but we need to look at those traditional theories untraditionally."[24] Possible new media research methods may be extensions of existing methods, but still "the new media researcher should consider alternative methods, or even multiple methods, and attempt a triangulation of methods."[25] Highlighting the range of methods employed in research on internet technologies, Schneider and Foot (2004: 119) show that "the emergence of the internet, and especially the web, has challenged scholars to both adapt familiar methods and develop innovative approaches." Jones (1999: xi) emphasizes that the internet is a "different sort of object" that requires a "conscious shift of focus" and method in an interdisciplinary approach—the kind Castells acknowledges in his "word on method" (Castells, 2000: 25), and utilizes. Calhoun (2002) also concurs that ICT research "will advance best if there are more researchers with serious knowledge of both information technology and social science." Although some scholars argue "there is a pressing need for descriptive and empirical work" given the rhetoric and hyperbole surrounding (simplistic) deterministic utopian predictions (visions) about immense social change brought about by technological developments (Howcroft, 1999: 277), others have indicated that "there are beginning to be interesting case studies to complement the usual journalistic anecdotes" (Calhoun, 2002). However, most of the empirical ICT research conducted (and data-backed commentaries written) so far focus on anywhere but Africa (e.g. Hill and Hughes, 1998 and 1999; Klein, 1999; Howcroft, 1999; Norris, 2000; Tsui, 2002; Hajnal 2002). Though empirical studies on ICTs in Africa come in a trickle of journal articles (e.g. Mercer, 2004), there have emerged some quite substantial edited volumes on Asia (Banerjee, 2003) and the Middle East (Eickelman and Anderson, 2003).

The call by Hacker and Van Dijk (2000: 220) for a break from the optimist–pessimist oppositions over digital democracy and an entry into "a phase of empirical research and conceptual elaboration" as well as the declaration by Uche (1998) that time is ripe for "empirical studies to ascertain the socio-cultural, economic and political ramifications" of ICTs on democracy in Africa could be a reaction to the fact that much of the writing on ICTs has focused too much on the digital divide and the optimist–pessimist debate (see also: Slevin, 2000; Abbott, 2001a and 2001b; Main, 2001; Hacker and Van Dijk, 2000: 220). Indeed Ott and Smith (2001) note that analyses of ICTs and the global information infrastructure (GII) have either been too technologically deterministic or overly focused on (American) imperialism and on the need for global governance. "Less has been said about the effect of growth in internet access on state-society relationship, particularly in the developing countries of Africa" (Ott and Smith, 2001). Significantly, Tomlinson points out that underestimating the media is "foolish" yet the entrapment of media-centeredness, or, worse, technological determinism, "is to risk losing a larger and more broadly enabling theoretical perspective provided by giving primacy of attention to 'deeper' social, economic and cultural transformations."[26] At the same time, Tomlinson censures the use of predominantly Western theories to explain research problems in the developing world. In fact some ICT authors have pointed out that Africa is "a region with very specific 'patterns of distribution' and a certain testing ground for the social impacts of new technologies" (Polikanov and Abramova, 2003: 43). Whether such regional uniqueness warrants questioning the relevance of "grand" theories and methods remains debatable. Clearly, more empirical research is needed to drive ICT policy, especially around the country strategies linked to the World Summit on Information Society (WSIS).

The distinctiveness of Africa is reflected in a number of recent writings presenting ICTs in general and the internet in particular as threats to the state, especially in Africa. As stated in the introduction, a number of scholars have noted that despite problems of access in Africa the impact of the internet is, paradoxically, much greater compared to more developed parts of the world where access is taken for granted. The resulting reconfiguration of the relationships between rulers and the ruled have led analysts to perceive ICTs as an impetus to the "third wave" of democratization (Hyslop, 1999; Huntintdon, 1991) in the continent. While comparative lack in relevant web content made e-mail the most common application used in Africa, especially in public access centers, social networking sites have become increasingly popular recently. With regard to the cell phone, text messaging is a popular application. Both applications cost less, especially in terms of time and bandwidth—which translate to monetary cost. These tie in with what Tsui (2002) terms legal, economical, social, and technical sphere that need to be taken into consideration in region-based ICT research. It is for this reason that this study takes a dialectical approach, cognizant of different kinds of informationality (or digitality), in different settings, with specific socio-cultural and political expressions (Castells, 2000: 5, 13 and 20–1; Van Audenhove et al., 1999). The focus is not just because the civil society as an urban phenomenon has been credited most for recent democratization efforts in Africa (Hyslop, 1999) but also because surveys indicate NGOs are some of the largest users of ICTs in the continent (Jensen in Ott and Smith, 2001; Polikanov and Abramova, 2003).

New Media and Democracy in Africa

Africa's postcolonial states are successors to profoundly anti-democratic colonial forms of governing, and the influence of that past is not negligible (this point is developed in chapter 4) (Haugerud, 1997: 5). In addition, many skeptics from academia and politics, including some African leaders, have argued that "African soil is infertile for democracy" due to "structural bottlenecks" (Dicklitch, 1998: 31). If this is a serious argument beyond a lazy search for a justification for continuing one-party rule, it raises questions about the continuing predominance of neo-patrimonialism and the parasitic and exploitative role of the political elite. It suggests that the social barriers to political development, including low levels of literacy, lack of strong civil society institutions, and an inability to access an effective electronic infrastructure, determine outcomes, a pessimistic view that needs to be tested empirically (and will be so tested in subsequent chapters). This is not to take the optimistic alternative a priori, but to argue that the possibility for democratization needs to be tested in detail against a sophisticated set of criteria.

Richard Sklar (1983: 12ff) provides four models for democracy in Africa. First, he observes the liberal-republican model, wherein government powers are limited by law, and citizens enjoy freedom of association to compete for office in free elections at regular intervals. Second, is guided democracy, a government by the guardians of the public weal who insist on political uniformity—a form of developmental dictatorship in a democratic cloak, Kenya having been an example. Third is social democracy, characterized by effective pursuit of an egalitarian social order, in addition to a government that is accountable to the people. Fourth is participatory democracy, which affirms the existence of a relationship between democratic political institutions and participative social institutions (see also Atieno-Odhiambo, 1987: 188). Sklar (1983) sees signs of the emergence of "developmental democracy," which accommodates the goals of social reconstruction implicit in socialist democracy, the resistance to authoritarianism implicit in liberal democracy, as in the struggle for trade union autonomy in Zambia, and the recognition of cultural diversity implicit in consociationalism, as in federal experiments in

Nigeria (see also Pinkney, 2003: 17). This provides a qualified, but relatively speaking more optimist view of democratic potential in Africa (Glickman, 1988).

Glickman saw prospects for the emergence of "nonliberal democracy" in several African states, with a general retreat of the state, intra-party elections in Zambia (subsequently followed by inter-party elections in 1991), the development of the ruling party as a watchdog over the government in Tanzania, the search for greater political participation in Ghana, and the growth of such groups as cooperatives, trade unions, and professional bodies (Glickman, 1988: 241–50; see also Pinkney, 2003: 18). Between 1990 and 1994, a wave of reform swept through Africa when 23 of the continent's 42 one-party states held competitive elections and installed nominally democratic regimes.[27]

> Using multivariate statistical analysis, the authors of one study [Bratton and Van de Walle, 1997] try to determine what political, economic, and international factors most convincingly account for patterns of mass protest, political liberalization, and regime transition. (Ibid.)

By contrast, Ayittey (1998) concludes a sometimes rather romanticized tour around African institutional weaknesses by arguing that the only solution to economic failure is radical political reform to rid Africa of its "vampire" states and to restore the accountability and democracy said to be characteristic of African political tradition. The agents of this transformation must be Africa's intellectuals, including those in exile (Ayittey, 1998). Whether this is entirely convincing, it does point to the role of networks—including electronic and virtual networks in the promotion of political and social change—which carries some real conviction. Pinkney (2003), more pessimistically, also suggests that there is a link between the new media and the more established and specifically "African models" of democracy, but holds that in this space, opposition parties contest elections but on terms dictated by their masters and deference to dominant elites carries into the new media. Civil society, for all its growing importance in social and economic life, is similarly told to know its place when it comes to constitutional matters. Some NGOs may enjoy influence in high places, but virtually all are required to register their existence, as if groups in society gain their legitimacy from the state rather than the other way round (Pinkney, 2003: 211). There have been cases where elements of the civil society have challenged authoritarian tendencies in government, but civil society's role is generally seen to have diminished when one moves from challenging authoritarianism to consolidating democracy (Pinkney, 2003: 212).

One might draw some of these threads together by suggesting that there was a great deal of dynamic change occurring in sub-Saharan Africa in the 1990s, but the nature of that change as well as the key actors involved must be clearly understood. These new democracies combine authoritarian and democratic methods of governance, ensuring primarily that economic liberalization occurs. NGOs and civil society fit into these new democracies as service-providers and legitimacy providers. Thus they have a limited, but important, role (see Dicklitch, 1998: 170). At this point, it is useful to ask what the sources of democratization in Africa are. They include "a complex process involving the interaction of agency and structural factors, domestic and international ones, and both economic and non-economic processes" (Van de Walle, 2001 239). From the 1980s legitimacy crises in Africa to 1990s with the end of the Cold War and economic challenges,

> restive populations were increasingly willing to contest central state power, notably through the fledging civic associations that had begun to emerge in response to state decline...protests quickly escalated into demands for regime change...governments found it harder to repress or accommodate the protesters...Leaders found it harder to sustain critical clientelist networks, with the result that the old political aristocracy was more likely to fractionalize. (Van de Walle, 2001: 239–240)

These new actors opened the arena for alternative communication. Political communications provide a system of rule as well as a system of dissent, and one can easily find examples in the past from across Africa where leaders such as Obote in Uganda, Kenyatta and Moi in Kenya, Kaunda in Zambia, and Nasser in Egypt developed a mastery of different kinds of media in order to exercise degrees of control over their peoples. This begs the question of whether the new media have the potential attributed to them by their optimistic proponents of resisting governmental manipulation as older media such as radio and cinema demonstrated. It is fair to say that the optimists have held the ring in the recent past; but it is also only fair to add that the debate has a long way to go.

Assessing the New Media and Democracy in Africa

Although the average number of internet users is limited[28] in Africa compared to other parts of the world (Mudhai, 2002; Jensen, 2002), the internet has made authoritarian rulers considerably more vulnerable there. At the least, they cannot control the flow of information any more (Laakso, 2000: 71). This is mainly because ICTs enable ordinary citizens to participate more directly in their politics and increases their role in policy-making at the expense of those Grossman[29] terms political "middlemen" (cited in Ott, 1998). But the increase in the range and accessibility of sources of information makes it much more difficult for the last word to rest with a Ministry of Information spokesperson in whichever country. It is not much wonder that *Newsweek* so hyperbolically proclaimed that Africans are "unleashing the power" of new networked media, especially the mobile phone (Ashurst, 2001). The "small media" of ICTs is one of the manifold ways by which African people exchange information of political significance without relying on the formal mass media—which are still not wholly free (Spitulnik, 2002: 177). Thus despite its shallow penetration, something is happening in Africa as a result of the internet that is likely to have a significant impact on international affairs in the future: the growth of a new group of internet communicators more readily able to converse with one another across international borders and even within nations and cities with frequencies and in ways not previously possible (Franda, 2002: 18). These new communicators constitute a relatively identifiable group (if not always a very homogenous one), whether they might seem more a "class," a "community," or a new elite to set alongside existing power elites. Apart from what one can describe as "the usual variables"—users are largely young, male, well-educated, above-average earners and English-speakers—most internet users in Africa are in NGOs, the news media, universities, and private companies (Jensen, 2000: 216ff; Mutume, 2000; Franda, 2002: 18, 37n35).

The average levels of internet use among respondents to the Economic Commission for Africa (ECA) survey was three to four pages of e-mail daily, with interaction most frequent with internet sites outside the continent. Surfing the WWW or downloading data are relatively minor activities for this new elite when compared to sending and receiving e-mail. This is primarily because the online time necessary for non-e-mail activities brings the cost to prohibitive levels (Franda, 2002: 18). Apart from personal and family use, the ECA survey identifies a number of broader online interests that have implications for organizational behavior, both within Africa and in the international arena. It profiles a group of young elites interested in international affairs and taking advantage of unprecedented opportunities to use internet technology to become more meaningfully involved with a wide variety of people from other countries (Franda, 2002: 18–19). The potential for increased internet use in Africa is undoubtedly substantial, but depends on further falls in costs as well as infrastructure growth and the spread of education. There is a widely held view that the libertarian culture accorded by ICTs shifts the balance of power between states and citizens, especially in developing countries (Loader, 1997; Tsagarousianou et al., 1998; Wheeler, 1998; Hague and Loader, 1999; Ott and Smith, 2001; Ferdinand, 2000; Spitulnik, 2002). Similarly, Ott (1998) proposes that access to electronic information can have a positive impact in promoting electronic democracy in Africa, by providing civil society with greater leverage vis-à-vis the state and political elites. While it could also be argued that there are already sufficient opportunities to provide political input in the United States and that the internet might become lost in the larger array of media available, in Africa, there are very few opportunities for political articulation, and it is possible that the internet could become a major tool by which NGOs and citizens exert political influence (Ott, 1998). This book will return to these hypotheses in later chapters.

It is not so difficult to suggest general connections between the trajectory of greater democracy in Kenya and Zambia and the growth of the new media. To suggest very specific points of causal connection is much more difficult. The effects of Kenya's 2002 free and fair elections continued to be felt as official transparency and accountability improved while civic and political life showed increased vibrancy. All these factors contributed to welcome incremental improvements in political rights and civil liberties. In both Kenya and Zambia, the combined if uncoordinated efforts of opposition parties and civil society have helped to end the ruling parties' overall majorities. Some people might see such developments as part of the unfinished business of transition rather than as an element of consolidation. But they have all occurred after the initial stage where authoritarian rulers came to concede multiparty elections (Pinkney, 2003: 203). Previously, both Kenya and Tanzania had allowed a choice between parliamentary candidates of the same party, a form of "intra-party democracy" that can reasonably be said to have bordered on out-and-out authoritarianism (Pinkney, 2003: 11). But the difference is that, unlike in an authoritarian system, contested elections are at least permitted as long as they do not threaten the power of the executive. This authoritarianism was not wholly selfish on the part of the rulers. It embodied a theory that had links to strongly held national ideologies that were seen to have triumphed with independence: society was perceived as an organic whole with common interests, in contrast to the uncontrolled aggregation of undifferentiated individuals' interests that took place in radical democracy. In the authoritarian nationalist system, leaders claim to know what these interests are (the general will), and the state exists to execute the general will without being inhibited by constitutional checks to protect minorities or—as in radical democracy—by majorities who have a false perception of their real interests. This rationale is not one that might reasonably be accepted; but it is important to note that the kind of authoritarian nationalism that preceded the moves to more genuine democracy did have *some* kind of rationale (Pinkney, 2003: 11). This rationale also reflected a view of the constraints of the level of economic development, a problem that remains.

As part of a national e-strategy, Kenya has embarked on an e-governance project that involves investing in computerization of government offices and launching of websites for each ministry. "The e-government will facilitate better and efficient delivery of information and services to the citizens," said National Security Minister, Chris Murungaru. It is hoped the project will enable the public to vote online in the next General Election.[30] A week to the December 27, 2002 general election, the Kenya government blocked a range of internet services from transmitting Jambonet, the internet backbone service and the only internet gateway in the country. State monopoly Telkom Kenya claimed the blocked ports were being used to transmit voice over IP (VOIP) traffic—which was illegal in the country. The blockage also cut off interactive internet applications such as MSN and AOL Messenger, Netmeeting, and a number of other chat utilities and most critically VPNs (Virtual Private Networks), which were mainly used by businesses. The ruling party, Kenya African national Union (KANU), was facing its first election defeat in nearly 40 years of independence.

There is also evidence to parallel these narratives from other parts of Africa. In Tunisia, eight young Tunisians were in the mid-2000s imprisoned for up to 26 years for downloading files from the internet in an alleged bid to plot for terrorism. Reporters sans Frontieres (RSF) awarded its first Cyber Freedom Prize to Zouhair Yahyaoui, an imprisoned Tunisian internet activist and online writer. RSF created the prize to honor internet users who, through their professional activity or principled positions, demonstrate their support for the free flow of information online. Zouhair Yahyaoui, whose pen name is "Ettounsi" or "the Tunisian," is the founder of the TUNeZINE.com internet magazine, an online journal used to disseminate information on the development of democracy in Tunisia. According to the PEN

American Center, Yahyaoui was arrested on June 4, 2002 by six plainclothes police officers who detained and tortured him for five days before he finally revealed the access code for his web site. The authorities were then able to remove TUNeZINE from the internet. His family members restarted TUNeZINE as a platform to campaign for his release (the site was available at: www.tunezine.com). Yahyaoui's fiancee, Sophie Piekarec, accepted the EUR 7600 award on his behalf at a ceremony in Paris on June 19. The event coincided with RSF's release of its new report, "The Internet under Surveillance—Obstacles to the free flow of information online," which documents the "attitudes to the internet by the powerful in 60 countries, between spring 2001 and spring 2003." Comparable uses of internet censorship in Zimbabwe are recorded in a variety of sources.[31]

The Kenyan Jambonet exchange point is said to be sometimes equipped with filters to prevent certain content material from being uploaded in Kenya. The very small aperture terminals (VSATs) used in Kenya are unidirectional for downloads only. In protest, Kenyan internet service providers (ISPs) built their own internet exchange point (IXP), but not without some fight with the regulator and the government. A week before the December 2002 Kenya elections, Jambonet blocked a number of its ports claiming that they were being used to transmit VOIP. The blockage seriously affected virtual private network (VPN) communication and also cut off interactive internet applications.

Conclusion

The new ICTs, especially the internet, have not been spared debates on democracy that characterized the introduction of early electronic media—radio, television, cable, satellite, video camera—in the twentieth century. The internet has been looked at both from the free-market libertarianism ideologies of neoliberalism as well as the Net libertarianism prism, from postmodernism (Ross in Miller and Slater, 2000: 16). The term "normative freedom" seeks to capture the apparent paradox by which no notion of freedom is really absolute, but necessarily takes the form of a normative structure, a social order (Miller and Slater, 2000: 16). This chapter has examined tools employed in the examination of the use of ICTs by CSOs in Kenya and Zambia as well as a number of other African countries.

The notion of the public sphere has been proposed as an analytical-empirical and normative tool. The public sphere, in the South, has taken on very different sizes and shapes in different historical periods, and in some cases media has been so controlled as to fall primarily into government space rather than public sphere (Berger, 1998: 606). Net-mediated public sphere, allowing plurality of viewpoints and multiplicity of actors, has been preferred to the exclusionary mass-mediated public sphere. Emphasis has been placed on the study of ICTs within a context. The central assumption in this study is that ICTs do not replace existing socio-political networks and face-to-face communication, but are added to them. Some attention is paid to Latour's work supportive of a comparative study that eschews simple relativism but maintains a skeptical attitude in the face of glib assumptions about what the internet "must" mean or do. A hybrid stance has been preferred in the examination of the concept of digital democracy in Africa although the dependency theory model and the fear of what Castells (2000: 18) would call informational capitalism of the new techno-economic system is not to be ignored in the analysis.

Despite the difficulties of the political theory, a number of key organizational players are more optimistic about the possibilities of the new media and their effect on democratization. The UN sees e-governance as presenting a historic opportunity, among them the opportunity to empower citizens for participatory democracy. There is a particular need to focus on "e-deliberators" or e-citizens, that is citizens with experience and comfort with online political conversation to promote its spread among groups and individuals (Clift, 1998; Raab et al., 1996). Although limited to a specific area and jurisdiction, the Minnesota E-Democracy project mentioned earlier relating to Minneapolis, St Paul's, and their surrounding area, offers some insights into the potential and working of e-democracy. It also offers some ideas on the appropriate (ethnographic, interview based, reflexive) ways to research this topic that has been developed and adapted to the distinct context that this book covers, notably in the later chapters (see Dahlberg, 2001).

CHAPTER 3

The "Wave" and "Spring" Metaphors in Networks' Struggle for Change

Introduction

In perhaps even more profound ways than the era of Gutenberg's movable type (1438), Morse's electric telegraph (1837), Bell's telephone (1876), Marconi's radio (1895), and Baird's television (1923), stories abound about the power and utility of new information and communication technologies (ICTs) as agents of socio-political change around the world. However, the "newness" of the new media presents researchers with methodological challenges in attempts to sift reality from rhetoric. The emergence of any new form of media is often associated with change, sometimes in hyperbolic terms by utopians and futurologists. Building on from theoretical exploration in chapter 1, this chapter provides the historical and contemporary context of marketing or branding such associations, with terms such as "wave" or "spring," to simplify or advance particular narratives or spectacles of media technologies or channels and socio-political change.

Communication Channels and Change

Following the discussion by Fagan (1966: 34–52) of the "Components of Communication Networks," this book considers the mainly urban civic actors and news media under study as "channels" of communication. Fagan (36) defines channels as "structures and institutions in the society [that] are, or might be, used to carry on communication of consequence to the gross functioning of the political system." He uses a fourfold classification: organizations, groups, the mass media, and special channels for interest articulation and aggregation (36). Although he warns that this typology is neither conclusive nor intellectually elegant, and draws no hard and fast distinction on communicational priorities, it is quite compelling and useful for our purposes.

In consideration of the classic Laswellian media research paradigm that the study of communications involves finding out *Who says What in which Channel to Whom* [*Why*] *with what Effect*,[1] this book examines the *process*, more than the *effects* or *consequences* of the use of ICTs media.[2] Significantly, it is important for our purposes to add, "in what context." The Laswellian model may appear hackneyed but in the absence of a more appropriate one, it remains key to communication research. Although examining broader issues of hegemony with regard to new media, Cline-Cole and Powell (2004: 5) assert that "the key issues must be seen as revolving around *who* uses the technology, *how* the technology is used, and to *what end* it is used." This leads us to ideas on power—even though the aim here is not to prove or disprove the power of the channel or the medium. All the same, power is implicit in the very idea of a political civic actor, the main focus of this book.

Indeed Fagan (1966: 18) defines political actors as "those whose significant role is to carry out 'political communication'—that is communicatory activity that is especially relevant to an understanding of political life. *Communicatory activity is considered political by virtue of the consequences, actual and potential, that it has for the functioning of the political system*" (Fagan, 1966: 20). This brings in *effects*, the fifth element in the Laswellian paradigm, which we examine later. In a similar vein, issues under consideration here revolve around the broader role of communication in social change so it is worth looking at some theoretical aspects of this phenomenon.

Rogers pronounced around the mid-1970s the "passing of the dominant paradigm," referring to Lerner and Schramm's post-WWII theory of communication and development (Schiller in Nordenstreng and Schiller, 1993: 470), but casual observers and expert analysts have never really given up on the media's potential for change. Indeed some authors envisage a clear replacement of the "development communication" take-off model with a *development informatization* model (Dordick and Wang, 1993: 20–4).

Fagan traces a communication formulation of political development to the work of Almond and Power[3] who define "systemic [political] change" as changes without necessary "direction" that affect in some basic manner the functioning of the national political system and result in structural, cultural, and performance patterns palpably different from those operating earlier (Fagan, 1966: 123). A subtype of this is political *development* which is *viewed primarily as a process of national integration, as a movement from less to more national unity*—resulting in a common frame of national political reference and action (Fagan, 1966: 124–5, 127).

> Political development involves extending central communication networks into and across previously isolated sectors of the society. The developing political system is characterised by new horizontal channels stemming from increased socio-economic interdependence and new vertical channels arising from increased pressures for political participation and administrative effectiveness...involves a structural expansion in the communication sector sufficient to make "national" politics possible. (Fagan, 1966: 128)

This is what Pye[4] calls the amplifying function of communication whereby "man-sized" acts are transformed into "society-sized" acts. Argues Pye: "Without a network capable of enlarging and magnifying the words and choices of individuals there could be no politics capable of spanning a nation."[5] However, this definition is far from complete as political development implies not only expanded communication capacity and increased homogenization of political images and identifications, but also the diffusion of particular types of behavior stemming from new ways of viewing self, politics, and the world (Fagan, 1966: 129). For this reason, Fagan (108–18) describes two models of communication and social change. Borrowing from Deutsch,[6] Fagan outlines three primary categories of events of "the model of exogenous change," linked as follows: (1) socio-economic changes with important communication concomitants in channels, content, style, opportunities, etc., lead to (2) new ways of perceiving the self and the world, which in turn lead to (3) behaviors which, when aggregated, are of consequence to the functioning of the political system—for instance the expansion of the politically relevant strata of the population and changes in the quality and content of services demanded from government (108–11). This model in its various guises informs much thinking and research on communication and political change. Such phrases as the "communication revolution" (referring primarily to developments in category one) and the "revolution of rising expectations" (referring primarily to developments in categories two and three) bear testimony to its pervasiveness in our current thinking (111).

In this model, change is seen as a result of developments that occur *outside of* (independently of) the political system that in turn comes to be affected by the new patterns of communication. Social-economic mobilization is the cause rather than the consequence of change in political system (Fagan, 1996: 108–11). Examples include technological innovations, for instance TV or ICTs, and how they influence politics in important but unanticipated ways.

In the "model of endogenous change," the starting point is *within* the political system itself: (1) Political strategies and forms of organization that directly or indirectly imply changes in communication patterns are selected and once in operation lead to (2) new ways of perceiving the self, the world, and politics (including new definitions of proper and improper political behavior), which in turn contribute to (3) changes in the functioning of the political system (although perhaps not the changes anticipated by those who implemented the new strategies and forms of organization) (Fagan, 1966: 112–13). There is purposefulness and directedness by leaders, to rectify "conditions" through either the creation of new political resources or the exploitation in an innovative manner of existing resources. Communication changes are both the instrument and the consequence of this policy-oriented leadership. Initial push from political sector and related communication development is confined or manifested there (113).

A full understanding of the relationship between communication change and political change cannot depend exclusively on either model, for both contribute to our understanding in most instances (Fagan, 1966: 123). However, exogenous and endogenous models are not the only two exclusive ways of describing change. Economic, sociocultural, political, and historical factors are always operative in communication change (albeit in more or less muted form) if only to establish limits beyond which change cannot occur (118). This is why some of the recent protests and uprisings end up being illusory, especially in Africa. I have singled out the instances in which *politics* is the prime mover (endogenous), holding them up for comparison against all other instances (the exogenous case) and we shall return to these models at the end. This provides a good starting point to launch into the third wave paradigm.

Third Communication Revolution and Information Society

As discussed above, models of communication-for-change are linked to the idea of the information society captured in the brief for the 2003 World Summit on the Information Society (WSIS) in Geneva:

> The modern world is undergoing a fundamental transformation as the industrial society that marked the 20th century rapidly gives way

> to the information society of the 21st century. This dynamic process promises a fundamental change in all aspects of our lives, including knowledge dissemination, social interaction, economic and business practices, political engagement, media, education, health, leisure and entertainment. We are indeed in the midst of a revolution, perhaps the greatest that humanity has ever experienced. (Cline-Cole and Powell, 2004: 6)

A markedly similar wording is discernible in the website associated with the G8 Okinawa Charter on Global Information Society that saw that "the essence of IT-driven economic and social transformation is its power to help individuals and societies to use knowledge and ideas." Among other things, "our vision of an information society is one that...work to fully realize its potential to strengthen democracy, increase transparency and accountability in governance, promote human rights, enhance cultural diversity, and to foster international peace and stability" (Mercer, 2004: 49). Envisaged is a society driven by knowledge and information. It is an idea whose earlier modern roots are in the writings of Madison: "A people who mean to be their own Governors, must arm themselves with the power which knowledge gives."[7] So it is not really as new as enthusiasts portray it.

Various authors have written about this "third wave" of information revolution marked by the internet—the first having been the printing press and the second radio and TV. The Japanese vision about it came in the 1960s when it was mainly seen as a postindustrial service and leisure society (King, 1984: 2; Lyon, 1988: 2). "It offers the possibility of a gradual replacement of the present top-down, hierarchical type of society to one which is less bureaucratized and in which entrepreneurial initiative can be more widespread within networks with strong horizontal linkages" (King, 1984: 2). There are those who visualized a radical shift, a major break. Futurist Toffler argues the first "wave" was agricultural, the second industrial, and the third, information society (Lyon, 1988: 2). He perceives a change of civilization, from hunter-gatherer to agricultural to industrial to post-industrial. The latter is the "so profoundly revolutionary" new civilization "bursting into being in our midst" (Toffler, 1980: 18), the "giant wave of change battering our lives today" (21). This grand metaphor, of colliding waves, is not original. Norbert Elias, in his *The Civilizing Process*, refers to "a wave of advancing integration over several centuries" (Toffler, 1980: 21). From culture shock Toffler coined "future shock" right back in the mid-1960s to refer to "too much change in too short a time" (Toffler, 1973: 4).

Tourane (1974: 3, 5) envisaged "new societies labelled post-industrial...They may also be called technocratic because of the power that dominates them. Or one can call them programmed societies...according to the nature of their production methods and economic organization." His main method is a focus on actors' interaction, exchanges, negotiations, and mutual influences (Tourane, 1974: 4). In a similar sense, Castells distinguishes the *capitalist mode of production* and development from the *informational mode of production* and development (Webster, 1995: 194). Castells' theoretical starting point, his reliance on the concept of "informational mode of development" easily drifts into a form of technological determinism found most frequently among techno-boosters who insist that the "information revolution" will transform radically the way we live (Webster, 1995: 213).

One of those falling in this camp, according to Webster, is American sociologist Bell (1999) but the latter refuses to be classified thus. "I am not a technological determinist, for all technology operates in a context not always of its making (such as politics and culture); yet technology is the major instrument of change (and instruments can be used well or badly) (Bell, 1999: xi, xiv, xviii). He however sees three different waves of societies:

> We are today on the rising slope of a worldwide third technological revolution. The first was the use of pumps, controlled chambers for locomotion, and machines. The second, about a century ago, can be identified with electricity and chemistry. The third, is about computers, telecommunications, and the like...Historically, every society has been tied together by three kinds of infrastructure, the nodes and highways of trade and transactions between peoples. The first is transportation: rivers, roads, canals, and, in modern times railroads, highways, and airplanes. The second is energy systems: hydropower, electricity grids, oil and gas pipelines, and the like. The third is communications: postal systems (which moved along highways), then telegraph (the first break in that linkage), telephone, radio, and now the entire panoply of new technological means from microwaves to satellites. (Bell, 1999: xlv, xxxii–xxxiv)

To Bell (1999: xlvi–xlvii), communications begins to replace transportation as the major mode of connection between people and as the mode of transaction and as geography is no longer the controller of costs, distance becomes a function not of space but of time; and the costs of time and the rapidity of communication become the decisive variables. Hence we are in an "information age," a coeval information or network society (Castells, 2000), a post-Fordist society, a broadband society or an information economy (Martin, 1995: 2).

More pessimistic writers like Douglas (1970), Schiller (1999, and in Nordenstreng and Schiller, 1993: 470), Beck (2001) and May (2002), emphasize risks. Schiller warns of a cultural and political pollution of the gargantuan private economic structures. From scarcity to blizzard/overload: The world seems so full of information that what is scarce is citizens' ability to make sense of it. There is the risk, exaggerated by Baudrillard[8] that citizens will become trapped in a never-ending information blizzard, without adequate free time to digest or make sense of the information flows that envelope them (Keane, 1991: 183).

The structuralist approach is a synthesis of extremes, introducing some sense of the complexity of the impact of social and technological change, and the likelihood that a diversity of interests, actors, and social structures would produce a variety of outcomes or, as Miles[9] put it, many possible information societies (Martin, 1995: 4). Continuity rather than discontinuity is what Giddens perceives although he does not write much about the "information society." It is not a concern of his to discuss the status of this particular concept, not least because he would surely be skeptical of the proposition that we have recently seen the emergence of this new type of society. Indeed, he has quite directly asserted[10] that "although it is commonly supposed that we are only now in the late twentieth century entering the era of information, modern societies have been 'information societies' since their beginnings" (Webster, 1995: 52). Consonant with this statement, Giddens' theorization leads one to argue that the heightened importance of information has deep historical roots, so deep that, while one may concede that information today—in an era of what he calls "high modernity"—has a special significance, it is not sufficient to mark a system break of the kind Bell conceives as "post-industrialism" (Webster, 1995: 52).

Dordick and Wang (1993: viii) point out that "defining information society is a difficult task"; they look at information society from the perspective of economic development. Almost all nations have chosen informatization as the most promising means for achieving the goal of joining global economy. "Those few of the least-developed nations in Africa, for example, are very likely to do so after they have achieved some measure of political stability. Indeed, many see economic growth as a means for achieving political stability. They will also choose informatization as the means by which to achieve this goal" (Dordick and Wang, 1993: ix). We cannot escape the impact of such wider social "revolutions" and scientific "paradigm shifts" (McQuail and Blumler, 1997: 22). Not when such a revolution is seen to drive such other related movements as the "third wave" of democratization.

The Third Wave of Democratization

The "third wave" of democratization, which started in Southern Europe in the 1970s and which, in one form or another, spread to most of Latin America, East and Central Europe, and parts of Africa and Asia, continued unevenly through the 1980s and 1990s (Huntington, 1991; Grugel, 1999: 1; UNDP, 2002). Factors driving its spread included the expansion and intensification of transnational communication systems (Held, 1995: viii); and the web of relations and networks that stretch across national borders (Held, 1995: ix). The demise of Communism meant that there was less inspiration and support for left-wing governments and political parties as Western governments now concentrated on the restoration of democratic elections with less fear of the "wrong" side winning. "The extension of democratisation was in many cases less than dramatic but the relationship between state and society changed significantly to introduce a more pluralist order" (Pinkney, 2003: 94).

> World politics have changed radically since around mid 1970s. At the beginning of 1975, (Freedom House reported) there were only 40 democracies in the world, and they were predominantly rich, industrialized nations of the west. In the mid to late 1970s, it was intellectually fashionable to dismiss democracy as a "luxury" poor states in the third and second worlds could not afford. From early 1980s, a democratic Zeitgist swept the globe as Spain crafted a democracy after recovering from the 36-year-old dictatorship of Francisco Franco, military withdrawal began in Latin America and military regimes gave way to civilian, elected governments in Ghana and Nigeria—albeit only fleetingly. (Diamond, 1997: xiii)

It was the beginning of a grand process that Huntington (1991) dubbed the "third wave" of global democratization. Democracy was restored in Turkey in 1983, in the Philippines in 1986, in South Korea in 1987, and in Pakistan in 1988. In 1989, communism collapsed in Eastern Europe or "the Soviet bloc," and a regional wave of democratic transition ensued there with the coming down of the Berlin Wall as the Cold War ended. Democracy was entrenched as the typical form of government as the number of electoral democracies—in which multiple political parties regularly compete for power through relatively free and fair elections—increased in the world from 76 in 1990 to 118 in 1996. The percentage increase was from 27.5 percent in 1974 to 46 percent in 1990 and to 61 percent in 1996 (Diamond, 1997: xiv). As indicated in the introduction, progress seemed to have stalled around 60 percent (Freedom House / Puddington, 2012: 29).

Diamond distinguishes features of the third wave democratization as changes in civil–military relations, international factors, civil society, and socio-economic development (Diamond, 1997: xxviii–xxxvi). Of crucial significance is the salience of international influences. As Huntington (1997) points out, international and especially regional demonstration effects played a crucial role in stimulating and providing models for subsequent democratic transitions. Also influential were a variety of more tangible international pressures and inducements, including the growth of governmental and nongovernmental forms of assistance to "democratic" actors, and the increasing emphasis on human rights and democracy promotion in the foreign policies of established democracies, especially the United States (Diamond, 1997: xxxiv). This is perhaps what leads Patomaki (2000: 1–12) to associate the "third wave" of democratization with the spread of harmful neoliberal world order. More positively, the internet and related ICTs have been seen by various authors (Ferdinand, 2000; Grossman, 1995) as a stimulant for a third great era of democracy; the first having been direct or classical Greek democracy and the second one representative democracy.

The spread of the "third wave" of democratization to Africa in the early 1990s represented the most significant political change in the continent since the independence period three decades before. Throughout the continent, significant political liberalization resulted in the emergence of a free press, opposition parties, independent unions, and a multitude of civic organizations autonomous from the state (Van de Walle, 2001 235; Bratton and Van de Walle, 1997). Voter turnout in founding elections was high in many African countries in the 1990s, exceeding 85 percent of registered voters in Angola, Burundi, Gabon, Mozambique, Namibia, Seychelles, and South Africa (Bratton, 1999: 549–50).

> The first half of the 1990s saw widespread political turbulence across the African continent... Transitions away from one-party and military regimes started with political protest, evolved through liberalization reforms, often culminated in competitive elections, and usually ended with the installation of new forms of regimes.... Together they amount

> to the most far-reaching shifts in African political life since the time of political independence 30 years earlier…From 1990, the number of political protests in SSA rose dramatically, from about twenty incidents annually during the 1980s to a peak of some 86 major protest events across 30 countries in 1991…African governments gradually introduced reforms to guarantee previously denied civil rights. (Bratton and Van de Walle, 1997: 3)

The year 1990 marked the beginning of a "second liberation" and the launching of the "third republic" in many an African country. By the end of 1994, 38 of the then 47 countries in SSA had held competitive multiparty elections for at least the national legislature and not a single de jure one-party state remained in Africa (Bratton and Van de Walle, 1997: 7, 8; Diamond, 1997: xiv). Within the space of a decade, scores of countries throughout Africa made an unsteady transition to some form of multiparty democracy. In the "Democratization" section of its *Africa Recovery* report of 1996, the UN indicated that in 1989, 39 of the 45 SSA countries had authoritarian forms of rule, but by early 1995, 31 of the 45 had democratic presidential or parliamentary elections. "Whether these changes are part of Huntington's 'Third Wave of Democratisation' or reflective of Fukuyama's 'End of History', or Africa's 'Second' independence there is a process of profound change occurring in SSA" (Dicklitch, 1998: 1).

> On closer examination, however, the scope of democratic progress in the world is partly illusory, for regular, free and fair elections do not ensure the presence of other important dimensions of democracy. Democracy may be the most common form of government in the world, but outside of the wealthy industrialised nations it tends to be shallow, illiberal, and poorly institutionalised…Clearly the third wave of democratisation has had much greater breadth than depth. The number of "liberal" democracies[11] increased during the third wave, although not as sharply as the number of electoral democracies. (Diamond, 1997: xiv, xv)

Approaches to the Study of Democracy: Reform Factors and the Third Wave

Alongside the "third wave" metaphor has emerged in the 1990s theoretical explanations about regime change—whether, how, and why democracies are installed and consolidated, raising paradigmatic issues that lie at the heart of social and political theory (Bratton and Van de Walle, 1997: 19). First is the structural or modernization (preconditions) model versus contingent (agency) approach, the first one probing whether regime transitions are a function of underlying preconditions at the level of the deep formations of economy and society and the second inquiring whether political change depends on the preference and choices of leaders and on their skills at mobilizing resources, counteracting opponents, and taking advantage of opportunities. A complete theory of political agency would also attend to the endeavors of ordinary citizens, the interplay between elite and mass actions, and the unintended as well as the planned consequences of political events (Bratton and Van de Walle, 1997: 19; Pinkney, 2003). Since third world countries lack democratic prerequisites (like material prosperity and a political culture of tolerance and participation),[12] the transition approach ("transitology") held sway especially in the 1990s as it sought to explain the "third wave" in terms of the ability of different political actors, whether inside or outside government, to consciously reach sufficient consensus on a new set of minimum procedural rules of the political game (Grugel, 1999: 5–8; Pinkney, 2003: 2).

Not everybody agrees to the efficacy of transitology as an explanation, nor do commentators necessarily all look at it in the same way. Grugel (1999: 10) argues that in insisting on "procedural minimum" for a functioning "democracy," transitology has devoted little time to the analysis of civil society, associational life, social and political struggles, and citizenship. Structuralism, by contrast, which failed to explain why the "third wave" of democratization began, "has proved more useful for examining the politics of the period after the collapse of authoritarianism [as] it conceptualizes democracy not as the result of luck, tactics and elite compromise, but as an outcome of social and class struggles" (ibid.). Democracy is not therefore located in a set of governing institutions; the institutions mediate social and class conflicts. Institutions make democracy functionally possible, but their mere existence does not guarantee democracy (Grugel, 1999: 10).

> Research on structural approach to democracy is also influenced by the normative tradition of political theory. In particular, it recognizes that, in order to be meaningful and substantive, democracy is required to have social as well as civil and political components...This approach emphasises the importance of structures, history and culture and takes into account authoritarian relations on the basis of gender, ethnicity and race. Democratisation, in sum, cannot be seen merely as the establishment of sets of governing institutions but is, more fundamentally, the creation, extension and practice of social citizenship

> throughout a particular national territory. This approach directs the observer away from an excessive focus on the state in isolation from society and towards the examination of state-society relationships. (Grugel, 1999: 10, 11)

In this regard, democracy exists when there is popular consent, popular participation, accountability and practice of rights, tolerance, and pluralism; the existence of formally democratic institutions alone does not guarantee or indicate the existence of democracy. It is long-term rather than short-term, and the quality of life of ordinary people is the litmus test; at micro-level of social relationships, not just at the macro-level of institutions (Grugel, 1999: 12). From the foregoing and taking into account African political games, this study favors a mixed approach that takes into account different aspects rather than straightjackets.

Anothersetofapproachesisinternationalversusdomestic-democratic, probing whether the trajectories of regime transition are best apprehended by paying attention to the separate and distinctive domestic histories of each country or whether a more holistic perspective that locates countries as parts of larger international systems, subject to powerful influences from beyond their own borders, should be adopted (Bratton and Van de Walle, 1997: 19). "In the end, it may be the external factors that will do most to provide a democratic opening...At first sight, the external forces seem to be on the side of repression both directly and indirectly (say, through)...ruling elite collaboration with global capitalism" (Pinkney, 2003: 40). However, it is worth noting that political entrepreneurs in Kenya and Zambia, among other African countries, have pursued interests that have reflected their needs much more than those of global capitalism, and Western powers have failed to subvert many rulers hostile to their interests. Once again, a mixed approach is favored here.

The third set of approaches is political versus socioeconomic considerations, probing whether the exercise of power gives shape to the social and economic world or whether politics is the dependent or independent variable (Brattton and Van de Walle, 1997: 20). Using this approach, one would argue that the structural adjustment programs in Zambia and aid conditions in Kenya weakened the economic realms and stimulated domestic unrest that in turn led to transition. It is such interplay of various factors that lead Bratton and Van de Walle to adopt a *politico-institutional approach*—based on *domestic political factors*, with attention given to both their *structural and contingent* dimensions. "We do so by discussing the notion of structured contingency, asking precisely how political agents and political institutions interact to affect one another. In short, we interpret the recent democratic experiments in Africa as the product of purposive political action in a context of inherited political regimes" (Bratton and van de Walle, 1997: 20). As analytical instruments, macroeconomic and international factors constitute contexts that shape political structures and precipitate political action but because of their secondary or supporting role, "our explanatory model concentrates on the processes and institutions internal to existing political regimes. A country's political prospects derive directly from its own inherited practices" (Bratton and Van de Walle, 1997: 41).

Approaches to Civil Society as Agents of Third Wave Change

Splichal et al. (1994) look at the information society in the manifestations of democracy through a global civil society. Diamond (1997: xxx) argues that

> perhaps no single factor more readily evokes the romance, excitement, and heady possibilities of democracy's third wave than the image of resurgent civil societies mobilizing peacefully to resist, discredit, and ultimately overturn authoritarian rule. Although democratic transitions are typically inaugurated and negotiated by political elites in both the regime and the opposition, civil society has played a crucial role in building pressure for democratic transition and pushing it through to completion.

To this extent, Pinkney (2003: ix–x, 3, 87–106) points out that the questions that scholars are asking about democracy have begun to change, with more attention turning to "the adequacy of civil societies to sustain democracy" or relations between the state and civil society.

> Civil society tended to be neglected in the earlier literature on democracy because it was frequently assumed [especially by transitologists] that most transitions involved negotiation between government and opposition, or elite and counterelite, with the wider society having little more than a walk-on role in the occasional riot or attempt at communal self-help. It is now widely acknowledged that there is a significant new relationship between state and society. Society has shown its willingness to challenge the state as it pressed for the ending of authoritarian rule, and the state has been forced to accept a more modest role as it suffers diminished resources for economic development,

> social provision, and the maintenance of order. More human activity now takes place away from the shadow of the state umbrella. Not all of this will be conducive to democracy, but the general effect is to establish a more pluralist political process. (Pinkney, 2003: 3)

Grugel (1999: 12) points out that identifying a central role in politics of civil society—the non-marketized sphere of associations, of networks, of agency and of resistance to the state—has led to the development of "civil society theory," traceable back to Plato and Aristotle, as we have seen in chapter 2. Here, civil society is examined as it relates to the third wave paradigm. That civil society has grown in all third world countries since 1980s is hardly in dispute (Pinkney, 2003: 99). It is generally accepted that the information revolution has led to a dramatic increase in civic scale in recent years, with the number of formally constituted NGOs (which do not tell the whole story) increasing from 6000 to approximately 26,000 during the 1990s alone, and news coverage in the recent past has reflected the growth of the NGO sector, with the use of the term "nongovernmental organization" or "NGO" increasing 17-fold in about a decade from 1992 (Nye Jr., 2004b: 90; Keck and Sikkink, 1998: 1–78).

Tellingly, Held (1996: 358) argues that democratization now requires "entrenchment in regional and global networks as well as in national politics" and Grugel (1999: 12) points out that non-state actors increasingly engage in operations across state borders as a way of effecting changes within states. Analytically, the first level of this NGO surge is global, leading to cosmopolitan democracy (Hamelink, 1993; Held, 1995; Patomaki, 2000; Patomaki and Teivainen, 2002). However, questions have been asked whether the norms of democracy should be applied to globalization, given that there is no world government (Patomaki and Teivainen, 2002) and democracy has largely been analyzed from a domestic point of view. The focus of the "new" [global] actors is often on a particular single issue.[13] The development of these kinds of NGOs or advocacy networks or movements is usually assumed to be mostly spontaneous. Instead of aiming at state power, they profess "cultural politics" or "extra-parliamentary politics." They are transnationally organized, and were among the early pioneers of the use of internet (Patomaki and Teivainen, 1995: 114).

Against the *monist* trend of globalization (imposing preferred, autocentric, and imperial set of values-norms and discouraging polycentric and divergent space), a *pluralist* globalism emerged among those social movements that seek to develop a "civil society" on a global scale (Hamelink, 1993: 384). The problem is that Hamelink seems to contradict himself by insisting on some kind of consensus "on basic values which can be shared across the globe—by all citizens of the world" (Hamelink, 1993: 385). Often these global NGOs aim at changes in the policies of particular states or corporations. Others, like Amnesty International,[14] attempt to enforce and also develop international law (Patomaki and Teivainen, 1995: 114). Greenpeace aims also include enforcement of international treaties and conventions, in particular by using media and the internet to make appeals to "international public opinion" (Patomaki and Teivainen, 1995: 114). These movements often relocate political space non-exclusively in less territorial terms. They reify or demonize the "enemy" (like WTO, IMF, the World Bank, or capitalism and unfair taxation) in ways that other NGOs do not. The main focus has been on being against something concrete (Patomaki and Teivainen, 1995: 117–18). It is discernible that they provided a model for domestic NGOs—as happened in the case of Occupy movement recently. For instance, political NGOs in much of Africa tend to be initiated or run by professionals such as lawyers.

At the second national and sometimes regional level, Dicklitch (1998: 123) informs us that NGOs and civil society have become increasingly important in Africa as harbingers of democratization from the 1990s—a phenomenon reflective of the dual processes of economic and political liberalization that propelled NGOs to the forefront as significant actors in the political and economic arena. How and why they are important is controversial, not whether they have become important. "The recent surge of interest in NGO activity in Africa calls for an examination of what role they actually play as opposed to what role they are expected to play in democratisation" (ibid.: 3). Given the traditional power systems as well as the strength and diversity of civil society organizations (CSOs) in Africa—including the churches and other religious formations, co-operative self-help associations, nongovernmental development organizations, and the like—the civil society becomes a very useful term to understand the complexity of African society (Jørgensen, 1996: 43). In Africa, CSOs also happen to be the largest ICT users thus making them an even more appropriate "channel" through which to analyze new media use for political networking. This analysis therefore leaves out political parties as a number of observers are reluctant to include political parties as organizations of civil society[15] especially given that in much of sub-Saharan Africa the general absence of a system of competitive and ideological party systems is regarded as an obstacle to the consolidation of democracy (Grugel, 1999: 13). It, however, is instructive to state that this study does not adopt an uncritical view about the influence of civic actors, including CSOs, or new media in politics.

Conclusion: Of "Waves" and "Springs"

The metaphor of "waves" or "revolutions" here takes into account what Williams (1961: x–xi) views in terms of the democratic revolution, the industrial revolution, and cultural revolution (including advanced communication). It is vital to note that

> there are two fundamentally opposing visions of an information or knowledge society. Put crudely, the first conceives of knowledge as something which can be objectified and controlled, and to which citizens or customers can then be given or sold access, so that they can gain benefit from the commodity. The second sees knowledge as essentially common property from which people and social groups gain value as they create it, exchange it, interpret it and adapt it. (Cline-Clone and Powell, 2004: 9)

The new ICTs, especially the internet, have not been spared debates on democracy that characterized the introduction of early electronic media—radio, television, cable, satellite, video camera—in the twentieth century. The internet has been looked at both from the free-market libertarianism ideologies of neoliberalism as well as the Net libertarianism prism, from postmodernism, and in terms of "normative freedom" paradox[16] (Ross in Miller and Slater, 2000: 16). The process and nature rather than the outcome of communication seem particularly important as new communicative forms are taking shape, which may alter the fundamental characteristics of mediated communication (Nowak, 1997: 38).

It is in this context that the "Spring" metaphor could be viewed in the same vein as the "wave," to capture particular trends—like the ones in North Africa and the Middle East in 2011. While critics like Alhassen (2012) find the term "seasonally inaccurate," "condescending," and "flippant," it is believed its coiners intended it to capture a "bloom" after "winter slumber," depicting a re-awakening or renewal. Whatever the debates, both "wave" and "spring" are not only convenient catchphrases but also intended to portray political reform.

CHAPTER 4

Civic Engagement, the African State, and Political Reform

For the developing world, it can be a challenge if crises of legitimacy, integration, and participation were to appear all at once instead of sequentially. Huntington[1] warned that if participatory politics intensified in conditions where institutions are weak (as obtained in Asia, Africa, the Middle East, and Latin America) then stability would be at risk (cited in Bienen, 1974: 10). By the late 1960s, the early association of participation with democracy had given way to this concern for stability (Bienen, 1974: 10). The assumption in liberal democracy is that a strong state and a strong civil society, each with a clear notion of its own role and limitations, are mutually reinforcing (Pinkney, 2003: 88), yet in most of tropical Africa the state is weak owing to colonial legacy, but civil society does little to provide an alternative basis for democracy, except at the most parochial level (Pinkney, 2003: 90). The retreat of the state in the face of retrenchment, privatization, the delegation of function to NGOs, and demands for greater respect for civil liberties may be seen as both a cause and effect of the promotion of more diverse interests and values (Pinkney, 2003: 98).

Dicklitch (1998: Pref.) argues that the failures of earlier statist development approaches "laid the foundation for the euphoric embrace of civil society and NGOs as the panacea for underdevelopment and authoritarianism" and that "the current fixation on NGOs as vehicles of empowerment, democratization and development falls within the parameters of neo-liberalism [which] advocates economic liberalization, the creation of a (minimal) liberal state and the adoption of multi-party politics as crucial elements of 'good governance' approach" (also Hydén and Bratton, 1992; Ndegwa, 1996: 15; Abrahamsen, 2000).

The legitimacy of Africa's "predatory" or "vampire" state has been called into question in recent times (Fatton, 1992: Ranger and Vaughan, 1993; Osaghae, 1994; Olukoshi and Laakso, 1996).[2] As a challenge to the legitimacy of state and party dominance, the urban civil society as a recent phenomenon sprang up in sub-Saharan Africa (SSA) due to a variety of factors: economic and political liberalization; the stoppage of donor assistance via states; change-euphoria around the world significantly linked to the fall of the Berlin wall, the end of communism, and with it the Cold War that freed donors from the East–West power balance that often propped undemocratic regimes particularly in Africa. The upsurge of civil society organizations (CSOs) is not unique to Africa. Throughout the 1990s, political parties as mass organizations lost much of their significance in the large European countries like Italy, Germany, and Great Britain. Their role as elements of political power-struggles waned, and they no longer had as much influence over societal discourses as they once did (Meyer, 2002: 100). However, civil society is not really such a new phenomenon only traceable to the early 1990s; it is just a new breed of civil society that emerged during that period in Africa. The African nationalism movements like Kenya's Mau Mau, though perceived as "terrorist groups" by the powers they fought, have been recognized in some quarters as resistance social movements. For instance, the Assembly of the Council of Churches for Britain and Ireland in their February 23, 1992 open letter wrote: "Africa's search for democracy is not new and has not merely stemmed from changes in Eastern Europe: it came out of the anti-colonial struggle" (Ranger and Vaughan, 1993: 259).

To a number of observers, the erosion of the postcolonial authoritarian-developmental African stateness is significantly attributed to the civil society's part in reconfiguring the post-1990s African political dynamics (Young, 2004). The notion of civil society has become so prevalent in Africa that even skeptics who doubt its relevance to African polities admit the concept is popular among Africans and Africanists (Chabal and Daloz, 1999: 17–30). Clientelist, patrimonial, and vertical networking in Africa make the idea of a politically salient cleavage between "state" and "society" misleading and an illusionary dichotomy. Warleigh (2001: 627) points out that governments and NGOs are interdependent particularly in Africa where the cadres in both circles often share similar backgrounds, education, and values.[3] Civil society in Africa is an evolving entity, an evolutionary concept (Gyimah-Boadi, 1997: 292).[4]

Among the forces that dislodged entrenched authoritarianism in Africa and brought about the beginnings of formal democracy in the early 1990s, the continent's nascent civil societies were in the forefront. Although external influences such as the fall of Communism and pressure from foreign donors were important, it was often the resourcefulness, dedication, and tenacity of domestic civil society that initiated and sustained the process of transition...civil society can take a large share of credit (Gyimah-Boadi, 1997: 278). Thanks to their efforts a number of African countries have become part of what Huntington (1991) calls democracy's "third wave" (Gyimah-Boadi, 1997: 278). "The third wave hit Africa in late 1989" with worker-trader demonstrations in Mali, then "similar phenomena became commonplace in other parts of Africa in the early 1990s, similar domestic forces...leading them" (Gyimah-Boadi, 1997: 279).

Trade unions and worker groups (including civil servants and teachers), religious organizations, and student groups protested autocratic and authoritarian policies and methods in Zambia, Mali, Niger, Ghana, Kenya, and Togo. "Religious based civil-society groups, in particular the ecumenical bodies, played key roles not only in starting but also in guiding the process of political opening. In several groundbreaking cases, the success of the transition to democracy owed much to the broad credibility, political skills, and commitment of Christian organisations and their leaders. In many cases they served as 'honest brokers' in bitter political conflicts between intransigent autocrats and impatient democrats" (Gyimah-Boadi, 1997: 279–80). Churches played a significant role in frustrating the Malawian government's attempts between 2001 and 2003 to secure a constitutional amendment to allow President Bakili Muluzi to stand for a third term in office (Ross, 2004). "Having played a prominent role as midwives of the democratic dispensation inaugurated in 1993–94 at the end of Kamuzu Banda's autocratic rule, the churches continue ten years later to play an integral role in the nurturing and development of democratic politics" (Ross, 2004: 91). A 1992 pastoral letter from Malawi's Catholic bishops, openly criticizing both political repression and the government's mismanagement of the economy, was a seminal event in a country that had long been a bastion of autocratic rule (Gyimah-Boadi, 1997: 279). Roman Catholic prelates such as Bishop Ernest Nkomo of the Congo and Monsignor Laurent Monsengwo of Zaire were pivotal in the transitions and national conferences of their respective countries. In Togo, when long-ruling President Gnassingbé Eyadéma agreed to convene a sovereign national conference to chart the country's political future, he named Archbishop Fanoko Kpodzro to head that body. And in Benin, Bishop Isidore de Souza became head of the interim High Council of the Republic, which presided over the successful multiparty elections of February 1991 and the transition to democratic rule (Gyimah-Boadi, 1997: 280).

However, as attention shifts to consolidation[5] and expectations regarding civil society's contribution run high, civil society remains too weak to be democracy's mainstay…the ability of civil society to help deepen democratic governance and put it beyond reversal remains in serious doubt (Gyimah-Boadi, 1997: 279).

> Civil society's weakness as a force for democratic consolidation is most glaring in the crucial area of ensuring public accountability. The relaxation of press censorship has allowed the emergence of independent newspapers with a zest for uncovering official misdeeds, yet these same papers typically lack the resources needed for in-depth analysis and sustained investigation. On the whole, civil society is too weak to redress state-society relations in favour of the latter. Despite the return to formal democracy and the promulgation of constitutions with all the usual checks and balances, officials retain enormous power. In all but a handful of Africa's new democracies, the threat of an "executive coup" is ever present. (Gyimah-Boadi, 1997: 280)

As Schmitter (1997) points out, civil society can contribute to democratic consolidation if other institutions are also favorable and if civil society actors behave in a "civil way." Schmitter also points out that a key post-transition dilemma is that the "primacy" of social movements and other democratizing civil society actors inevitably declines after the transition, as the authoritarian state disappears, political parties and more established interest groups take center stage, and people turn to more private concerns (Diamond, 1997: xxxi). What has followed the democratic revolutions in East Central Europe, Russia, and Africa has not been so much adaptation as retreat and dissipation of civic energy. The broad fronts of religious, professional, student, labor, and other associations broke up once their common goal of bringing down a despised regime had been achieved. Class and ethnic divisions once again fragmented society, and the leadership ranks (and thus operational capacities) of civil society organizations were rapidly depleted as activists were drawn into politics, government, or business (Diamond, 1997: xxxi). The civil society has also been affected by the lack of a culture of free collective activity and the harsh economic realities of 1990s, which have driven people to the exigencies of daily survival (Diamond, 1997: xxxii).

Often, the civil society in Africa and the south depend on external funding. This way, donors are able to determine many policies and priorities without the need for consent from either the indigenous population or its elected representatives (Pinkney, 2003: 105). It is an interesting observation by donors on the political nature of civil society in African countries that bringing civil society into the reform process will not undermine it but strengthen it. Donors apparently see civil society as a potential ally in their "free marketeering," which suggests that civil society is not a very deeply rooted locus of opposition to the free market (Pinkney, 2003: 101).[6] Yet others argue that because of the financial and political weakness of civil society in Africa, direct international assistance to NGOs and the cooperative linkages that Schmitter (1997) terms "transnational civil society" loom increasingly large in the quest for democratic consolidation. Such international support and linkages have been especially important in encouraging new types of NGOs (and critical media) that seek to reform and deepen democracy as they "foster group and individual autonomy from the state" (Gyimah-Boadi, 1997).

At the local level, some argue that the initial rise of civil society belonged to the authoritarian era of the 1970s and 1980s. Much of it had less to do with democracy than with personal survival in the face of falling living standards and the inadequacy of state services (Pinkney, 2003: 102). The pressure for democratization and democratic consolidation may come from a small counter-elite of religious leaders and urban intellectuals who have only tenuous links with the wider society, as in Haberson's description of Kenya.

As currently structured, NGOs are not viable vehicles for African democratization. Their democratic promise is impeded by inhospitable structural conditions, historical legacies,[7] regime restrictions, and internal (NGO) limitations. (Dicklitch, 1998: 3). The author makes this judgment based on a study in Uganda. First, she argues, rather interestingly, that "the current political economy of neo-liberalism in Africa, which encourages privatisation, and the supremacy of the market, significantly undermines the empowerment function of NGOs" (Dicklitch, 1998: 3). Second, that "NGOs are increasingly relegated to service-provision and gap-filling activities by the retreating state, but those supportive functions are not matched with increased political efficacy" (Dicklitch, 1998: 3). NGOs are also fundamentally constrained by regime impediments and the current political-economy of development. They are often discouraged from performing more politically sensitive advocacy or empowerment roles by the regime as well as the International Financial Institutions (IFIs) (Dicklitch, 1998: 3). These constraints reinforce internal NGO shortcomings including a heavy reliance on foreign aid, a tendency towards competition rather than cooperation between NGOs, weak coordination, relative youth, a lack of democratic decision-making, and paucity of finances, which in turn leads to external dependence. For the most part, NGOs fail to empower their constituencies or wider community, and fail to provide a stable source of pressure on the regime for democratic transition and consolidation (Dicklitch, 1998: 3–4).

It is therefore not surprising that Li (1999) warns against civil society determinism and urges limits on predictions about the prospects for democracy on the basis of a non-state civil society. "Flourishing non-state sectors *may* benefit pro-democracy forces but not necessarily ensure democratisation" (Li, 1999: 418). One should sort out the forces or elements that are either conducive or hostile to democracy in non-state civil society, rather than referring to them as the precondition of democratization in authoritarian developing countries (Li, 1999: 418). The potential of a non-state civil society to deter democracy should not be underestimated. Based on a Chinese case study, Li suggests that efforts to promote democracy should focus on pro-democracy forces rather than non-state civil society as a whole (Li, 1999: 418). It is those pro-democracy forces, rather than non-state sector in general, that we focus on here.

Statist approaches have admittedly been too focused on the state to the exclusion of other societal actors and forces, but the current focus on NGOs and civil society as the vehicles for empowerment and democratization is also overstated and unrealistic (Dicklitch, 1998: 169). As long as the state remains at center stage in African politics, most advancement in popular political and economic empowerment by NGOs and civil society will be contingent on state acquiescence. In other words, the parameters within which civil society and NGOs can operate are defined by the regime in power (Dicklitch, 1998: 169). The author judges NGOs and civil society in Uganda as "weak" and further points out that they are not unique in their weakness. "In Zimbabwe, Kenya, Zambia, Ghana, the Gambia and Senegal few NGOs have established structures that widen participation"[8] (Dicklitch, 1998: 169). "Democracy and civil society are mutually dependent. In order for democracy to be consolidated and deepened, an effective and democratic civil society must be in place. In order for civil society and NGOs to make a democratic difference, there must exist a minimum level of democracy" (Dicklitch, 1998: 170). The reliance on the state to provide enabling conditions makes this a continuing challenge that information and communication technologies (ICTs) alone cannot resolve.

CHAPTER 5

Power and Influence in the Digital Age: New Challenges to State Hegemony

Today, the Internet rests on servers located in specific nations, and various governments' laws affect access providers. The real issue is not the continued existence of the sovereign state, but how its centrality and functions are being altered.

(*Nye Jr., 2004: 84*)

Introduction

Three interconnected questions run through both academic literature and practitioner debates about the political impact of the new media. What can the new media influence in contemporary societies, and how do they do so? What can civil society and its organizations influence in drawing on the potentialities of the new media? How do these two combine to aid and/or shape cosmopolitan democracy and cyberactivism at the global level and cyberdemocracy at the national level? These complex questions point towards a fourth, which grows out of the discussion in the previous chapters: how is the public sphere reconstituted, and how is the public conversation redrawn, in a given society under the impact of the new media? To answer these questions is to raise issues that are all couched in the language of power and influence.

This chapter probes these questions looking primarily at theoretical debates, and so laying the foundation for the empirical analyses of the succeeding chapters. It performs an interdisciplinary analysis of both the state and of new media and the activism that it is said to involve. The chapter starts with ideas of power and influence, and then looks briefly at debates on power and influence in the media, including arguments about the role of technology change in the media as drivers of political change. Next it turns more specifically to the new media, and the nexus of relationships between media, technology change, political organization, and political action that they evidence. It evaluates some of the mythologies of the new media, including the notion that they erode state power. The chapter goes on to examine the direction of the discourse on the "effects model" following the emergence of the new information and communication technologies (ICTs), especially the internet.

Reference is made to conflicts over state "hegemony," with potential theoretical connotations not fully pursued here, meant in a general sense as the domination of the state and its institutions over social and cultural arrangements, including civic actors. A reduction in state hegemony implies an opening of civil society influence. To move from the rather closed and controlled societies of the 1970s to a more democratic future after the 1990s, challenges to state hegemony are necessary (but not sufficient) conditions of change. Development of, and consequences of, conflicts between state and civil society, is looked at using a loosely Weberian notion of those terms. Thus "hegemony" as it is used here does not, for example, refer to a specifically Gramscian or related conception of power relations.

Power and Influence

The concept of power is central to claims made about the state, about non-state actors, and about their relations with the media and civil society. The meaning of media power, particularly where and how it manifests itself, remains debatable. For instance, the distribution and exercise of media power in dictatorships and democracies cannot be the same. Media content and form may not have the same effect on users. In the relational sense of power, as the capacity that A has to get B to do something they would not otherwise have done, media "power" refers to who controls the media and their content, and about what effects such controls have (Street, 2001: 232). Street identifies three forms of such mainstream media power. First is *discursive* or ideological or knowledge power, the way media privileges particular discourses and constructs particular forms of reality. Second is *access* or gate-keeping power, the way in which the operation of mass media controls (acknowledges or excludes) the range of voices (identities) or interests. Third is *resource* power, the way in which media owners (industry) can affect the actions of governments and states.

The media have the potential to play key roles in the power balance in civil society if we accept that civil society functions as the citizens' curb on the power of the state and its tendency to try to dominate (Hayes, 2001: 43). This notion originates in the work of Alexis de Tocqueville, who first realized its importance as the space within which the struggle for democratization takes place (Cohen and Arato, 1992 16; Hayes, 2001: 43). Civil society is thus traditionally viewed as a means both to limit state power and to promote intra-citizenry solidarity (Warleigh, 2001: 619). In this context, in developing nations, the international donor community is increasingly turning to civil society as a political territory separate from (although connected to) that of the state, in which citizens are able to make demands and exert some control over the use of state power (Pankhurst, 2000: 156). The UN and the World Bank have come to refer explicitly to NGOs as key actors in the process of constructing a new civil society as a necessary condition of transformation towards development (Warleigh, 2001: 625). This implies the existence of a nexus of power operating in civil society in which the media play a central role. This is hardly contentious, given some well-established examples.[1]

This begs the question of what is meant by power more generally, before the specific forms of power in the communications media are discussed. Although the concept is widely contested, one standard definition is that power "is the ability to influence the behavior of others to get the outcomes one wants" (Nye Jr., 2004b: 2). In this context, Nye Jr. has defined "soft power" as the ability to get what an actor wants through attraction or seduction or persuasion rather than through out-and-out coercion or direct inducements such as payment (Nye Jr, 2004a: 5; Nye Jr., 2004b: x, 5). "When you can get others to admire your ideals and to want what you want, you do not have to spend as much on sticks and carrots to move them in your direction...many values like democracy, human rights, and individual opportunities are deeply seductive" (Nye Jr., 2004b: x).

Power and Influence in Communications Research

After 1945, the field of communications research (like, perhaps a little later, that of International Relations) was dominated by American paradigms of causal, behavioral, scientific, quantitative, and empirical research drawing on epistemologies and methodologies from the natural sciences and applied to social and psychological research questions. Central to the application of this paradigm was the model of communication as a transmission process in which a message was intentionally sent and received, with predictable and measurable changes or impacts on the receiver (McQuail and Blumler, 1997: 21). From the late 1960s, new critical (especially linguistic and cultural) researchers rejected especially the functionalist and positivist approaches as new theories, methods, and objects of study emerged. However, developments in media technology have also promoted conceptual change, since fundamental properties and effects of "new media" are said to diverge from those of "mass communication" (McQuail and Blumler, 1997: 21). A proliferation of approaches to the impact of media and communications technologies on politics included those of Morley, Curran, and Rosengren but the most reviewed ones include Katz's 1959 functional "uses and gratifications" approach contested with Klapper's 1960 *The Effects of Mass Communication*, and Gerbner's 1970s "cultivation analysis" that rivaled Hall's "encoding/decoding model," which emphasized different accounts of how audiences received or read and interpreted the mass media (cited in Lewis, 1991: 11–44; Nowak, 1997). At the same time, perceptual–cognitive theories of communication effects emphasize the importance of the receiver's subjective perceptions and experiences of the message as well as the situation in which the text and the reader meet (Nowak, 1997: 33).

This plurality of approaches has at least one element in common: the most enduring of all concepts in the political lexicon, the concepts of power and influence, are understood as inextricably linked to communication. In the field of international relations, "the exchanges of documents, people, goods, and even violence that take place across national boundaries can almost all be considered forms of communication" (Fagan, 1966: 6). As one of the most influential "conventional" liberal models asserted, political interactions of various persons and groups are constituted by patterns of *influence* and *power*, manifested in and affected by *symbols*, and stabilized in characteristic political *practices* (Lasswell and Kaplan, 1952: 53).

Social, political and cultural power may rest on various bases, differing not only from culture to culture, but also within a culture from one power structure to another. Power and influence are wielded not only by public authority but also by private interests, including interest groups.[2] Democracy is shaped, and may be enhanced, but not necessarily compromised by such interests, so long as they do not provide an "alternative state." That proviso is, however, clearly an important one.

The Media Influence Debate in Context

The influence of the media not only causes people to do what they might otherwise not do, but it also shapes perceptions and world-views, alters agendas, excludes argument, demonizes individuals and groups, and transforms the metaphors and language used to make sense of the world—such as the "Arab Spring." The field largely began with a set of practical and policy-relevant questions concerning both the unintended effects of the new mass media (print, film, radio, and later television) and also the potential for intentional effects, especially education, advertising as well as propaganda (McQuail and Blumler, 1997: 20). Those who emphasize content stress common codes and their disciplinary power, and ascribe to the media a considerable shaping capacity in influencing consciousness and action, while those who focus on audiences stress course-outcome variations, assign the media less (or at least qualified) power and adopt a socially and culturally differentiating perspective (Nowak, 1997: 35–6). The extended power of the most intrusive electronic medium, television, has been described as an "ideological octopus" (Lewis, 1991). Debates on the impact and significance of the new media need to be set alongside the existence of widespread continuing debate about the capacity of the old media to shape our lives, questions that are not yet resolved.

During the early years of the electronic mass media, the 1920s–1940s, sweeping assumptions were made about the power of the mass media to influence behavior, especially through propaganda (McQuail, 2000; Defleur and Ball-Rokeach, 1989; Cumberbatch, 1989: 3). The basic assumptions were that media messages are received in a fairly uniform way by every member of the audience and that the messages trigger immediate and direct responses (Cumberbatch, 1989: 3). "The early students of mass communication were interested in the process of remote social control" (Cumberbatch, 1989: 3, quoting Katz, 1988). To explain the media's limited power on behavior change, a number of theoretical notions were developed. Most importantly, the problem was turned round (Cumberbatch, 1989: 3): instead of asking what the mass media "do" to people, why not examine what different people do with the mass media? This approach, more generally called the "uses and gratifications" approach, became fashionable. Among early research was the work of Herzog from the mid-1940s to mid-1950s on the motivations and gratifications of listeners to daily radio serials. Another example is Berelson's 1948 study, "What Missing the Newspaper Means" (carried out during a newspaper strike: Cumberbatch, 1989: 3). A second concept in the 1940s and

1950s was "personal influence" and "diffusion," the two-step flow theory where opinion leaders play a major role in shaping ideas and behavior (Lazarsfeld et al., 1968; Katz and Lazarsfeld, 1955; Rogers, 1995; Cumberbatch, 1989: 4). Much of the post-war research then shifted to selective influence, taking into account various intervening variables in the form of psychological and sociological factors–religion, sex, education, race, and social relationships (De Fleur and Ball-Rokeach, 1989: 195). By the late 1950s, there seemed a reasonable consensus among mass communication researchers that the media ordinarily had very little effect. Media reinforced prejudices and opinions, but rarely changed them. This may be counter-intuitive, and was a conclusion counter to what both most media professionals and most commentators believed, but it was a strongly framed view of the limited influence the media really exercised. Nonetheless work continued within this field. For instance Signorielli and Gerbner (1988) listed 784 annotated bibliography on violence and terror in the media. However, other scholars looking over such research effort have found it lacking both methodologically and in its scope (Lowery and De Fleur, 1995: 3). This reflects uncertainty as to appropriate paradigms, but also a conflict between disciplines involved in what has always been an interdisciplinary field.

New Media and Power: Technologies of Freedom?

The new media are significant as a major symptom of economic and structural change, including the growth of the knowledge economy in the shift from resources as factors of production; knowledge capability also affects security (Nye Jr., 2004a: 75–6). Nye draws attention to the capacity of NGOs to exercise soft power, to share information, and to make themselves believable at times when governments may lose public trust (Nye Jr., 2004: 31). A number of other authors make the connections between civic actors and new or alternative media (Smith and Johnston, 2002; Waltz, 2005; Brooke, 2011; Carty, 2011; Earl and Kimport, 2011; Khan and Lee, 2011; Lievrouw, 2011; Olesen, 2011; Loader and Mercea, 2012).

It has been suggested that the most powerful engine of change in the "relative decline of states and the rise of non-state actors is the computer and telecommunications revolution" but that they can also have "the opposite effect, amplifying political and social fragmentation by enabling more and more identities and interests scattered around the globe to coalesce and thrive" (Mathews, 1997: 51; see also Franda,

2002: 19). However, this argument about the decline of the state is at once mistaken and over-simplifying. Non-state actors of different kinds can evolve, and can acquire real political leverage, without necessarily taking away from the state's power; but this probably cannot be the case without a reformulation of the nature of the state.

The internet poses particular issues among the new media. It is no longer uncommon to come across expressions alluding to the power of the internet, such as "cyberpower" (Jordan, 1999) and "cyberimperialism" (Ebo, 2001). Jordan (1999) conceives of three interconnected levels of power in relation to the internet: individual control, technosphere defining the limits of cybersocieties, and collective imagination of cyberheaven (e.g. the immortality of silicon) and cyberhell (complete surveillance).

This resource is of course not evenly distributed: Americans represent one-twentieth of the global population total, but nearly half of the world's internet users (Nye Jr., 2004b: 30). The existence of cybercafes and public telecommunications facilities of different kinds means that people who may not themselves have a private telephone line or who cannot afford to buy a computer may nonetheless be able to gain access. This has sparked concerns about the influence of the net, which encompasses fears about pornography, and the ability of terrorists to circulate ideas (or bomb recipes). In some respects, these debates echo those surrounding the older question about the influence of TV, but in other respects they are quite new, reflecting concerns and potentialities in the new technologies themselves.

Ithiel de Sola Pool wrote:

> Electronic media, as they are coming to be, are dispersed in use and abundant in supply. They allow for more knowledge, easier access, and freer speech than were ever enjoyed before. They fit the free practices of print. The characteristics of media shape what is done with them, so one might anticipate that these technologies of freedom will overwhelm all attempts to control them. Technology, however, shapes the structure of the battle, but not every outcome. While the printing press was without doubt the foundation of modern democracy, the response to the flood of publishing that it brought forth has been censorship as often as press freedom. In some times and places the even more capacious new media will open wider the floodgates for discourse, but in other times and places, in fear of that flood, attempts will be made to shut the gates.[3]

Drawing on the famous phrase coined by McLuhan, Castells declares that "The Network is the Message," in the opening sentence of

The Internet Galaxy (2001). Castells goes on to make some extravagant claims for the impact of the net, including that the net has the capacity "to distribute the power of information throughout the entire realm of human activity" (2001: 1), and that "we are entering, full speed, the Internet Galaxy in a state of informed bewilderment" (2001: 4). McLuhan's deterministic "medium is message" view is seminal in the debate on the impact of the new media (see Levinson, 1999). How far do the new ICTs act as technologies of freedom, or, equally, perhaps, of control (see also Pool, 1983 and Keane, 1991)?

The new information technologies facilitate political learning and alternative news by civic actors acting regionally and globally (see Patomaki, Teivainen and Rönkkö, 1992). Their influence does not lie only in the message, nor in the medium alone, but in the ways they can be used. This begs questions about the sustaining hardware and software, and how far that is in turn capable of being manipulated by competing interests. But much of the literature assumes that computer hardware is available freely to deliver the internet and e-mail via their respective software, while the cell phone hardware can also be a platform for delivery and transmission of the internet, e-mail-like text messages, and pictures.

The Internet: Myths and Realities

In the first chapter of his edited volume, Steve Jones (1999: 1–27) examines research on the perception of ICTs or computer mediated communications (CMCs) as engines of social change and the internet in particular as an information highway. He concludes that "the Internet is . . . an engine of social change . . . (but) our metaphors have led us astray: The internet is not an information highway" (Jones, 1999: 2). In the case of Africa, in particular, the cell phone and the e-mail are popular applications worth focusing on. But these specific applications need to be seen in a social and technological context.

It is less often that scholars go one stage further back to enquire what it is about the internet that has led to the idea that it might be a powerful democratic instrument at all? Graham (1999: 62–71) examines "the advantage of the email and the power of the web." Some of this democratic potential existed in the minds of early users who idealized the properties of the system. This may blind one to a possible totalitarian potential. Some of the earlier claims have turned out to be myths as Curran (2012) has pointed out. "It is impossible for outsiders like governments to intercept [messages] en route without destroying most of the technology's efficiency gains" (Ferdinand, 2000: 12). Other properties of the internet continue to make it a formidable tool.

Whereas older technologies like the TV have limitations on target and scope, the internet's "freedom from national politics, its non-affiliation with any one individual interest group, and the absence of physical and jurisdictional boundaries have all made it the best global outreach medium with the greatest potential to influence global cultural changes" (Kizza, 1998: 25). The major difference the internet has brought to international relations at the beginning of the twenty-first century is a vast reduction in the cost of communicating and sending data across great distances in the most developed parts of the world (Franda, 2002: 7). While some of the most extensive uses of the net are still government and military as well as big business, it creates a system in which power over information is much more widely distributed, although it is hardly a "flat" system without any concentrations of power. Compared to the radio, television, and newspapers, controlled by editors and broadcasters, the internet creates unlimited communication: one-to-one, one-to-many, many-to-one, and many-to-many (Nye Jr., 2004a: 82).

These features have led many specialist writers to maintain that the internet has "a momentum, a force of its own. It's damn near unstoppable" (Mann and Stewart, 2000: 1). They go on to suggest that it has the potential to revolutionize political activity far more profoundly than the telephone or television ever did, for it offers the possibility of direct two-way interaction between the citizens and politicians (Ferdinand, 2000: 1). This may underestimate the impact of both the older technologies in political debate, but it points to a high degree of transformational capacity on the part of the net. We might say that there are four particular dimensions in which the internet can expand the scope of democratic communication and action, although it does not supersede the dominant role of mass-media communication. First, the net dramatically enhances the access activist groups have to internal information from various institutions and the centers of political decision-making. Second, the internet can also be used directly or indirectly to set up independent group initiatives, or as the starting-point for intervening in politics along more traditional lines. In either case, the net multiplies opportunities for political participation. Third, the internet has already proven to be effective in organizing local and regional citizens' action networks in civil society–even if authoritarian political leaders can now impose blockades. Finally, activist internet communities can put neglected public issues on the "conventional" mass media's agenda, and thus make political actors aware of them as well (Meyer, 2002: 122).

The internet has had a major impact on many areas of life, from e-commerce to distance education. The availability of government documents on the internet has changed not only the access issue, but also the way information is now provided (McPhail, 2002: 227). It also appears to be the case that, with internet use, public opinion polls are becoming more accurate as people are becoming more informed and knowledgeable. However, the internet retains the potential to amplify the voice of those who use it, and if those voices are already dominant, then it has the potential to become an agency of what McPhail calls "electronic imperialism" (McPhail, 2002: 236).

Social Media: Second Generation Internet Democracy?

As indicated in chapter 2, the idea of the public sphere has recently been challenged by the emergence of personalized media forms. "Despite these [public sphere notion] setbacks to digital democracy, a fresh wave of technological optimism has more recently accompanied the advent of social media platforms such as Twitter, Facebook, YouTube, wikis and the blogosphere" (Loader and Mercea, 2012: 2). The user is much more of focus in this kind of media than most others. The fact that Facebook founders recently used its one billion users to sensationally commercialize their business, with an ambition of raising US$100 billion to become one of the world's richest companies by market capitalization, makes one wonder where the power really lies. Citing Mosco, Loader and Mercea (2012: 2) wonder whether the recent popularity of social networking sites (SNS) is "a further latest incarnation of Internet mythology-making…Or do they offer new opportunities for challenging dominant discourses and privileged positions of power?"

Loader and Mercea (2012: 2) "contend" that the increasing ubiquity of social media will augment "their potential to shape social relations of power…yet such influence is likely to be in ways that are indeterminate and contingent upon a multitude of clashes" given it is difficult to judge if recent "disruptive activity," whether Egypt mobilization, spread of WikiLeaks disclosures, and challenge to privacy legislation in the United Kingdom, indeed tip power balance.

The Electronic Mail (e-Mail)

The e-mail is one of the most commonly used service of the internet (Mann and Stewart, 2000: 9; Kizza, 1998: 15), but in recent times SNS have increased in popularity. E-mail is one of the many technologies that has the *potential* to enhance participation not just via computers but also other devices, including cell phones. The ability of computer users to send multiple messages far outpaces the ability of those using traditional communication to send multiple messages. In addition, e-mail may be subject to censorship by e-mail providers (Meadow, 1993: 447–8). At the same time, the very commonality of e-mail use means that the technology has provided a powerful new metaphor for other forms of expression, and a focus for other kinds of cultural attention (e.g. the film *You've Got Mail!*).

Cell Phones: "Let Freedom Ring"

Surman and Reilly (2003: 60) argue that most civil society organizations (CSOs) had not moved much beyond e-mail and basic web sites, and identify six "emergent" technologies–such as mobile and place-based mapping technologies like GPS. Cell phones offer great potential, especially in the area of mobilization–especially in poorer parts of the world, such as Africa. Cheaper or second-hand smartphones with picture, video, and audio capabilities are finding their way to Africa where technology is maturing in some parts to allow faster connection. In a converged ICT environment, the cell phone works well with other technologies and is just one of mobile communication technologies (MCTs) that could connect to the internet with some impact on society (Dalpino, 2000: 52–72; Cooper et al., 2002: 288; Katz and Aakhus, 2002).

Myerson (2001) links the communication visions of Heidegger and Habermas to recent hype around a "mobilized" world. Even if not overly reinforcing Myerson's thesis, Rheingold (2002) points out that the 1980s PC wave and the 1990s internet revolution would be overtaken by the twenty-first-century mobile explosion–with the fast, sophisticated, always-connected smart MCTs (cell phones, PDAs, pagers, and other portable internet devices).

The theoretical aspect is explored at a deeper level by Katz and Aakhus (2002) who argue that functional and structuration[4] theories fail to deal with or account for some core aspects of the way people use mobile and other forms of personal communications and the way they make meaning from them and their use. In particular, they point out that the former is instrumental and goal-oriented at the expense of the symbolic while the latter emphasize process at the expense of the values that animate process (Katz and Aakhus, 2002: 315). They propose the *Apparatgeist* perspective, with its logic of perpetual contact, which sees mobile phones as both utilitarian and, even more, symbolic and spotlights how personal technology can be used creatively to empower some individuals, often at the expense of others (Katz and Aakhus, 2002: 315). The *geist*, German for spirit or mind, of the *apparat*, Germanic and Slavic for machine, influences both the designs of technology as well as the initial and subsequent significance accorded by users, non-users, and anti-users (Katz and Aakhus, 2002: 304–17).

The fact that mobile phone use far exceeds landline and internet use in developing countries is one of the most commonly cited ICT phenomena even though these references hardly go beyond a passing mention. Perhaps the most phenomenal cellular phone growth rate has been witnessed in African countries–mainly because they were late or initially slow adopters and because governments were more forthcoming in liberalizing cellular markets than loosening decades-old stranglehold on the fixed networks. Cell phones cannot yet rival the radio as the mass media of Africa and other developing regions but rural penetration, even if still limited in certain parts of Africa, makes them a little more accessible than computer internet. White (2003) notes that the mobile coverage is moving beyond the big towns and is often reaching populations ahead of telephone landlines, mains electricity, and drinkable water–even in collapsed African states, like Somalia, Liberia, and the Democratic Republic of Congo.

No doubt statistics conceal the stark realities of disparities within countries (urban versus rural), regions (for instance southern and northern Africa versus the rest of the continent), and globally (the North versus the South). Yet as Surman and Reilly (2003) point out, access is not a major issue for CSOs as they tend to be much better resourced, even if operating in rural settings, than the ordinary member of the public. Short message service (SMS) remains the most appropriate application and a cheap handset is the most practical option that can be easily appropriated by CSOs for their activities especially in developing countries.

Even for ordinary people, including those in villages, cell phone technology has in some cases been used to empower people with knowledge–for instance with market information. In Senegal, where 70 percent of the population lives in rural areas and very few would normally access market information, Manobi, a joint venture between Senegalese and French entrepreneurs, uses teams to independently gather information about the prices of foods and goods being sold in the markets in and around the capital, Dakar, and then upload prices to a central database using mobile phones that dial in to the server (BBC, 2002).[5] This greatly improves price transparency and guards against exploitation of illiterate and semi-literate farmers by middlemen. Prices are kept low and farmers pay for the service as part of a deal between Manobi and the national telephone company. This model has been applied in socio-political realms as well, for instance to monitor elections and relay data as has happened recently in a number of African countries. For instance, in Kenya and Zambia, NGOs–some with official mobile phone policy–used their field observers to monitor elections and gather data and then relay information instantly to their head offices in the capital cities where the data and analyses were disseminated to media houses for immediate broadcast, say by the recently licensed private FM radio stations. While this worked well in the 2002 election in Kenya, the 2007 elections were rigged and chaotic despite extensive use of cell phones by members of the public–some of whom circulated alarmist messages fanning violence.

The increasing mobile phone presence, for instance through "the umbrella people"[6] of Nigeria, has led to the assertion in the *Financial Times* that Africa's cell phone boom is "sweeping up all levels of society" and that "no other technology, not even the internet, has changed lives and work in Africa as much as the mobile phone has" (White, 2003). Two years earlier, the *Newsweek*, in a report titled, "Africa's Cell Phone Boom: The New Technology Is Causing a Revolution on The Old Continent" and subtitled, "Changing Africa: Let Freedom Ring," explained "how Africans are unleashing the power of the mobile phone" (Ashurst, 2001; Mudhai, 2003).

It is not just in Africa where the mobile phone is being used for social change, in the same way as the fax was used by Chinese dissidents to coordinate the 1989 Tiananmen Square demonstrations, or the internet by Indonesia's anti-Suharto demonstrators in 1998. The Philippines distinguished itself as a hub of mobile phone activism. For instance, text messaging played a key role in the January 2001 downfall of President Joseph Estrada. Minutes after the collapse of Senate impeachment proceedings against Mr Estrada for plunder charges, hundreds of thousands of Filipinos passed around a message via SMS to gather at a religious shrine–forcing Estrada to step down after four days of intense rallying at the shrine (Tan, 2002; Rheingold, 2002). Later, an environmental watchdog NGO called BK (Bantay Kalikasan in Tagalog) held a campaign in mid-2002 to report vehicles that choke with exhaust fumes[7] and force the government to implement the country's Clean Air Act 1999. The Smoke Belchers campaign involved any cell phone user reporting to BK any vehicle they see emitting black smoke (Tan, 2002). At the end of each week,

BK compiled a list of vehicles with five or more complaints against them and sent it to the Land Transportation Office (LTO)–the licensing arm of the Department of Transportation and Communications. The LTO would then summon the offending vehicle owners to their offices for an exhaust test. Those that failed were required to clean up their engines in a garage and those that did not comply lost their licenses (ibid.).

Earlier and recent examples exist in other parts of the developing world. For instance in Bangkok in 1992, members of the Thai professional classes–dubbed "mobile phone mobs"–coordinated anti-military demonstrations with student leaders and with one another, using cellular phones (Dalpino, 2000: 70). In the October 2003 "Gas War"[8] in Bolivia, cell phone coordination enabled ordinary people from different parts of the country to lay a week-long siege on La Paz–facilitating the biggest indigenous siege of the capital in about 300 years (Plath, 2003). When women went on hunger strike in churches the mobile communications network made it a coordinated act (ibid.). Being South America's poorest country, not many Bolivians have direct access to mobile phones so their case is nowhere near the so-called smart mobs phenomena. "The groups were well organised with cell phones used to co-ordinate between the leadership of existing organisations and networks" (Plath, 2003). This third-party or two-step flow tactic undermines concerns over access and underscores the value of more strategic use. The Bolivian use of community radio outlets like Pio Doce (whose transmitter in Oruro was bombed) provides yet another lesson, that such technologies as the mobile phone amplify best when combined with other more established forms of communications as well as organic social networking.

Some critics contend that the invasion of poor villages by ICT tools like the cell phone is part of the imperialist and capitalist schemes by Westerners, especially Americans, to influence the developing world. Citing common "network fail," Akhter (2001) argues that the famous Bangladeshi Grameen mobile phone project "is a conduit for undesirable access to poor people by multinational corporations and their products." While these sentiments are valid, it is difficult to wholly reduce the rapid expansion of ICTs to a strategic game rather than economic pursuits–especially when users fully embrace the technology and even gain from it. Hermida (2003) provides testimonies of previously impoverished village "phone women" proudly praising the transformation in their lives as a result of the Village Phone (VP) project.[9] Although, for sustainability, the VP project is based on a commercial model, its network can be easily appropriated for socio-political use. Going by the Malaysian internet expansion experience, one can postulate that the Bangladeshi VP services, including electronic funds transfer, internet access, market information, and cell broadcast (of disasters, etc.) are adaptable to fit in the four ICT activities identified by Surman and Reilly (2003)–especially mobilization and observation–in times of socio-political crises. All it would take is some kind of strategy, especially by CSOs.

The above illustrations reinforce Surman and Reilly's observation that most existing examples tend to be local and national due to the nature of cell phone systems and infrastructure. Transnational Civil Society successes have mainly been attributed to ICTs in general or "the Internet" in particular as demonstrated by the definition by Ulrich (2002) of Arquilla and Ronfeldt's 1997 coinage of "NGO swarm" as a "large number of diverse NGOs focusing on an issue through the use of the Internet." In a rare case of specificity, Rheingold (2002) indicates that the "Battle of Seattle" demonstrators in the late 1990s relied on cell phones to coordinate action and evade barricades. Increasingly, cell phones are becoming tools for mobilization in Africa.

Participation: Civil Society Power and Influence

For interest groups and CSOs, "power and influence is manifested in the clamour for political participation" (Bienen, 1974: 8–18). Bienen distinguishes between political demands and political participation. For instance, people may get what they want with relatively low participation. Second, participation can also have a supportive rather than a destablizing effect on a regime that imposes controls on political life by encouraging specific forms of participation and curtailing others.

To take this argument further, it is necessary to consider the conditions under which networks have influence. To assess the influence of advocacy networks, we must look at goal achievement at several different levels. Keck and Sikkink (1998: 25) identify the following types or stages of network influence: (1) issue creation and agenda setting; (2) influence on discursive positions of states and international organizations; (3) influence on institutional procedures; (4) influence on policy change in "target actors," which may be states, international organizations like the World Bank, or private actors like Nestle Corporation; and (5) influence on state behavior. Keane (1988) argues for the extension of the process of democratization from the political sphere (where individuals are regarded as citizens of a state) to the civil sphere, where individuals are regarded variously as men and women, entrepreneurs and workers, teachers and students, speakers and listeners, producers and consumers. Struggles over *where* citizens can vote should be given as much priority as the struggles in the nineteenth and early twentieth centuries over *who* can vote. Keane (1991: 171–2) goes on to claim that:

> In *Public Life and Late Capitalism*, I argued (against Habermas and others) that democracy should not be treated as a form of life guided by substantive normative principles. I questioned the view, associated with various forms of "Socratism" (Kierkegaard), that argumentative reason can separate truth and falsity and produce a consensus among speaking and interacting subjects... I further proposed that democracy can survive and thrive without philosophical presuppositions, that it is best understood as an implied condition and practical consequence of the recognition that our modern world is marked (however imperfectly) by trends toward philosophical and political pluralism.

Free speech and equal access to the means of communications are crucial to genuine open democracy, based on Habermas' conception of republican democratization. In a similar vein, Arendt argued that political action and speech–by definition pluralist–aid resistance to social control so are conditions for not just democracy, but also emancipatory social exchange, itself an object of democratization (see Gordon, 2001). These debates point to potential roles that the new media may play in shaping not just the fact of democratization but also the specific of the processes whereby it comes about in particular instances.

In both Kenya and Zambia, there has been regular and periodic change of leadership through elections from the 1990s, although before then both countries could be seen as having more of autocratic-totalitarian regimes. In the process, one can observe civil society attempting to define political problems that were ignored, discredited, coerced, or repressed. At times, a "circus" was offered to divert public attention (Fagan, 1966: 29). Citizens, except relatives and cronies, had little room to participate or be consulted in policy-making affecting them. The scope of allowable criticism was very narrow or non-existent, conforming with claims by Fagan that the standard method of limiting public criticism is punitive: citizens, groups, and media that step out of line are subjected to swift and severe punishment that is meant to be a deterrent to others. Thus although licensing, censorship, and harassment are used to contain those who would speak out against the regime or its policies, the most important control is fear of incurring the displeasure of the rulers with all that might follow in physical and fiscal discomfort (Fagan, 1966: 30).

Sovereignty: Cosmopolitan Democracy

Around the world, governments (especially authoritarian ones like Cuba and Iraq, as well as some less closed ones like China, Iran, and Malaysia) have variously sought to either shut down the internet or restrict its access by populations, especially in moments of crisis (Simon, 2002; Samii, 2003). All the same, it does not follow that more internet access and use necessarily translates to less sovereignty (Everard, 2000; Giacomello and Mendez, 2001). Dahlberg's important study of CMC in Minnesota provides an interesting comparison, not least in its methods and question formulation, even though one immediately accepts that there are considerable differences between the African and provincial US contexts (Dahlberg, 2001). A second US example, the Computer Professionals for Social Responsibility (CPRS), was inspired by their 2000 symposium "Shaping the Network Society: The Future of the Public Sphere in Cyberspace" to launch the "Public Sphere Project" based in Seattle–the venue of the groundbreaking 1999 anti-WTO global civil society protest (Schuler, 2000).

Dahlberg, in his 2000 Doctoral Dissertation in Sociology at New Zealand's Massey University, "The Internet and the Public Sphere: A Critical Analysis of the Possibility of Online Discourse Enhancing Deliberative Democracy," draws on Habermas to develop a public sphere model with six sets of normative conditions (Dahlberg, 2001). These include autonomy from state and economic power, exchange and critique of criticizable moral-practical validity claims, reflexivity, ideal role taking, sincerity, and discursive inclusion and equality. He uses this template to evaluate the extent to which online deliberation is facilitating the public sphere in his case study of the Minnesota E-Democracy project. Dahlberg gives a persuasive vision of the criteria one might employ in thinking through the interaction of the new media and civil society.

Using the writings of Rogers and Marres, Dean (2002:169–71) suggests an emphasis on "issue networks" resulting in neither a set of norms and procedures, nor a democratic public sphere, but configurations that she terms "neo-democracies," an idea derived from

Castells. These networks arise not through the relatively liberal or open debate suggested by other writers on cyberspace as public sphere, but through contestation and conflict. The fantasy of unity or harmony of shared interests is rejected for the antagonisms that animate political life. In making these points, Dean (2002: 170) clearly holds that the naïve aspiration towards political harmony in the cybersphere guts social life of its essential political (and essential conflictual) dimensions. Indeed, not only is Dean suspicious of the notion of "public sphere," but also of the idea of the public as such. And since the notion of the public, though important to utopian imaginings of democracy, was "co-opted by a communicative capitalism that has turned them into their opposite," it may well be necessary to abandon them–if only to realize them. Hence, instead of prioritizing plurality, inclusivity, equality, transparency, and rationality, neo-democratic politics emphasizes duration, hegemony, decisiveness, and credibility (Dean, 2002: 172). In this conception, "neo-democratic" politics are struggles for hegemony; they are partisan, fought for the sake of people's most fundamental beliefs, identities, and practices (Dean, 2002: 173). The replacing of transparency by decisiveness follows from the critique of publicity as ideology. The politics of the public sphere has been based on the idea that power is always hidden and secret. But clearly this is not the case today. All sorts of politics processes are perfectly transparent. The problem is that people do not seem to mind, that they are so enthralled by transparency that they have lost the will to fight. With this in mind, neo-democracy emphasizes the importance of affecting outcomes, and rejects an emphasis on process as key to democratic potentiality (Dean 2002: 173–4). It matters more whether outcomes such as WTO or World Bank interventions can be changed or reversed than whether the procedural structures of democracy work in exactly this or that way. This approach also qualified the emphasis on rationality in other ideas of cyber democracy and the public sphere. It is not my purpose in outlining Dean's account here to say necessarily that this is the only way of developing an effective cyber democracy. Rather, it is more my intention to point to the existence of a real debate over the conditions of re-imagining democracy under conditions of global technoculture, a project that is only just beginning.

Linked to these debates about democracy is a set of concerns about the impact of cyberpolitics on the sovereignty of the state. Of course, some writers may point to the decline of the state and regret it, while others may celebrate it; but are either camp correct? Giacomello and Mendez (2001) conceive a *techno-driven* hypothesis (an enhanced internet leads to less state sovereignty), while others advocate a *politics matters* hypothesis (that internet growth does not inevitably lead to a decrease in state sovereignty: it depends on political action and how the impact is felt). In the former group we can put authors like Grossman (1995) and Negroponte (1995) while in the latter we may include Margolis and Resnick (2000), Everard (2000), and Keohane and Nye Jr. (1998, 2001). Nordenstreng (1993, citing Rosas) conceives a shift to a third stage in the evolution of the concept of state to one where the civil society plays a crucial role.

Attempts at regulation and control of the net are recorded by Mueller (2002) and Kizza (1998: 66ff). They list areas of concern identified by the European Commission. These include: national security (bomb-making, drugs, terrorism); protection of minors (violence, pornography); protection of human dignity (racial hatred, discrimination); economic security (fraud); information security (hacking); protection of privacy (electronic harassment); protection of reputation (libel, comparative advertising); and intellectual property and copyright theft (Slevin, 2000: 223). From the mid-1970s to the 1980s, many other governments started getting worried that the transnational data flows (TDF) via computers, particularly by American-based transnational corporations (TNCs), could jeopardize national sovereignty and independence on economic, legal, and socio-cultural fronts. In 1978, delegates from 78 governments reported that TDF "could place national sovereignty in jeopardy." The phenomena posed in 1979 "was possibly the most dangerous threat to Canadian sovereignty"; the Commission of the EC was worried in 1979 that TDF threatened "a reduction in [Europe's] independence in decision-making"; and French President Francois Mitterand said in 1982 that TDF use for the "dissemination of information processed and largely controlled by a small number of dominant countries could cause the rest to lose their sovereignty" (all reported in Drake, 1993: 259ff). But until the 1990s, there was little government-initiated regulation of internet access and content (Slevin, 2000: 220). Most countries started regulating the internet using existing laws but it was reported that most governments also realized that "the capacity for the negative regulation of communication systems has generally been slipping away" (Slevin, 2000: 221).

Surprisingly, or perhaps not, an African country–Kenya–was one of the few countries around the world that have made moves to manage their own national top level internet domain name system (Highway Africa news dispatch from Africa Telecoms, Cairo, May 2004). However, the Kenya Networking Commission Centre would have to overcome numerous bottlenecks before it became operational and credible. Quite apart from the question of the regulation of allegedly "undesirable" material, however, it is worth noting that states still play a big role in financing, building, and maintaining telecommunications infrastructure. They also generally play a critical role in licensing operators and service providers, and this includes those with the most impeccable "neo-liberal" credentials. Kenya too retains a high degree of involvement in the national telecommunications infrastructure, and this provides an important resource for intervening in communications on both the internet and mobile phone system if it is seen as necessary. In 2012, the regulatory body Communications Commission of Kenya sought legislation allowing monitoring of internet content.

At the same time, new media are economic systems, and provide key actors with the opportunity to raise income (governments through licensing and fees as well as corporations). Sassen (1996: xii, 1–31).) argues that the formation of new economic systems centered on cross-border flows and global telecommunications and computer networks "has affected two distinctive features of the modern state: sovereignty and exclusive territoriality." She further coins a concept of "economic citizenship" that "does not belong to citizens" but "to firms and markets–specifically, the global financial markets" (Sassen, 1996: xiv, 33–62). In a different paper (Sasssen, 1998: 551), she points out that transnational corporation intranets and encryption behind firewalls "represent private appropriations of a public space."

Hacktivism (using techniques of internet-based activism including but not limited to hacking into other systems to make protests) provides a particular focus of global protest, using the internet and e-mail systems to challenge established power, a focus for most Global Civil Society protesters. Nye Jr. notes that the information revolution makes states more porous, and more vulnerable to such action. Governments now have to share the stage with actors who can use information to enhance their soft power and press governments directly, or indirectly, by mobilizing their publics (Nye Jr., 2004b: 91). Throughout the 1990s, transnational or global civil society seemed both to be strengthening and to have major impacts on some aspects of international decision-making. One example lies in the 1992 Rio de Janeiro Earth Summit, where NGOs roused enough public pressure to push through agreements on controlling greenhouse gases. Another is provided by the 1994 protesters who dominated the World Bank's anniversary meeting with a "Fifty Years is Enough" campaign, forcing a rethink of the Bank's goals and methods. In 1995, Royal

Dutch/Shell, although technically in the right, was prevented by Greenpeace, the most media-savvy of all NGOs, from disposing of its Brent Spar oil rig in the North Sea (Franda, 2002: 20, citing the *Economist*). It was not Greenpeace's near suicidal interventions at sea on their own that made the difference, but their ability to commandeer media space on both conventional and new media to promote their argument that made the difference.

In his various work, Lipschutz (1996, 2006) advances the argument that there are emerging de-centered networks of domestic, transnational and global civil societies focused on the self-conscious constructions of knowledge and action, and that easily cross the reified boundaries of Space. This argument may well make some sense. However, it requires specific testing and detailed analysis in particular contexts of political action and social structure rather than the kind of generalized discussion it often receives.

The Resilient State: State Control and Censorship

In 1977, when the internet had barely emerged, Keohane and Nye (2001) concluded that "modernists point correctly to...fundamental changes now taking place, but they often assume without sufficient analysis that advances in technology and increases in social and economic transactions will lead to a new world in which states, and their control of force, will no longer be important" (Franda, 2002: 228). "The prophets of a new cyberworld...often overlook how much the new world overlaps and rests on the traditional world in which power depends on geographically based institutions...classic issues of politics–who governs and on what terms–are as relevant to cyberspace as to the real world" (Keohane and Nye, 1998: 82; also see Franda, 2002: 228). Political sovereignty and legal regulation work within specified territorial jurisdictions. And to at least some considerable extent, greater than some cyber activists readily concede, the cyberworld too depends on this (e.g. for the management of intellectual property disputes). Arquilla and Ronfeldt caution that prevailing hopes of peace-enhancing tendencies of interconnectivity in the new media must be tempered by a realization that the information revolution augurs a new epoch of conflict, in which, they suggest, new modes of armed combat and social upheaval will emerge (Arquilla and Ronfeldt 1998). There have been a number of occasions in the past when interconnectivity was hailed as the end of warfare, that war had become unthinkable. However, by the mid-2000s more than 30 nations had developed aggressive computer-warfare programs

(Nye Jr., 2004a: 85), and these capabilities had been used in different conflicts, including the war in Afghanistan as well as between China and Taiwan. Furthermore, the technologies create new insecurities and vulnerabilities: every night, American software companies send work electronically to India, where software engineers can work while Americans sleep and send it back the next morning (Nye, 2004a: 86). Thus it would appear that an info-warfare race is already taking on the proportions of the Cold War era nuclear arms race. China's cyber-war attempts and capabilities have been in public domain but as early as mid 2001, there were widespread reports of imminent cyber attack of the United States by Castro's Cuba and in early 2012 there were reports that Cuban, Venezuelan and Iranian diplomats discussed such attacks.[10]

Anne-Marie Slaughter (1997) has sought to rebut the claim that the state was in decline and that global politics were increasingly fragmented, while acknowledging the role of ICTs in general and the internet in particular in expanding CSO allegiances and reach. She argues that the "new mediaevalists" miss two central points: one, that "private power is still no substitute for state power"; and two, that "a gain in power by non-state actors does not necessarily translate into a loss of power for the state" (Slaughter, 1997: 184; Franda, 2002: 20). This is especially significant in the African context. Although the internet and other aspects of IT have enabled a small elite class of Africans, Asians, and Latin Americans to organize somewhat more effectively than had been the case previously, they have not been able to overwhelm or supplant state power, and their ability to pressure governments and international organizations on specific issues has been dependent on considerable support–especially funding–from organizations (including government organizations) in the developed world (Franda, 2002: 20–1). These so-called pro-poor interventions by global-Northern NGOs that bypass the state in Africa cannot replace or significantly weaken it, activists Jenny Rossiter and Robin Palmer suggest: "NGOs cannot seek to replace the state, for they have no legitimacy, authority or sovereignty and, crucially, they are self-selected and thus are not accountable" (cited in Ranger and Vaughan, 1993: 260). Franda (2002: 21) agrees, that NGOs may be guilty of exaggerating their own influence, and their impact in mobilizing and ordering civil society organizations "have been marginal rather than central to the purposes and dominance of the governments of most nations."

Information technologies have provided the state with the ability to collect, analyze, and utilize unprecedented quantities of data associated with the running of both the state apparatus itself and the civil society...[hence] some analysts have referred to the "self-reporting state" [although] there is little convincing evidence that these data flows are significantly enhancing the internal autonomy of the state, which is a necessary condition for sovereignty (Camilleri and Falk, 1992: 120). Governments of course also have access to the web, and as Everard (2000) has pointed out, it is governments who have much the greatest technological capacity if they choose to deploy it. More simply, governments have their own web sites, and their own information management teams. Cyberspace is not an arena dominated by anorak-clad hacktivists, much of it is a territory held by expensively suited consultants who are willing to work equally hard for clients from the cyberworld, from opposition, from corporate power or from the state, providing only that they are suitably paid. Thus it is undoubtedly the case that the same technologies could reinforce control and surveillance powers of centralized authorities that pose threats to individual privacy and democratic rights (Raab et al., 1996: 283). Central surveillance has proved highly effective, although it has needed to be targeted (hence the effective prosecution of child pornography, at the cost of huge state resources, while other forms of pornography remain largely unregulated). In specific target areas (the war against terror is presumably another, although its history is yet to be written), central surveillance is possible, but governments that aspire to control information flows through control of the internet face high costs and many frustrations (Nye, 2004a: 82). It may also be that not all states can manage either the technology or the resources to do this; but it is in principle not outside the capability of many states to do this if they choose, at least within certain limits. Thus the uses of the US Patriot Act of 2001 and China's campaigns against cyber cafes both illustrate state power against the web community.

Alternatively, instead of seeing the net as undermining the sovereignty of the state, in the case studies by Franda (2002), the nation-state has been conceived as the gatekeeper of technological innovation, particularly in matters related to IT (Franda, 2002: 230; Calhoun, 2002). This gatekeeping notion does not escape some of the issues raised in the debate about control, but it does at the same time capture some of the salient features of the networked polity and the complexity of relations between state and civil society.

Conclusions

This chapter has explored a wide range of issues relating to power, which form both conceptual and practical grounds for the book as a whole. Research has over a long period of time explored what the media do to people or what people do to or with the media (message). This work has not necessarily thrown up any definitive conclusions, but it has at least been influential in defining questions that are widely asked about the power of the media. The question of the relationships between the media, the state, key elites (as they change and restructure), and civil society is complex and requires an approach that is multi-leveled, non-reductive, and open minded. It also requires an approach that is sensitive to the African context without allowing that context to provide excuses for the unacceptable.

Among the civil society responses, at the Geneva WSIS PrepCom3, to Senegalese President Abdoulaye Wade's Digital Solidarity Fund proposal, was one that the fund should envisage tools that go beyond the internet. The cell phone is clearly one such tool, and its potential as a factor in African political and social organization is considerable. Rheingold (2002) states that text messaging in particular is one of the fundamentally new ways that people use to engage in collective group action (both of traditional and new forms). The focus, especially with regard to the developing world, should not be on the next leap-frogging craze or on the buzzwords of the expensive frontier technologies, but on basic phones offering basic services–especially text SMS.

Another significant point is the fact that mobile phones need to be used, and understood as being used, strategically within the wider framework of other related ICTs rather than in isolation. Besides the internet, the private and community FM radio remains a vital tool–especially for local and national NGO activism–for the developing world. It is cheap, easily usable, and available to much larger numbers of people than any of the new media. In fact the digital 2G and 3G-4G cellular networks themselves are part of the radio spectrum that includes PAMR (public access mobile radio), FWA (fixed wireless access), and public data and mobile satellite services (MSS). At the same time, users have to realize that these are state-controlled resources and as CSOs embark on mobile phone "swarms," governments will respond accordingly. Plath (2003) cites the case of India where texting has previously been shut off at critical points to stem the spread of rumors and coordinated race riots during communalist uprisings around the mid-2000s. Cell phone network shutdown has happened in Nigeria and been ordered in Kenya in recent years. In such cases, there may be reasonably good motives to interfere with the medium, but the examples do at the same time emphasize how fragile the power and "independence" of the new media actually is. Hope lies in the fact that governments also need the mobile phone network infrastructure for business and for their own communications.

This chapter has raised questions of how new media technologies and their use affect the state. It has suggested that the state's formal sovereignty is little affected, that the state's capacity to act may be changed, but that it is not necessarily diminished. At the same time, if one does not see the state as inevitably constituted in predatory opposition to civil society, the new technologies open the possibility of a move towards a version of Arendt's conception of performative politics, and of an agonistic public sphere seems to offer a more productive way forward (Lacey, 1996: 15). However (whatever other issues arise) this is not possible unless questions of unequal access, cultural diversity, and multiplicity of agents of power are addressed. This debate hovers on the frontier between the successor ideas of 1950s liberalism and 1960s critical theory in an interesting but not wholly satisfactory way (unsatisfactory because so hard to resolve, and so hard to apply in the specific African context). However, there are significant limitations for contemporary critical theory in any conception of the public sphere that requires a sharp separation between civil society and the state, a requirement that characterizes both the Habermasian and the Arendtian accounts of the decline of the public (Benhabib, 1992: 72–81; Fraser, 1992: 132–6; Lacey, 1996: 226). Mouffe's sense of the possibility of a dialogic democracy or contested dialogue may provide a different (because not grounded in a liberal discourse) way of coming to a possible acceptable form of public conversation in which realities of power and conflict are not neglected alongside an increased consociationalism.

Reviewing the debate concerning the retreat or resilience of the state, Nye suggests (in the passage used as the opening quotation of this chapter): "complicating the task of national governance is not the same as undermining sovereignty. Governments adapt. In the process of adaptation, however, they change the meaning of sovereign jurisdiction, control, and the role of private actors" (Nye, 2004a: 84–5). Private systems such as corporate intranets or worldwide issue-specific newsgroups "do not frontally challenge the governments of sovereign states; they simply add a layer of relations that sovereign states do not effectively control...If we restrict our images to billiard ball states, we miss this layer of reality" (Nye, 2004a: 84). The state is changed–arguably transformed–by the new media, as Everard (2000) argues, its potential is enhanced in some respects as it is limited or pushed back in others, but it is not necessarily reduced *as a whole*. Even in economic terms, although the nation's role in the goods economy is diminishing, its role in the services sector is stronger than ever. Empirical research work indicates that both the utopian and the dystopian narratives about the immense social change brought about by ICTs have some force; the question is how to balance out both processes (Howcroft, 1999). Or, as Van Dijk (1999: 79) has argued, "networks can lead to either a more powerful state, through concentration of political power, or more power for citizens and social interests, through dispersion of political power." This happens in part through state-controlled infrastructure and the state's ability to conduct research and manipulate commercial technology producers through its purchasing capacity. Thus the vast legal, administrative, military, and ideological apparatuses of the state remain powerful and functional, albeit somewhat weakened to varying degrees. The conclusion drawn by Giacomello and Mendez (2001) that more internet activity equals more politicization provides a more fruitful research agenda, and a starting point for empirical enquiry, rather than the rather empty and one-dimensional argument about the "decline of the state."

PART III

Continental Trends and Networks

CHAPTER 6

Platforms and Applications Diffusion: Civic Engagement and ICT Trends

> *Trying to understand the Internet by simply counting terminals and technical infrastructures leads to a dead end. This is particularly true in Africa. Only a dual approach, based both on the possibilities of technologies and actual ways of using the Internet, makes it possible to broaden the framework and to understand the impact of the Internet on the whole of the environment which supports the life of humankind.*
>
> *Cornu, 2002*

Introduction: The Digital Divide in Context

Tambini (1999: 306) points out that "as long as access to the new media is restricted, it will be impossible to realise their democratic potential." Heralding the internet as a means of freedom, productivity, and communication comes hand in hand with the denunciation of "the digital divide" induced by inequality on the internet (Castells, 2001: 247). To this end, information and communication technologies (ICTs) may be seen as tools for capitalism, imperialism, and "electronic" or "virtual" colonialism (Schiller, 1999; Ya'u, 2004), a weapon for the rich and the powerful, which will smother the voices of the small and the weak (McLean, 1989: 1; Ya'u, 2004). Mercer (2004) describes the relative failure of donor initiatives to introduce ICTs into NGOs in Tanzania, with the aim of achieving externally desired changes to local organizational practices. The findings of her study, focused on the better-connected cities of Dar es Salaam and Arusha, support other ICT studies that suggest that if they are to work, ICTs must be structured around the needs and perspectives of their users. Such users are situated within broader social, cultural, and political contexts (Cline-Clone and Powell, 2004: 7). While pointing out that "access to ICTs has to some extent facilitated networking among Tanzanian NGOs whose advocacy and lobbying activities have had some impact upon national policies," she concludes that donor engineering of elite civil society leads to "ICT fetishism" and therefore likely to result in a case of misplaced optimism.

This view of the information revolution and the information society becomes clearer on reading Guy Berger's assertion regarding modernization's "infrastructural focus on the reach of media" with the reality that "much media in the South did not, and still does not, reach beyond the elite" (Berger, 1998: 601). This very short chapter examines two areas, in an attempt to establish continental trends. The first is the use of select new media platforms and applications and the second is civic engagement trends and factors.

Select New Media Platforms

A select few new ICT media platforms and applications have become very popular recently among civic actors across Africa. They are the ones that can, and have, become a source of headache for some rulers.

One of the most common platforms is that of web logging, or blogging. Radical bloggers were a constant source of irritation in North Africa before the recent uprisings. Many of them were arrested and jailed or harassed by police, but that did not stop the tide of events that finally ousted dictatorial regimes.

Let us take one example from a country that is not too well known for radical activism. Tanzanian media and political analyst Elsie Eyakuze runs the Mikocheni Report (http://mikochenireport.blogspot.co.uk/), focusing on the intersection of feminism and politics. She writes for the *EastAfrican* newspaper and her blog won her a third runner-up place in the first Tanzanian blog awards in the category of best political blog.

Another popular trend is the use of social network sites, such as Twitter – widely credited for catalyzing the 2011 protests in Egypt. Arguing that focus on Twitter use in North Africa "has obscured the explosion in its use across the rest of Africa," Karanja (2012) notes that this social networking site (SNS) "has been adopted enthusiastically by young people right across the continent...part of a revolution which poses challenges not just for Governments." Figure 6.1 shows how popular this medium is across the continent.

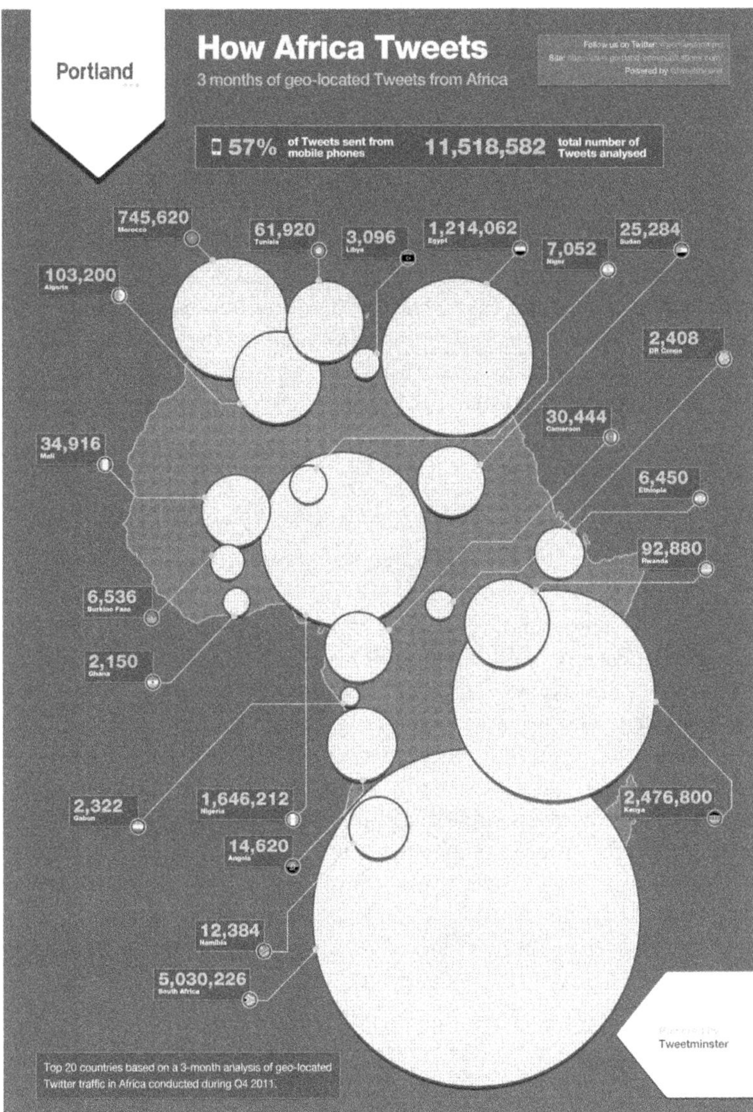

Figure 6.1 How Africa tweets

Pointing out how "the continent as a whole is often totally ignored when global surveys are done" about Twitter adoption, Karanja (2012) highlights the results of a survey commissioned by London-based Portland Communications that "examined only those Tweets which made clear their authors were living in Africa." Specific peculiarities include adoption by young audiences, with 60 percent in their twenties (compared to thirties for Europe and North America), predominant use of cell phones "which makes it all the more likely that the Twitter revolution has only just begun", and less emphasis on usage by high-profile personalities (Karanja, 2012).

In South Africa, the more popular SNS is MXit (www.mxit.co.za), which youths there have popularized. The platform's creator is Namibian developer, Herman Heunis. On the web site, it is promoted as South Africa's largest SNS mainly used for chat and instant messaging, and that it is java-based, mobile-based, and practically free (Mudhai, 2011a). The creators say on their website that it "turns any old phone to a smart phone," and the youths there prefer it to Facebook and Twitter—although reliable usage data are hardly available.

Civic Engagement Trends and Factors

There is an argument in some quarters about civic apathy in Africa. Ibelema (2008: 45ff) characterizes this as civic cynicism, a breakdown of values, which in politics includes corruption, vote-rigging, violence against opponents, and purchase of votes—"that bear negatively on the viability and consolidation of democracy." Ibelema (2008) notes that "in general, the task of reversing the culture of civic cynicism in Africa falls upon several institutions" (55) but "of all units of civil society the task of civic education and value reorientation falls especially on the press and religious organizations" (56). Although a recent survey of civic engagement in the world picked only a few African countries, it shows that the level for Africa is generally low—consistent with the trend in the developing world (Table 6.1).

A rather narrow range of factors, mainly looked at from a Western perspective define what constitutes civic engagement. Whatever the case, there is no clear relationship between the free status of a country, its civic engagement, and other related factors such as ICT access and development status. This is something that still needs a closer look.

One of the most common questions following the so-called Arab Spring is whether it would spread to the rest of Africa. Kenya-based Ugandan journalist Onyango-Obbo points out that "one issue that has been discussed more than the rest is whether the North African uprisings can happen with the same result in sub-Saharan Africa" (Mudhai, 2011b: 326). Opinion is divided between two camps, one that believed that the Arab Spring would spread to the rest of Africa

Table 6.1 Comparative measures of freedom, civic engagement, ICT, and development

Freedom Rating (FR)[1] *[1–7]*	*Country / Territory*	*Civic Engmt Index*[2] *[%Avg]*	*Indiv. Intrnt Usage*[3] *[%Ppn]*	*Households with*[4]		*Mobile Cellular Subs per 100*[5]	*HDI Index*[6] *[Value]*	*HD rank*[6]	
				Home Intrnt access	*Mobile cell phones*				
Free (2011)									
1	Cape Verde	—	30	—	—	74.97	0.568	133	Medium
1.5	Ghana	44	9.55	0.3***	—	71.49	0.541	135	Medium
1.5	Mauritius	—	28.33	20.2**	82.8**	91.67	0.728	77	High
2.0	Benin	—	3.13	—	—	79.94	0.427	167	Low
2.0	Namibia	—	6.5	3.3***	52.4***	67.21	0.625	120	Medium
2.0	São Tomé & Príncipe	—	18.75	—	—	61.97	0.509	144	Low
2.0	South Africa	26	12.3	8.8*	83.2*	100.48	0.619	123	Medium
2.5	Botswana	—	6	—	—	117.76	0.633	118	Medium
2.5	Mali	23	2.7	—	—	48.41	0.359	175	Low
Partly Free (2011)									
3.0	Lesotho	—	3.86	—	—	45.48	0.450	160	Low
3.0	Senegal	31	16	4*	85.7*	67.11	0.459	155	Low
3.0	Seychelles	—	41	10***	—	135.91	0.773	52	High
3.0	Sierra Leone	—	0.26*	—	—	34.09	0.336	180	Low
3.0	Tanzania	—	11	0.6***	—	46.8	0.466	152	Low
3.5	Comoros	—	5.1	—	—	22.49	0.433	163	Low
3.5	Kenya	34	25.9	2.2***	—	61.63	0.509	143	Low
3.5	Liberia	47	7	—	—	39.34	0.329	182	Low
3.5	Malawi	41	2.26	—	—	20.38	0.400	171	Low
3.5	Mozambique	—	4.17	0.9***	—	30.88	0.322	184	Low
3.5	Niger	26	0.83	0.1**	31.9**	24.53	0.295	186	Low

continued

Table 6.1 Continued

Freedom Rating (FR)[1] *[1–7]*	*Country / Territory*	*Civic Engmt Index*[2] *[%Avg]*	*Indiv. Intrnt Usage*[3] *[%Ppn]*	*Households with*[4]		*Mobile Cellular Subs per 100*[5]	*HDI Index*[6] *[Value]*	*HD rank*[6]	
				Home Intrnt access	*Mobile cell phones*				
3.5	Tunisia	24	36.8	5**	—	106.04	0.698	94	High
3.5	Zambia	32	10	0.6***	28***	41.62	0.430	164	Low
4.0	Burkina Faso	23	1.4	—	21.6***	34.66	0.331	181	Low
4.0	**Guinea-Bissau**	—	**2.45**	—	—	**39.21**	**0.353**	**176**	**Low**
4.0	**Nigeria**	**47**	**28.43**	**6****	**49.7****	**55.1**	**0.459**	**156**	**Low**
4.5	**Morocco**	—	**49**	**20***	**67***	**100.1**	**0.582**	**130**	**Medium**
4.5	Somaliland	—	—	—	—	—	—	—	—
4.5	Togo	—	5.38	—	—	40.69	0.435	162	Low
4.5	Uganda	34	12.5	—	—	38.38	0.446	161	Low
5.0	Burundi	12	2.1	—	—	13.72	0.316	185	Low
5.0	Central African Rep.	—	2.3	—	—	22.25	0.343	179	Low
5.0	Guinea	—	1	—	—	40.07	0.344	178	Low
5.0	Madagascar	—	1.7	—	—	37.23	0.480	151	Low
Not Free (2011)									
5.5	Algeria	19	12.5	7.2*	94.1*	92.42	0.698	96	Medium
5.5	Angola	—	10	—	—	46.69	0.486	148	Low
5.5	Congo (Brazzaville)	—	5	—	—	93.96	0.533	137	Medium
5.5	Djibouti	22	6.5	1.7*	—	18.64	0.430	165	Low
5.5	Egypt	27	26.74	25.3*	58.7*	87.11	0.644	113	Medium
5.5	Gabon	—	7.23	—	—	106.94	0.674	106	Medium
5.5	The Gambia	—	9.2	—	—	85.53	0.420	168	Low
5.5	Mauritania	—	3	—	—	79.34	0.453	159	Low
5.5	Rwanda	16	13	—	—	33.4	0.429	166	Low

5.5	South Sudan	—	—	—	—	—	—	—	—
6.0	Cameroon	33	4	1.2***	45***	44.07	0.482	150	Low
6.0	DR Congo (Kinshasa)	22	0.72	—	—	17.92	0.286	187	Low
6.0	Côte d'Ivoire	—	2.6	0.5***	—	76.13	0.400	170	Low
6.0	Ethiopia	—	0.75	0.1***	—	8.26	0.363	174	Low
6.0	Swaziland	—	8.02	—	—	61.78	0.522	140	Medium
6.0	Zimbabwe	—	11.5	2.5**	—	61.25	0.376	173	Low
6.5	Chad	27	1.7	—	—	23.83	0.328	183	Low
6.5	Libya	—	14	—	—	171.52	0.76	64	High
7.0	Equatorial Guinea	—	6	—	—	57.01	0.537	136	Medium
7.0	Eritrea	—	5.4	—	—	3.53	0.349	177	Low
7.0	Somalia	40	1.16*	—	—	6.95	—		NR
7.0	Sudan	37	10.16**	—	—	40.54	0.408	169	Low
7.0	Western Sahara	—	—	—	—	—	—		NR

Sources: Freedom House / Puddington (2012), Gallup / English (2011), ITU (2011), UNDP (2011).

Notes on Indices: See original sources/tables for technical notes and additional data. Dash (—) indicates data not available. 1. Freedom House's Freedom Rating (FR) is an average of Political Rights (PR) and Civil Liberties (CL) ratings, from 1 (most free) to 7 (least free), ranked overall as Free (1.0–2.5), Partly Free (3.0–5.0) and Not Free (5.5 to 7.0), based on events from January 1, 2011 to December 31, 2011 (Freedom House / Puddington, 2012); 2. Gallup's Civic Engagement Index (CEI) is an average from the responses of a sample of about 1000 adults (aged 15 and older) in each country surveyed in 2009 and 2010 on telephone / face-to-face on three areas – donated money, volunteered time, helped a stranger – resulting in rankings from 60 (highest), reflected in the United States and Ireland, with error margin of between ±1.7 and ±4.7 percent (Gallup / English, 2011). [Result for "Somaliland region" entered here for both Somali and Somaliland. Sample was higher in 3 of the 130 countries]; 3. Data for 2010 from ITU (2012) table on Percentage of Individuals using the internet, 2000–2010. Asterix indicates most recent pre-2010 data available, 2009 (*) or 2008 (**); 4. Proportion of households data from ITU (2012) table, Core Indicators on Access to and Use of ICT by Households and Individuals. Asterix indicates data for 2009(*), 2008 (**), 2007 (***); 5. Data for 2010 from ITU (2012) table, Mobile Cellular Subscriptions per 100 Inhabitants; 6. Human Development Index (HDI) covers life expectancy at birth, schooling, gross national income per capita, and non-income elements. Based on global scale, highest value being 0.943 for Sweden, ranked number 1, and lowest 0.286 for DR Congo, ranked 187. 1–47 is Very High HD, 48–94 is High, 95–141 is Medium, 142–187 is Low. NR = Not Ranked.

and another that dismisses that point of view on grounds that conditions are different.

Manji and Ekine (2012) envisage a revolutionary wave across the continent, targeting especially the Not Free countries. However, others think differently. "No—the conditions are completely different," argues a senior coordinator of one of South Africa's most active civic network in the recent past.[1]

Journalist Mwaura Samora, in an opinion in a Kenyan newspaper, argues that the Arab Spring and, in particular, Gaddafi's humiliation "has inspired down-trodden people across Africa," even though he recognizes that "few Zimbabweans had the courage to celebrate [Gaddafi's downfall] publicly, preferring to exchange messages via social networks and other discreet platforms" (Mudhai, 2011b: 326).

As I have argued elsewhere (Mudhai, 2011b: 326), small windows of freedom in sub-Saharan Africa (SSA) make contagion difficult in that part of the continent but major battles of reform cannot be ruled out long-term. Figure 6.2 shows the possible outcomes of intervention, especially in youth civic engagement, that could have implications for activism. Kenya's National Council of NGOs chairman Ken Wafula

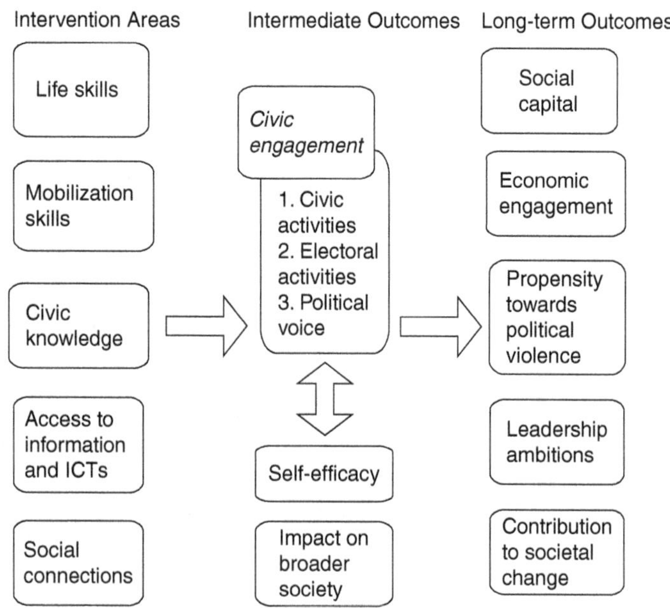

Figure 6.2 Conceptual framework on youth civic engagement[2]

cautioned at a China-Africa forum in Nairobi that "it was becoming increasingly clear [that] economies that grow without [a] corresponding expansion in democracy will sooner or later collapse...Libya is a good example in Africa" (Mudhai, 2011b: 327).

Onyango-Obbo, writing in August 2011, thought analysts had phrased the Arab Spring–SSA contagion question wrongly: "I was one of those who early in the year asked whether the Arab revolt could spread to the rest of Africa. I was mistaken. I asked the wrong question." He appears to suggest that it is the Arab North that is catching up with the struggles for freedom and democracy that have been going on for decades in SSA (Mudhai, 2011b: 327).

Following reconstruction in Arab Spring casualties such as Libya, Onyango-Obbo envisaged "a possible new pattern...in which the most democratic and wealthy nations in Africa are the bottom of the continent (South Africa, Botswana, Mauritius, Cape Verde, Zambia), and its tip (Tunisia, Egypt, Libya). The poor and repressive ones will be clustered in the middle. Sub-Sahara Africa as a political and economic concept will make less sense" (Mudhai, 2011b).

Conclusion

Some degree of freedom in media and communication ecology limit "Arab Spring" domino-effect in SSA but intensification of agitation for reform in the long run cannot be written off.

CHAPTER 7

Identity and Issue Networks: New Media, Politics of Belonging, and Change

Grassroots movements have harnessed the potential of the Internet to forge solidarities, organize displays of resistance, and articulate alternative visions of world order...the growing visibility of networked civil society demonstrates how ICT have precipitated an explosion in transnational communication.

(*Crack, 2008: 2*)

Despite limitations of resources and cost of Internet access, larger numbers of African NGOs, both on the continent and in the Diaspora, are making effective use of Internet communications tools, including email and the web.[1]

Introduction

Through the informational activities of some of Africa's mainly urban political civic actors, the new information and communication technologies (ICTs) are largely perceived to offer unprecedented plurality that challenges the hitherto excessive powers and influence of the continent's ruling elites. Before the advent of ICTs, many African leaders tightly controlled information dissemination—allowing only dominant political views. Alongside chapters 6, 9, and 10, this chapter examines the perceptions that in Africa the impact of ICTs is, ironically, disproportionately greater than their overall spread, and that the libertarian ICTs, as impetus to the "third wave" of democratization, shift the balance of power between states and citizens, especially in hitherto autocratic developing countries (Mudhai, 2003, 2004a, 2004c, 2005 – citing Ott 1998, Ott and Rosser 2000, Ott and Smith

2001). To borrow from Keck and Sikkink (1998: x), the goal here is more than highlighting the presence of civil society organizations (CSOs); delving into the experience of particular civic actors hopefully generates a more powerful understanding of their conception, strategies, limits, and effectiveness, making it possible to situate them within the rapidly changing configuration of activist politics. These networks are not mutually exclusive.

ICTs, Civil Society, and Democracy

Civil society can be expected to stimulate both a renewal of the mass media in the direction of more appropriate reporting and the emergence of other complementary forms of public communication (Dahlgren, 1996; Meyer, 2002: 137).[2] When it comes to new media use, Northern CSOs have embraced ICTs far more easily, and relatively effectively in certain cases, than their Southern counterparts. In the mid-1990s, the 150-member American Council for Voluntary International Action published an internet guide for CSOs due to "myriad requests for information we were receiving from international NGOs that were eager to join the information age" (Parada, 1997: 4). Contributors to a volume edited by Peter I. Hajnal (2002) give case studies on how transnational civil society organizations (TNCSOs), like Amnesty International, Oxfam International, the International Campaign to Ban Landmines, and Médecins Sans Frontières, have made efforts to use ICTs strategically in their operations and especially for campaigns on the policy areas of security, development, international law, human rights, and humanitarian assistance. Other authors, like Rodgers (2000 and 2003) and Beier (2003), have done related or divergent research on these and other TNCSOs. In recent years, a number of authors, such as Tai (2006) on China, have looked at specific countries in their study of CSOs–NGOs and new media.

The UN Rio Earth Summit in 1992, attended by more than a thousand NGOs in the parallel Global Forum, saw the first mass use of ICTs to interconnect and network such an enormous gathering. One of the most significant documents to emerge from the Global Forum was the "Communication, Information, Media, and Networking Treaty" that declared the right of communication as a basic human right (Hassan, 2004: 108). These "com-activists" or critical social movements or what Surman and Reilly (2003) call "social tech" movements, like Indymedia (born at the "Battle at Seattle"), Association for Progressive Communications (APC), Communication Rights in the Information Society (CRIS), and Computes for Social

Responsibility, have used ICTs to create a network of individuals and NGOs supporting communications rights and also fairly successfully involved many actors from the developing world and employed decentralized networked command-and-control strategies (Mudhai, 2004b). These groups promote DIY "tactical media" of ICTs and use such strategies as "culture-jamming" (brand-bombing of America), "warchalking" (hitching free rides on institutional and business wireless hot-spots), and other forms of digital direct action.

There have been other cases of successful NGO collaboration that focus on human rights and development in general. One well-known "swarm" case of NGO collaboration is the support given to information operations to prevent the Mexican government from harassing the Zapatista rebels in Chiapas (Garrido and Halavais, 2003). "Were it not for the innovative use of ICTs by their leader 'Subcommandate Marcos' in promoting their struggle against the Mexican government and military, then the Zapatista movement may well have remained an obscure rebellion that was quietly, but no doubt viciously, crushed" (Hassan, 2004: 108). Through use of fax, laptop, e-mail, and the internet, the movement connected rapidly with sympathetic groups and movements around the world (Hassan, 2004: 108–9). In another case, Northern NGOs have networked using ICTs to help Brazilian resistance movements, the Yanomami Indians as well as rubber-tapper communities, the *seringueiros* and the *empates*, to call for extractive reserves and sustainable development to protect their livelihood at the Amazon forest area. New communication networks that connect indigenous groups with NGO networks create discursive space for indigenous groups previously excluded from public discussions. There are also unconfirmed reports that most of the 100,000 activists who met to critique neo-liberal globalization at the World Social Forum in Porto Alegre, Brazil in 2003 were from developing countries' NGOs—which hints to not only greater ICT networking but also real-life collaborative action (Todd, in Mudhai, 2004b).

Since transnational advocacy networks are not powerful in the traditional sense of the word, they use the power of their information, ideas, and strategies to alter the information and value contexts within which states make policies. Keck and Sikkink (1998: 16) propose a typology of tactics that networks use in their efforts at persuasion, socialization, and pressure: (1) *information politics*, or the ability to quickly and credibly generate politically usable information and move it to where it will have the most impact; (2) *symbolic politics*, or the ability to call upon symbols, actions, or stories that make sense of a situation for an audience that is frequently far away; (3) *leverage politics*, or the ability to call upon powerful actors to affect a situation where weaker members of a network are unlikely to have influence; and (4) *accountability politics*, or the effort to hold powerful actors to their previously stated policies or principles.

> A single campaign may contain many of these elements simultaneously. Information binds network members and is essential for network effectiveness. Many information exchanges are informal—telephone calls, e-mail, fax communications, and the circulation of newsletters, pamphlets and bulletins. They provide information that would otherwise not be available, from sources that might not otherwise be heard, and they must make this information comprehensible and useful to activists and publics who may be geographically and/or socially distant. (Keck and Sikkink, 1998: 18)

Non-state actors gain influence by serving as alternate sources of information and the media is an essential partner in network information politics. To reach broader audiences, networks strive to attract press attention (Keck and Sikkink, 1998: 19, 22). In an increasing number of cases, the internet has proven extremely useful in monitoring membership and mobilizing members behind NGO programs but, as we have already seen, this does not necessarily translate into an all-powerful tool compared to states (Franda, 2002: 21).

In Africa, most of the NGOs emerged in the last decade or so and receive a great deal of donor support. Whether they are effective in using ICTs as political tools is a matter keen watchers are just beginning to investigate. Although not much has been done empirically or written academically about African CSOs and their use of ICTs for political purposes, a small body of work is just beginning to emerge. From a theoretical and a pan-Africanist perspective, Herman Wasserman (2003) explores "the role that new media technologies might play in facilitating an African public sphere in which civil society organizations from different African countries might co-operate in influencing public policy." Niombo (2003a, 2003b) provides a glimpse into the situation in the Democratic Republic of Congo. Mwesige (2003) focuses on the use of cyber cafes in Uganda by a predominantly urban cyber elite, from a digital divide perspective. Within the context of what she terms the "Zaptista effect," in an allusion to the well-known "CNN effect," Mercer (2004) points out that "access to ICTs has to some extent facilitated networking among Tanzanian NGOs whose advocacy and lobbying activities have had some impact upon national policies," but donor engineering of elite civil society leads to "ICT fetishism" and is likely to result in a case of misplaced optimism. More recently, some of the contributors to a volume edited by Nwokeafor and Langmia (2010) touch on the civic role of new media but by far the most apt are Manji and Ekine (2012), and Ekine (2010).

Digitally Enabled Identity and Issue Networks

Formal groups, such as registered NGOs, and informal networks have coalesced based on issues or their identity to fight one cause or another of common interest, and their advocacy, campaign, support structures, and general activities have been made possible and easier by new digital media. Some have achieved their goals, but others are still fighting—if not given up. Some of the most common issue-identity areas include: politics-elections and human rights; resource-economic rights; information and communication; civic-online journalism; gender; sexual orientation; youth and young persons; labor; diaspora-exile; intellectual—academic and professional; religious; cultural-ethnic; peasant-rural. The list is not in any particular order, the typology is not exhaustive, and the categories are not mutually exclusive, given that a number of civic actors straddle the issues and identities. However, they are a helpful way of fathoming what brings the actors together. We will examine a selection of these.

Political-Electoral and Human Rights Networks

New media alone could not have resulted in recent changes in North Africa, but their use contributed to some of the actions that helped bring change. One case is that of the Facebook page, "We Are All Khaled Said,"[3] which was used by Google executive Wael Ghonim to mobilize fellow activists in Egypt anonymously from Dubai in mid-January 2011—making him one of the world's most influential people (Elbaradei, 2011). "He quickly grasped that social media, notably Facebook, were emerging as the most powerful communication tools to mobilize and develop ideas" (Elbaradei, 2011). "I was optimistic... from the 14th to 25th... everyone was working out a plan to convince more and more people to go to the street... A lot of people were making fun of it on Twitter, saying that this is the first revolution where the time, location, date was pre-announced" (Ghonim, 2011). It did not all happen on the internet. His emotional TV appearance[4] and his personal presence at, and address to, the Tahrir square crowd added to the strength of his advocacy.

In his firsthand account of the events, El Ghayesh (2012: 86) describes how "we walked around downtown Cairo and checked Facebook and other social websites trying to find out where the protests were... Another call for protests was made on Facebook for what would be known as 'The Friday of Rage' on 28 January." He points out that given "the call for protests through Facebook had been going on for three years and it never really worked out for Egyptian activists," the protest worked partly because the timing was right in relation to Tunisia. Digital connections were not without frustrations, though, as Ghayesh recalls: "suddenly, phone calls to my friends at Tahrir Square wee all met with the same message: 'This phone cannot be reached at the moment.' The government had managed to shut down all cell phone communication in Tahrir Square."

From Egypt, let us examine the Right 2 Know campaigns by anti-secrecy coalitions in South Africa (www.r2k.org.za) and Nigeria (www.r2knigeria.org). In South Africa, they were up against the ruling African National Congress bent on misusing its majority in Parliament at the expense of fundamental rights and freedoms of ordinary people. Disputed features of a proposed Protection of Information Bill include: no protection, with harsh sentences of up to 25 years, for whistleblowers and anyone who helps them; draconian jail sentences, of up to five years, for coming across "state secret" without passing it on to the police or security agencies; shielding security agencies from any scrutiny or accountability; no independent appeals mechanism, for instance against unjustified secrecy classification (R2K press release, November 21, 2011).

The main demands of R2K SA, which could be gleaned from their web site and various communications, included the withdrawal of the "secrecy" bill, and its replacement with legislation based on public interest and effective public consultation. For their campaign, structurally R2K had a national coordinator, and four regional coordinators for Gauteng, Western Cape, KwaZulu Natal, and Eastern Cape. They used a variety of platforms. Apart from their web site, they were on Facebook (www.facebook.com/Right2Know), Twitter (@r2kcampaign) and they recruited campaigners via SMS word "TRUTH." On November 22, 2011, a day before the final presentation of the secrecy bill in parliament, they staged six protest pickets in Johannesburg, Vereeniging, Soweto, Pretoria, Durban, and Cape Town. "We are not anti-ANC, but we're anti-secrecy," said one of the campaigners, an academic.[5] To win more public support, they issued press releases—for example one ahead of the November 22, 2011 protests.

As part of their protests, the group used e-mail to coordinate events. One such e-mail was sent in relation to the November 22, 2011 protest.

> This week, as the National Assembly prepares to vote on the Secrecy Bill without heeding our call to protect South Africa's right to know, the R2K campaign is calling on all provinces to stand up against this attack on our democracy. As the ANC reneges on its commitment to meaningful public consultation, R2K activists are organising a series of pickets to give the public a voice: we reject the Secrecy Bill![6]

The e-mail provided specific venues, meeting times, and contact persons with their cell phone numbers. It also appealed for volunteers to assist in organizing other protests.

One strategy was to send e-mails to party Chief Whips to influence parliamentarians to vote against the bill. More than 50,000 people flooded the inboxes of the four influential MPs via a link provided by R2K partner, Avaaz, ahead of a September 20, 2011 parliamentary vote.[7] On September 15, 2011, Avaaz urged the public thus:

> In **four days, MPs could pass an outrageous secrecy bill that undermines the constitution and South Africa's democracy**—helping the government keep wrongdoing from the people and enabling cover-ups of corruption and human rights abuses. But there are **four people that could make or break this bill:** the Chief Whips.[8]

Part of the strongly and carefully worded two-paragraph two-sentence letter read thus: "As Chief Whip you have the power to persuade our MPs to protect our democracy and our Constitution". Convergence of platforms was evident in the way the "Support the Right 2 Know Campaign and Stop the Secrecy Bill!" posters were distributed. In smaller print at the bottom of the poster, one is directed to go online to download it, and to sign up for the campaign. The poster was circulated via e-mail with a brief on what recipients should do as part of the November 22, 2011 protests.

> Please send this on to anyone that you know. The idea is that people should print out this simple A4 poster, and put it up in a visible place—a car window, office door/window, in front of their home…ANYWHERE! Also, remember to print a few extra copies and pass them on to fellow South Africans! Especially those who don't have access to internet/printers! Lets cover South Africa with this poster and show the government we won't tolerate them trying to hide anything from us![9]

Following campaigns from 2010 to September 2011, the government withdrew the draft bill and promised further public consultation on the secrecy bill. A day before the September 20, 2011 parliamentary vote, and following a flood of e-mails to Chief Whips and R2K protests on 17 September, R2K partner Avaaz declared:

> **The Protection of Information Bill has been withdrawn from the parliamentary programme for tomorrow's vote.** ANC Chief Whip Mathole Motshekga said the legislation had been withdrawn for "further consideration". Public pressure is working! Now let's make sure the Bill is redrafted to respect our Constitutional rights.[10]

The bill was re-tabled in parliament two months later. "It is crucial to point out that whatever amendments made to the Secrecy Bill prior to the finalised version now tabled in parliament were all the result of the demands and sustained pressure from a range of civil society organisations, including the R2K Campaign."[11] The R2K campaign recorded and remembered political undertakings.

> the ANC Chief Whip's office promised a transparent and clearly road-mapped process to "ensure that as many people as possible, regardless of their political allegiance, get an opportunity to have a say on the draft legislation before it is passed into law." Communities were promised ample notice of upcoming meetings to express their views on the Secrecy Bill.[12]

However this promise was a brief victory. It turned out to be hollow. "Any public engagement has now been rendered meaningless by moving the Bill back to parliament, showing the Chief Whip's promises to be utterly empty."[13]

The R2K's seven-point Freedom Test remained unmet by the bill—but some victory could be claimed by the fact that four were, at least partially, met by late 2011 in the view of the movement.[14]

Twitter and Facebook were R2K SA's primary campaign tools, in addition to the popular South African text-based platform, MXit, and to some degree YouTube.[15] By around mid-May 2012, they had 3454 Twitter followers and 6360 Facebook friends but had no figures for MXit whose use they had to scale down when some payment was needed to keep the heavy usage. "Evidently it was phenomenally successful,"[16] an R2K co-ordinator said. "Twitter has been very useful in connecting us with SA journalists/editors and helping shape the discourse around the Bill. FB connects us to the middle-class section of our support base." The coalition commanded following from 25,000 individuals mainly recruited via social media, and about 400 civic organizations. "Every public action we take is coordinated and communicated in the main through social media. So I'd say their contribution has been essential to our success."[17]

An interesting formal grouping in this category is the African Democracy Forum (ADF), launched in Abuja, Nigeria, in October 2000, as regional network of democracy, human rights, and governance organizations seeking to consolidate democracy "by providing opportunities for democrats to openly express their views while also acting as a platform for mutual support and the sharing of resources."[18] Organizations and individuals working on democracy issues in Africa through ADF activities have increased from 120 around 2004 to 450 in 2012. The organization, hosted at the Pretoria offices of the Institute for Democracy in South Africa (www.idasa.org), is affiliated to the World Movement for Democracy (www.wmd.org). Its activities include ICT support.

Conclusion: Enhanced-Efficiency and Partial Efficacy in Africa

The central assumption in this chapter is that ICTs do not replace existing socio-political networks and face-to-face communication, but are added to them. ICTs are merely trend amplifiers rather than radical tools of social change. The civic actors also use other media, like land lines, faxes, letters, postal services, radio, TV, leaflets, village meetings, workshops, and conferences as well as corporeal interactions.

There are many civic networks in Africa that are hardly online, especially in the rural areas and in countries where internet access is still prohibitive—whether via computers or cell phone. An example is Ticheze a Malawi (TaM), a membership-based outreach grouping with limited online presence. A hint of their activities can be gleaned from an entry via cell phone on their Facebook account on their first anniversary in November 2011: "TaM as a group has close to 100 members. We meet every Friday at Lilongwe Hotel and MASM [Medical Aid Society of Malawi] in Blantyre. Please send your e-mails for more info." To which a member adds: "Monthly contribution is MK1000."[19]

PART IV

A Tale of Two Countries—Kenya and Zambia

CHAPTER 8

La Luta Continua: Transition and Disillusionment in the "Second Liberation" and the "Third Republic"

In Kenya we see a debate about whether pressure from outside, or protest from below have done more to undercut the one-party state; we wait to see whether "moral ethnicity" or "political tribalism" will triumph; we watch as women are mobilised in the cause of democracy.

(*Ranger and Vaughan, 1993: 261*)

Introduction

Questions remained whether Kenya would follow the example of Zambia, "sweeping away after three decades of rule the party that had secured independence" (Throup and Hornsby, 1998: 1). A combination of internal protest, external pressure for change, and a series of mistakes by the government's elite between 1988 fraudulent party elections and 1991 forced the Moi regime to allow multiparty politics (Throup and Hornsby, 1998: 2). Kenya's "democracy wave" started with the *Saba Saba* (Seven Seven) uprising of July 7, 1990. Donor pressure, including the 1991 Paris Consultative Group's decision to withhold US$1 billion aid pending political reforms, ultimately led to repeal of section 2(a) of the constitution in 1991 and the controversial 1992 multiparty general election (Ajulu, 1998: 275). This initiated a process of gradual, and not always smooth, transition.

In Zambia, the second republic demonstrated a highly flawed rhetoric of popular democracy, according to Burnell (2001a) who recognizes the significance of Hargeud's analysis of the so-called historical divide, with a turning point around 1990. In the Zambian case, as in a number of other countries in the region, there appeared to be a trade-off between stability and democracy.[1] To move towards a more genuine democracy is to seek ways of breaking this (apparent) bind, and 1990 represents a move away from that apparent obstacle to a more popular and open form of governance which was a precondition for later transformations.

There are strong enduring patterns in Zambian political behavior, not least in an enduring political culture (Van Donge, 1995: 194). For example the "big man" syndrome, clientelism, megalomania, ethnicity, and economic mismanagement were all manifest in the political system under Kaunda, and this was not simply a politics of the center. It was reflected at lower levels of party and government structures. This kind of political culture proved highly resistant to more transparency or accountability, perhaps not surprisingly. At the same time, as Burnell has suggested, Zambia was a haven of political stability in a very troubled region (Burnell, 2002: 1107). So too was Kenya—save for the early 1990s' politically-instigated "ethnic" clashes, the surprising 2007/08 post-election violence, and the recent threats of terrorism due to Nairobi's political-military cohabitation with the United States and Britain. The former British colonies (Northern Rhodesia and British East Africa), each ruled by a strong man president after independence in 1963 (Kenya) and 1964 (Zambia), were among the first African countries to repeal their constitutions and to embrace multiparty politics in 1991. These moves included the imposition of presidency term-limits. Whereas in Zambia, the former trade unionist Chiluba beat Kaunda in the 1991 multiparty election, Kenya's divided opposition twice (1992 and 1997) "voted Moi back in, in spite of the electorate voting him out."[2] Both countries created constitutional review commissions while, at the same time, the incumbents (Chiluba and Moi) realized they had given in to pressure and tried to amend the constitutions to rule beyond their two terms. In other words, the late 1990s was a turning point marked by unprecedented public debates on democracy compared to the first quarter-century after independence. This atmosphere of debate and of the potential for realizing a more effective democracy was itself one of the factors that made the transition from the "old" politics possible.

The reluctance with which incumbents opened the doors to pluralism meant that civil liberties would still not be guaranteed. Most commentators judged multiparty Zambia as a one-party dominant system, almost a *de facto* one-party state (Burnell, 2002: 1106) under the Movement for Multiparty Democracy (MMD) that returned to power—albeit with the compelled retirement of President Chiluba in favor of his former Vice President Levy Mwanawasa—in the December 2001 general election. It could be said that a similar predominant-party-system existed in Kenya until President Moi's Kenya African National Union (KANU), which had ruled since 1963 independence, was unseated by the now deeply wrangling National Rainbow Coalition (NARC) in the December 2002 general election. While one could detect a shift in power within a ruling elite, this represented only a limited opening of the elite, and certainly not a movement towards a more ideal form of democracy. On the other hand, it did register a shift in so far as it marked a move towards a more open form of government and towards a greater involvement of press and public. There was a sense in each country that, if not fully accountable, government was nonetheless more accountable than had hitherto been the case.

Kenya

In the Kenya of the 1960s and up to around the mid-1980s, "clear norms and procedures were evolved for regulating the relationship between state and society—norms that were accepted by both the rulers and the ruled, and that remained constant over time" (Barkan, 1992: 168). This relatively authoritarian system of governance made sense in a patriarchal and relatively traditional society, although it frustrated the dream of fuller democracy, which had been part of the struggle for independence in many people's minds. Both social and political stability seemed to be guaranteed by this order; but there were considerable costs to be borne. Not least, this form of political order in effect encouraged the growth of an endemic pattern of corruption at all levels of administration. Although corruption is a deeply embedded social malaise permeating every sphere of life in both Kenya and Zambia, it is the high-level official corruption that has had the most devastating effects on the economies and the people. Apart from being repeatedly ranked among the top most corrupt nations by Transparency International, Kenya had a crucial $205 million loan suspended in 1997 by the International Monetary Fund (IMF) due to corruption. The IMF's action resulted in the slashing or stopping of aid by other multilateral lenders, like the World Bank, and by bilateral donors.

At the same time, much of the effort to maintain the existing system and to resist the pressure for a more democratic system of government centred on the established parties of the ruling elite. This necessitated the prevention of the emergence of new political parties and movements. But this could also be counterproductive. The Kenyan government's banning of the Kenya People's Union (KPU) in 1969 and the subsequent period of *de facto* one-party state could have planted the seeds for multiparty struggle. In 1982, then Constitutional Affairs Minister Charles Njonjo rushed through Parliament a bill, seconded by then Vice President Mwai Kibaki, that made Kenya a *de jure* one-party state. They did this to counter attempts by George Anyona and Jaramogi Oginga Odinga to form a political party. This action in turn precipitated the fight for political pluralism and the expansion of democratic space in the country.

However it is fair to say that the fight for pluralism continued with its aspiration unsatisfied and its leaders, including many journalists, gaoled or exiled or otherwise neutralized, until transformation elsewhere in the world provided additional impetus for change. Fear of economic sanctions from multilateral donor institutions and bilateral Western donor nations had some impact. But the transformation of the global political and social environment associated with the ending of the Cold War was the most significant change. It is not an exaggeration to say that the transition to democracy in Europe had a compelling effect on the expectations of many African people, but also on their sense of what was possible. If Poland or even, in a limited way, Russia, could seem to become democracies accountable to their people, running open economies and removing an old and deeply entrenched (and deeply corrupt) elite, then surely such changes could happen anywhere. In the Cold War era, corrupt African leaders were propped up by their Western "allies" if they had the "right" credentials as opponents of "communism" and its influence. After 1990, it became apparent both that western governments' priorities had shifted and that new threats had overtaken communism. Some of those threats could best be countered, it seemed to be felt in western capitals, by abandoning the old allies and looking for changed political structures. It is wrong to say that African democratization was dictated from outside, but foolish to ignore the impetus of outside events in its emergence.

In post-1990 Kenya, a candidate has to win at least 25 percent of votes in at least five provinces before being declared President. This is designed to promote ethnic balancing. But it also promotes party alliances and coalition building. This is not seen as undesirable, but as a mechanism which, if it can work, provides a framework for a different basis for political stability than that offered in the one-party state: political stability has certainly not ceased to be a main goal of political managers and of the state.

Parties, Clientelism, and Corruption

Following the 1960 end of an eight-year state of emergency, which in turn followed a 1952 armed Mau Mau insurrection, Kenya African National Union or KANU (transformation from a district association, Kenya African Union) and Kenya African Democratic Union (KADU) were formed in 1961 for that year's election. However Kenyatta's regime triumphed in the 1963 election and took over from the British colonial authority. The new government starved KADU of state resources, and co-opted its leaders a year after independence. Following the resulting collapse of KADU, its deputy leader, Daniel arap Moi, was made KANU's vice president. Kenya became a *de facto* one-party state. Kenya's Socialist-leaning Vice President, Jaramogi Oginga Odinga, resigned, protesting against Kenyatta's capitalist *modus operandi*. He formed the Kenya People's Union (KPU) in 1965. But Odinga and 29 other defectors from KANU were forced to seek a renewal of their mandate in the Little General Election of 1969 in which 20 of the dissenters lost their seats. KPU was then banned in 1969, making Kenya a *de facto* one-party state once again. Complementing Kenyatta's commitment to a professionally run single-party state was Kenyatta's tolerance of a relatively free press and the emergence of autonomous associational life, as long as they did not challenge Kenyatta's authority directly (Barkan, 1992: 174).

Thus within these norms of permissibility, a wide range of associational life made its presence felt in Kenyan society. These included professional associations and economic interest groups such as the Law Society of Kenya, the Chamber of Commerce, the Kenya Manufacturers Association, the Kenya Farmers Association, and the Central Organization of Trade Unions. It also included church organizations of various denominations. Kenyan-based NGOs such as the National Council of Churches of Kenya, *Maendeleo ya Wanawake* (the Women's Development Association) emerged. Powerful ethnic welfare associations, including the Gikuyu Embu Meru Association (GEMA) and the Luo Union played a significant role in social and political life. And community self-help development organizations, known as *Harambee*, evolved (Barkan, 1992: 175). It is therefore fair to say that there was a great diversity of social organizations and civil society organizations (CSOs) of different kinds. But all this was under the condition that they engaged in politics only in a limited way, and that they did not come to be seen as a direct threat of any kind to the existing regime and the elite the regime supported.

Whereas professional and economic associations served mainly urban constituencies, a distinctive feature of other associations was the extent to which they established linkages between the Kenyan state and rural society. On the one hand, these organizations broadened the social base of the Kenyatta regime. On the other hand, they served as counterweights to the state and fostered a process of bargaining and mutual accommodation between the regime and civil society (Barkan, 1992: 175). Thus, although Kenyatta's regime was an authoritarian one, especially during its latter years, and while he ruthlessly repressed any direct challenge, it was not a system marked by the excesses of personal rule found elsewhere in Africa and later in Kenya itself. Kenyatta never sought to monopolize all sources of authority, and he did not fear the emergence of a social debate across the nation, providing its political impact was muted (Barkan, 1992: 175).

When Kenyatta died in office in August 1978, Vice President Moi took over as the constitution required. But he was faced with serious economic pressures. "The end of the world coffee boom in 1979, the dramatic rise in the price of imported oil in 1980/81, the world recession of 1981/82, and the continuation of a 3.9 percent annual rate of population growth combined to slow 15 years of economic advance. Severe droughts in 1979–80 and again in 1984, which necessitated large importation of food, further complicated the economy" (Barkan, 1992: 178). Despite these pressures, and partly in response to them, Moi embraced a populist approach to governing based on what he termed his *Nyayo* (initially Kenyatta's footsteps then his own from 1979) philosophy of "peace, love and unity."

As part of this approach, Moi cracked down on corruption, ordered ethnic associations like GEMA to wind up, focused attention on the small tribes that had been in his defunct KADU, and adopted personal rule. "Public debate of new policy initiatives was discouraged and ultimately forbidden. Only praise was acceptable" (Barkan, 1992: 180). By 1982, the semi-free press that had operated throughout Kenyatta's tenure came under intense pressure and began to practice self-censorship as KANU established its own newspaper, the *Kenya Times* (Barkan, 1992: 180). A process of gradual but significant closing down of channels of communication and debate took place.

After the elections of 1983, dissenting MPs—who did not *fuata nyayo* (toe the Moi line)—were expelled from KANU and the legislature.

"With uncertainty came both fear of the president and sycophancy to ward off his suspicion" (Barkan, 1992: 180). The system became increasingly monarchical, and often increasingly arbitrary in its use of power. To consolidate his powers, Moi put in motion institutional changes such as the measure already mentioned of getting parliament to amend the constitution to make the country a *de jure* one-party state in May 1982 (in response to Odinga's attempt to form an opposition party in the 1980s). The resulting press criticism and an attempted military coup that August only made the regime more manipulative and repressive (Barkan, 1992: 180).

From then onwards, leaders viewed as a threat to Moi such as Charles Njonjo, the former Attorney General (and then Constitutional Affairs Minister), and G. G. Kariuki, Minister of State in the Office of the President, and former Vice President Mwai Kibaki (now the President), were hounded out of office, and removed from the party and parliament by the KANU machinery. Some, like the prominent Kikuyu politician Kenneth Matiba and former Nairobi Mayor Charles Rubia, were detained after calling for the abolition of the one-party state following their expulsion from KANU (Barkan, 1992: 181). It is against these significant levels of authoritarian and arbitrary uses of power that the subsequent moves towards democratization mapped later in this thesis need to be measured.

Zambia

By contrast, democratization in Zambia can be considered a success story—or much more than a success story. It is reasonable to suggest that democratic culture has been more evident in the behavior of the Zambian political elite at least in some respects from the beginning (Van Donge, 1995: 193). This cultural basis in the elite has been important since independence, although one cannot say that Zambian politics has altogether lacked some of the features that have characterized Kenyan party and intra-elite relations. Formerly "Northern Rhodesia," Zambia became the 36th independent African country on October 24, 1964, when it also became the 20th member of the Commonwealth. Compared to Kenya, Zambia is sparsely populated, although the urban areas have a high density of population and a high level of political and social exchange and communication.

It did not take long before Kaunda's rule degenerated into urban riots in protest against rising food prices, which led to more serious instability, with some clashes like the one in 1987 resulting in 15 deaths (van Donge, 1995: 197). But the balance between perceived stability and perceived central control was different in Zambia compared to Kenya. Thus there were several coup attempts. The most important one in 1980 was foiled at the last minute (Van Donge, 1995: 197).

One of the most important factors in Zambian political difficulties has been the very high level of dependence on copper exports. This in turn makes the polity dependent on world copper prices. The disastrous decline—especially since the mid-1970s—of copper prices has seriously impaired the underlying strength of the Zambian economy (van Donge, 1995: 198). It has also had an impact on the very considerable growth of international indebtedness, and on the government's ability to deliver on promises, and expectations of increasing welfare. As these pressures piled on, two trade unionists called for a referendum on the one-party state in February 1990 and Kaunda consented two months later, a month ahead of the formation of the MMD. This new political party, featuring prominent lawyers like Roger Chongwe and Levy Mwanawasa, as well as trade unionists like Frederick Chiluba of the Zambian Congress of Trade Unions (ZCTU), took centre stage in the opening up of political activity away from the established parties. On November 30, 1990, parliament voted to re-introduce multipartyism (see Ihonvbere, 1995 and 1996; Rakner, 2003).

In the elections of October 31, 1991, Chiluba and the MMD won 125 of the 150 parliamentary seats. Only a quarter of the voters (24.2%) voted for Kaunda. Turnout at the polls was low (45%)—due to a defective registration system and to voter apathy (Van Donge, 1995: 202). Nonetheless, even if the result was hardly a ringing endorsement of the new party and its incoming government, it was a decisive rejection of the old established political system and the party, which had up to then predominated. From this moment onwards, an emergence of greater and more genuine democratization seemed more possible and more desirable, although it probably could not be seen as inevitable. There was also a climate that encouraged rather more debate after Kaunda had left office: the public space was more open, and the public conversation less restricted, relatively speaking.

In 1995, the Zambian constitution was amended to read that "non-indigenous" Zambians could not contest presidential elections; and that both parents of a candidate must be native-born Zambians. This was to bar Kenneth Kaunda, whose parents were born in Malawi. The aim was to ensure that Kaunda did not contest the elections and that Chiluba be re-elected in 1996.

General Observations and Comparisons

To some early 1970s observers, Kenya was a post-independent African political and economic "success story"—one of the most stable and open societies in Africa (Bienen, 1974: 3; Kaplan et al., 1976: 213). To others—especially western nations pursuing strategic political interests, Kenya was until as recently as the early 1990s a "beacon of success," an "economic miracle," and "a showpiece of economic prosperity and political stability," before the burnished image became tarnished almost overnight (Haugerud, 1997: 4).

Kenya is an atypical African country. It does not exhibit patterns of coup and countercoup[3] that characterize a number of African states, and it is relatively well endowed (Bienen, 1974: 195). It has had a relatively stable social structure, and sophisticated elite, and quite significant economic resources (including the bases for a strong tourism industry). Unlike Zambia, it is not dependent on a single crop or commodity, although coffee exports have been an important source of external earnings.

Kenya had a politics that involved more participation both at local and national levels, and among elites and non-elites alike, than most African states (Bienen, 1974: 195). It had the preconditions for a move towards a more open democracy, including a tradition of debate and dissent in the political culture. Although the political leadership looked for deference, the political culture was not deferential as they might have wished.

Postcolonial Kenya opted for national capitalist economic development rather than for an emphasis on redistribution. This policy was based on a determination to retain ties to Western countries and companies, and to gain foreign aid and investment. This thus encouraged private ownership and the growth of a middle class (Bienen, 1974: 3–4; Kaplan et al., 1975: 213; Ajulu, 1998; Throup and Hornsby, 1998: 3). In turn, this had effects on patterns of social and political communication: there were more channels of communication and there was more demand for communication in the political system as a result of this social formation.

Aid conditions by the United States and the World Bank were also relatively favorable. Kenya has always been the most favored for British aid in Africa (Throup and Hornsby, 1998). Set against this, one must emphasize that the political economies of both Kenya and Zambia have been dependent on multilateral and bilateral donors as well as on MNCs (Nzomo, 1994). Kenya's growth has always been a hostage to levels of foreign investment, aid, and other external items like tourism. Critics, including Kenya's own first Vice President Oginga Odinga, in his book *Not Yet Uhuru* (1967), have pointed out how seriously this was limiting the development of autonomous business and autonomous economic development. These disadvantages are not redressed by the continuing high profile of Kenya in the western media (Throup and Hornsby, 1998: 1), although western attention to Kenyan developments, both successful and unsuccessful, could be said to give the country an advantage over other more ignored African societies.

It is worth setting these political, social, and economic development patterns in the context of overarching political philosophies articulated by the ruling elites. *Harambee*, Kiswahili for "let's pull together," was a rallying call to pool resources for self-help (Thomas, 1985). This happened through funding drives across the country. But too often, funds looted from public coffers were given to politicians. The Moi government wanted to win elections so that they could "donate" parts of this funding for development projects in their areas and thus become popular. Moi combined Kenyatta's *harambee* with his own ambiguous motto, *Nyayo*—the shortened form of *fuata nyayo*, Kiswahili for "toe the line."[4]

These political events unfolded within the context of a formal set of relationships between the state and state power. It has been said that the African state, from the beginning of colonialism, was charged with the duty of establishing and maintaining "law, order and good government" (Atieno-Odhiambo, 1987, citing Allot). The evolving nature of the African state has promoted a burgeoning literature, much of it very critical. One of the things that we can say Zambia and Kenya have in common is that they are not characterized, and have not even nearly been characterized, by failing statehood. It may be that state power has been used unwisely at times, and on occasions dictatorially too. But the framework of state, law, and authority has remained intact, and has provided a jurisdictional and political continuity from independence.

The political process, having been participatory in the era of decolonization, had found itself depoliticized and canalized into mainline one-partyism, as well as into personal loyalty to the presidency. This regimentation has involved increased control by the state of the political processes, legally, administratively, or at times extra-legally. In sum, there is regime control of the rights to free speech and assembly, the agenda of parliament, voluntary associations, and party politics, particularly in Kenya. This might betoken a problem that the state is too strong rather than "failing." These impositions have had to contend with the struggles of institutions and individuals, who have fallen back on the received notions of democracy and the traditions of dissent to contest their legitimacy (Atieno-Odhiambo, 1987: 189). Control largely rested in the hands of a leader and his authoritarianism, aided and supported by a small group around him with strong ethnic ties with each other (Bienen, 1974: 3–4; Throup and Hornsby, 1998: 3). This created a structure of politics that has been characterized by what one author has described as the ruling elite's "benevolent elitism."[5] This pattern of authority cannot be wholly detached from the colonial past: Kenya was under the control of a strong neo-colonial elite influence. Patterns of administrative style, language, social discipline, and authority carried over from the polity before independence. This, together with a parasitical elite of top politicians and civil servants bereft of any conception of development, or even of national interest and dignity, or a sense of nationhood, shaped the emergence of a strong but corrupt centralized political apparatus (Bienen, 1974: 4–5). They arrogated to themselves the wisdom to choose the development path on the grounds that citizens were ignorant. "Curtailing effective mass participation is thus justified. Organized dissent is not allowed and the heavy hand of civil administration and, if need be, police and riot squads are used to put down opposition" (Bienen, 1974: 5). Paternalism certainly did not end with formal decolonization. And the paternalism of Kaunda and Kenyatta, although modified, did not disappear with their removal from the political stage.

This was so despite tensions that led to the ban on the opposition KPU in 1969, and the assassination in the same year of the popular politician Tom Mboya, which later led to direct demonstrations against Kenyatta resulting in turn in the police killing 43 protesters in Mboya's regional town of Kisumu. Earlier in 1965, radical Asian politician Pio Gama Pinto had also been assassinated. The attempted coup in March 1971, and the assassination in mid-1975 of Josiah Mwangi Kariuki, a popular figure within the opposition wing of KANU, can also be traced directly to reaction against the forms and impacts of state power at the time. These actions on the part of the ruling elite and its henchpersons seem to have had profoundly contradictory effects, for they were devised to ensure the continuation of the ruling party and the stability of the system it maintained, but could at the same time be seen as undermining both.

All the same, in many estimates, "Kenya's politics had been noteworthy for the continued tolerance by the government to a considerable degree of public criticism of its leaders and programmes...the press and the members of parliament felt free to criticize, condemn, and call for major changes" (Kaplan et al., 1975: 214). This judgment may be seen as somewhat generous, but it does capture one dimension of openness in the Kenyan polity. The same author suggests that the large and weakly organized single ruling party, KANU, "was open enough to contain nearly all shades of Kenyan political opinion" (Kaplan et al., 1975: 214). An adherence to the practice of secrecy and collegiality kept from public view the method of operation within Kenyatta's cabinet that exercised effective political control of national power (Kaplan et al., 1975: 214). This was reflected in the closeness, as well as the closedness, of the inner elite. Bienen (1974: 21–2) argues that "the Kenyan regime 'works' for a large number of Kenyans despite the gross disparities in power and income between individuals and groups,"[6] and that "Kenya is a participant society in important respects despite a curtailing of political competition and a fall-off in voting turnout." He claims that "Kenya's leaders are sensitive to rural demands despite the real limits on participation that exist," and that despite myriad economic and political problems "Kenya has maintained a stability of regime" as the ruler–ruled relationship "remained relatively unchanged in the decade since independence." While this is a reasonably accurate picture, it is hardly a desirable one, and it points to the context of clientelism, corruption, and the detachment of many people from their government and from politics altogether, which characterized both countries under one party rule and its often very watered down alternative up to the mid-1990s. Nonetheless, Kenyan politics appears more stable and more capable of satisfying people's aspiration when compared to some other countries in the region.

It was the formation of classes and new class fragments that would affect stability. Kaplan et al. (1975: 213) observe that from around 1975, the country "was certainly facing newly strengthened forces of dissent" over government policies, especially "disagreement over the distribution of political power and economic gain in the modernised centre of the society." New cleavages were slowly beginning to replace the basic political division along ethnic lines. Kenya became an increasingly authoritarian state during the 1980s and the ruling party, KANU, developed into a key apparatus of political control—harassing dissenting politicians, church leaders, and lawyers who dared criticize it (Widner, 1992; Throup and Hornsby, 1998: 3). But this could not contain the emergence of new groups, most significantly in the larger cities, for the emergence of a stronger middle class and of more active political groups especially in the urban environment helped to bring about change despite the domination of old elite single-party politics.

Nyangira (1987) has argued that both ethnicity and class are important in gaining a balanced view of politics in Kenya. Turning first to class, Kitching (1980: 453) argues that "the structural situation of the rich, the poor and the middling groups in Kenya's distribution of income and wealth justifies theoretically the view not only that Kenya's ruling class is a petit bourgeoisie, but that Kenya is predominantly a petit-bourgeois society and economy." Kitching however modifies his theoretical approach and points out that Kenya's society cannot be divided into what he views as Althusserian Marxist class analysis of "exploiters" or (bourgeoisie or capitalist class) and the "exploited" (proletariat or working class). Engaging with the debate in the writings of other Kenyanist scholars points to the triangular relationships between the Kenyan bourgeoisie, external capital, and the state—with the last playing at least a significant, and sometimes a dominant, role.[7]

The Kenyatta regime inherited a state, but it also inherited a society characterized by class contradictions. The representatives of various class interests saw in the state a potential instrument for extending the hegemony of their specific class interests on the rest of society (Atieno-Odhiambo, 1987: 190). Together with these specific concerns, the ideology and practice of "regime-building" shaped a quest by the leading elite for hegemony by the state in all spheres of national life (1987: 191). Goran Hyden argues that in a peasant society such as Kenya, where the economic base is fragmented, "the most common political response to these structural contradictions has been to create a unified, usually coercive political superstructure" (Atieno-Odhiambo, 1987: 191). This suggests that the countryside, as well as the cities, were characterized by increasing diversity of wealth, consumption, and expectations.

Turning to questions of ethnicity and diversity, Zambia is one of the most ethnically and linguistically heterogeneous nations in southern Africa, with 73 distinct ethnic groups and over 80 identifiable languages, including seven official languages (Reynolds, 1999: 42). The four main cultural groups are: (1) The Bemba (Chiluba's tribe), dominant in the Northern, Copperbelt, and Luapula provinces; (2) The Nyanja (Kaunda's tribe), originally from the East, now majority in Central Province and the capital, Lusaka; (3) The Tonga, from the agricultural south; (4) The Lozi of the Western Province. Despite this cultural and ethnic diversity, Zambia avoided "significant inter-ethnic strife" throughout the First and Second Republics (1964–91).[8] Ethnic differences have always shaped political behavior, and have often been sources of conflict, which has challenged the stability of government and state alike. Chiluba's MMD came to power in 1991, riding a multi-ethnic backlash against Kaunda's failed one-party state. But Chiluba's administration quickly opened up ethnic and regional cleavages that had been successfully contained by Kaunda's policy of "regional balancing," which had been a transparent effort to balance tribal differences rather than a simple geographic formula. The majoritarian electoral system provided the incentives for increased ethnic mobilization and polarization (Reynolds, 1999: 274). As a result, Zambia went ahead with multiparty elections in November 1996 with a fragmented and ethnically based party system. This gave an impression of ethnic breakdown of the pattern that has occurred in other states in central Africa and the Great Lakes region, but that conclusion goes much too far and is oversimplified. It is true that Chiluba's cabinet was increasingly dominated by Bemba ministers. Furthermore, the deeply flawed 1996 general elections did not merely illustrate general alienation from the political system (only 28% of the voting age population turned out to vote), but Kaunda's Nyanja-based United National Independence Party (UNIP) retained the sympathies of the Eastern Region even though they boycotted the official vote (Reynolds, 1999: 275). Thus provincial and ethnic distrust continue to complicate and undermine the give and take of democratic competition in Zambian multiparty politics (Reynolds, 1999: 40–4). But this was a challenge rather than a breakdown to both state and society.

Kenya is one of the countries where ethnic hostilities have increased, and become electorally codified, as elite entrepreneurs react to the new incentives of a winner-take-all multiparty constitutional dispensation (Reynolds, 1999: 274). Kenya has about 40 tribes; three tribes, the Kikuyu (otherwise the so-called GEMA: Gikuyu, Embu, and Meru), the Luo, and the Luhya together form about 50 percent of the African population, while two smaller tribes, the Kamba and the Kalenjin form about 10 percent of the populace. At the same time, ethnic aggregation can be misleading, for there are crosscutting cleavages within groups and mutually self-serving relations between members of different groups (Cohen, 2001). True to Moi's "prediction," the advent of multiparty politics sparked off "ethnic clashes" in the Rift Valley and coastal areas where at least 1000 people from "opposition tribes" were killed and at least 30,000 evicted from their land ahead of the 1992 general election (Cohen, 2001).

To use the language of "class" is problematic also because while it is possible to distinguish class divisions, they overrun ethnic and other divisions. Furthermore, class fragments are deeply divided against each other. Thus it has been claimed that the bourgeoisie in Kenya was factionalized, and that the factions or fragments pursued different interests in a struggle to co-opt the state. There have been several instances in which various factions have organized themselves and attempted to grab power. These have included the so-called change the constitution group, a collection of prominent politicians from Central Kenya whose objective was to amend the constitution in such a way that the vice president of the republic did not automatically assume power upon the demise of the serving president (Nyangira, 1987: 25). More recently, there was another group of prominent politicians who coalesced around Charles Njonjo, with the aim of staging a constitutional coup. Their object was to promote a vote of no confidence in the then head of state (Moi) followed by installing their man in power (Nyangira, 1987: 25). Although the support of the Kikuyu was more or less assumed automatic, the most ardent beneficiaries were just not ordinary Kikuyu, but the Kikuyu bourgeoisie who looked to him for patronage in business and in bureaucratic jobs. At this same level Njonjo received widespread support from the bourgeoisie of other ethnic groups (Nyangira, 1987: 25–6). Again, one can see that political cleavages cut across the social, ethnic, or class divisions that one might predict as the dominant factors in shaping political behavior. This is not to say that those older divisions no longer matter, but that the political context is more complex than an emphasis on either class or ethnic or regional allegiances on their own might suggest, and that this complexity has grown rather than diminished in the last twenty years.

Political Rights and Civil Liberties

Freedom House provides a composite measure of civil liberties and political rights that gives a useful guide to the trajectory of political decency and tolerance in each of the case studies (Reynolds, 1999: 31). Zambia did not manage to move into the *Free* category despite continuous periods of multiparty competition since 1991 (Table 8.1). The country was considered free during 1991–92, but state respect for individual liberties and rights rapidly worsened, returning the country to the *Partly Free* category between 1993 and 1996. In 2011, Zambia was in the *Partly Free* category.

These categorizations are imperfect, and lump together very different countries with different problems in their categories. Nonetheless, they do provide a rough but significant measure of the direction of movement of polities, and they demonstrate the fragile nature of

Table 8.1 Freedom House ratings (Political Rights, Civil Liberties, "Free" Status)

	1994	*1995*	*1996*	*1997*	*1998*	*1999*	*2000*	*2001*	*2002*
Kenya	6,6NF	7,6NF	7,6NF	6,6NF	6,5NF	6,5NF	6,5NF	6,5NF	4,4PF
Zambia	3,4PF	3,4PF	5,4PF	5,4PF	5,4PF	5,4PF	5,4PF	5,4PF	4,4PF

Source: Compiled from country data at Freedom House, www.freedomhouse.org

Notes: First figure is for Civil Liberties and second is for Political Rights; NF = Not Free; PF = Partly Free.

Table 8.2 Subjective indicators of democracy

	Polity score[a] 2000 (-10 to 10)	*Civil liberties[b] 2000 (7 to 1)*	*Political rights[b] 2000 (7 to 1)*	*Press freedom[c] 2000 (100 to 0)*	*Voice and accountability[d] 2000–01 (-2.5 to 2.5)*
Kenya	–2	5	6	70	–0.68
Zambia	1	4	5	62	–0.17

Source: Compiled from UNDP (2002: 40–1).

Note: The measures are based on different methodologies. a. University of Maryland's polity score reflects the presence of institutional factors necessary for democracy—whether laws and institutions allow democratic participation—but not the extent of participation. Scores range from –10 (authoritative) to 10 (democratic); b. Freedom House designations for civil liberties and political rights: 1–2.5 (Free, F); 3–5 (Partly Free, PF); 6–7 (Not Free, NF); c. Freedom House designates free space as follows: 0–30 (Free Press); 30–60 (Partly Free Press); 61–100 ((Not Free Press); d. The World Bank's tool based on statistical compilation of perceptions of the quality of governance, based on a survey covering a large number of respondents in industrial and developing countries as well as NGOs, commercial risk taking agencies, and think tanks. The index ranges from around –2.50 to around 2.50 (higher better). [UNDP, 2002: 41).

the limited measure of democracy in both Kenya and Zambia in the recent past as well as its imperfections.

The Kenyan elite clearly considered it unnecessary that there should be any popular political participation other than through representative government, especially through voting. This presents a very limited idea of democracy (see chapter 3) where governments are elected, but expect public conversation to be silent and the public space to be closed between elections to allow the elite to rule as they choose (see Table 8.2) (Barkan and Okumu, 1979: 27); in the eyes of the leadership, any meaningful participation beyond election day would threaten political order because the country and the people were "not ready." This is not only a rejection of any more genuine or participatory democratic form; it is also a curious echo of the language of colonial administrators into the 1950s.

2003	*2004*	*2005*	*2006*	*2007*	*2008*	*2009*	*2010*	*2011*
3,3PF	3,3PF	3,3PF	3,3PF	3,3PF	3,4PF	3,4PF	4,4PF	3,4PF
4,4PF	4,4PF	4,4PF	4,4PF	4,4PF	4,3PF	3,3PF	4,3PF	4,3PF

After the 1982 attempted coup, in a climate of political tension and immanent violence, Moi's ruling regime adopted an intimidating new set of electoral procedures, like queue-voting or *mlolongo*. At the same time, the government instituted a systematic reduction in press freedom. This containment of potential democratic aspirations lasted throughout the 1980s. But it came to clash not only with internal activism, but also with external political and economic forces. Eventually, in the changed climate of the post-Cold War years, "aid agencies imposed an aid condition requiring the government to (1) amend the Constitution to end the one-party state and allow a multiparty system; (2) establish an impartial elections board, reinstate the secret ballot, redistrict where population shifts require it, and update voter registration roles; and (3) relax direct and indirect state censorship of the press" (Cohen, 2001: 102). Other international organizations, including NGOs, put similar although less effective pressure on the regime. The conditionality pressure on Kenya was led by the US government, whose so-called rogue ambassador, Smith Hempstone, a former Texan journalist, mingled easily with local people and local CSO groups, much to the chagrin of the ruling regime.

Further pressure to democratize, and to move the existing institutions to a more genuinely and effectively democratic basis, came from other outside groups, including well-funded ones. Steered by the academic Joel Barkan, USAID's $7 million "Kenya Democracy and Governance Project" was aimed at strengthening parliament, the Auditor and Controller General's offices, and civil society, among other institutions and networks. The government showed little interest for some time, and was reluctant to add its own funding, but eventually found itself forced to adapt to at least some of these pressures (Cohen, 2001: 104). Civil society funds were used to sponsor conferences on "democracy in a multi-ethnic society," support local human rights groups in their efforts to track "state-sanctioned ethnic cleansing," and study "weaknesses in civil society," giving particular attention to the "Asian-African split" and "ethnic divisions among Africans."[9] When Smith was replaced as US ambassador, his successor, Aurela E. Brazeal, adopted a somewhat more conciliatory approach. But US pressure on Kenya did not diminish. And the German and Japanese ambassadors, along with the Australian High Commissioner, continued to exert pressure, at their governments' behest, to promote democratization (Cohen, 2001: 104).

Political change in Kenya owed something to the activities and economic and social pressures of powerful external actors, as well as to the persistence, and often the courage, of civil society activists. Many of these changes have their origins, as this discussion has suggested, well before the new media started to have a significant impact. The new media came to overlay these existing forces for change and to push the changes that had occurred significantly further.

Conclusion

In Kenya, the national movement was betrayed by postcolonial elites who were at the same time deeply rooted in colonial experience, so we can speak of them without tautology as forming a neocolonial elite. They accepted and protected—and benefited from—the norms of the old rulers, resulting in bitterness and exacerbating tribal tensions among citizens who fought and died for freedom (Bienen, 1974: 4–5). In Zambia, a ruling elite did some of the same things, although for rather different reasons and with less effective impact in stifling democracy. It is ironic, but also perhaps not surprising, that in the country with a greater tradition of social dissent of the two, Kenya, a greater effort was made to suppress dissent, while in the country with a weaker tradition of dissent, Zambia, a more open democratization came more easily. Some of these failings can certainly be attributed to the shortcomings—vanity as well as hunger for personal power—of individuals. But the political system, the institutions, and the elite fabric, all participated in the maintenance of forms of government, which worked against popular representation and open accountability. To change this was going to take a significant effort in both elite and broader society, and required a change in the terms of social and political discourse to which, it can be argued, the new media made a significant contribution.

CHAPTER 9

Civic Actors and the Struggle for Change: Precursors to New Social Movements in Kenya and Zambia

Although no harm was done as such to European or colonial officers or missionary officials, "riots and treason which took place in Zambia under the slogan of *Cha Cha Cha* caused heavy losses to public and government property" (Virmani, 1989: xiv). These marked the peak of African protest against colonial exploitation and racial oppression and defined the eventual formation of an African national party. To protest the treatment of African Christians as inferior in the eyes of the whites, a crop of Zambia's African evangelists claimed to have a link with the Watch Tower Movement (WTM) that had grown in Europe and later spread to the United States and Australia. Followers of the WTM preached disobedience of existing authority because the world was going to end so the African evangelists stressed on the disobedience of the white people's administration and the chiefs of the Native Authority. They stressed that the new world was going to start soon where the oppressed people of the black race would be the first beneficiaries and would enjoy the best things of life (Virmani, 1986: 46). A desire was cultivated among the followers of the WTM to throw away the yoke of civil authorities of the whites with the hope of curing their social and economic ills. They also demanded equality with white people (Virmani, 1986: 46). However, the WTM met opposition in part from other groups, like the Mwenzo Welfare Association in the mid-1920s. "On the whole, WTM was a weak movement... However, it had brought momentarily people of all ethnic stocks into one fold against the white colonial government and enabled the Africans to demand indigenous control over the religious matters" (Virmani, 1986: 47).

Unlike Zambia of the 1950s and 1960s where mine workers' riots and mild agitations by the African National Congress (ANC), led by Harry Nkumbula and Kenneth Kaunda, represented the main forms of opposition to colonial policies (Mulford, 1967), Kenya's was much more organized and often violent. Nyangira (1987: 16–18) examines "the era of the associations" and "ethnic alliances in national movements" from early twentieth century. Keck and Sikkink (1998: 39–78) classify efforts by Western missionaries among the Kikuyu of Kenya in 1920–31 as one of the historical precursors to modern transnational advocacy networks.[1] This qualifies for what Nortje Marres (2006: 5) calls "issue networks" given the comparison by Keck and Sikkink (Keck and Sikkink, 1998: 39–41) of these advocacies to "noncampaigns" or related issues around which activists did not organize, for instance "the absence of a campaign among other cultural groups like the Maasai that also practised female circumcision was a puzzle even to reformers at the time." One way of viewing this is that the campaign started by Protestant missionaries (especially the Church of Scotland Missionary Society, led by Dr. John Arthur) was meant to counter the equally transnational freedom struggle that manifested itself most prominently among the central Kenya communities that experienced British settlement earlier in a larger scale compared to other parts of the country. The missionaries countered freedom fighters by discrediting cultural practices associated with communities actively involved in it and using local collaborators.

The campaign, in the context of what Kenyan historian Bethwel Ogot and others recall as increasing African opposition to British colonial practices,[2] partly bred counter-movements such as the Kikuyu Central Association (KCA) (Keck and Sikkink, 1998: 69). Advocacy by the emerging young mission-educated African elites, led by Kenyatta as KCA secretary general, turned the missionary anti-cut campaign into "a symbol for colonial attempts to impose outside values and rules upon the population" (Keck and Sikkink, 1998: 70). It is worth noting that Kenyatta used his British-life experience and anthropology training at the London School of Economics in the mid-1930s to take the fight to the enemy, employing advocacy tactics such as bypassing local missionaries to present a formal petition directly at meetings in London with top Scottish Prebysterian church authorities as well as senior UK political and government leaders all of whom cherished the opportunity to hear the other side of the story from the horse's mouth (Keck and Sikkink, 1998: 70).[3] The second strategy was to use the British press. In a convincing letter to the London *Times* on five other key issues, he argued that the repression of native views was a "short-sighted tightening of the safety valve of free speech which must inevitably result in dangerous explosion—the one thing all men wish to avoid" (Keck and Sikkink, 1998: 71).[4]

Communication strategies changed on the local front, where pro-circumcision forces "circulated a satirical song that ridiculed missionaries, chiefs, and officials, and praised Kenyatta" (Keck and Sikkink, 1998: 71). The authors do not, however, mention the vernacular newspaper, *Mwigithania*. The government and missionaries, fearing a threat to public order, repressed the singers, flogging them, sentencing them to detention camps, and prohibiting public meetings (Keck and Sikkink, 1998: 71).[5]

> Kenyatta and his organisation had helped reframe the debate from one about health and Christianity to one over nationalism, land, and the integrity of traditional culture.... by the mid-twentieth century African intellectuals like Kenyatta were holding up an idealised version of the traditional past as an alternative to Western lifestyles and "progress" that they feared were inappropriate for their countries. The anti-circumcision campaign became associated with colonialism and interference, and the practice of female circumcision with independence, nationalism, and tradition. (Keck and Sikkink, 1998: 71–2)

The result was that the colonial rulers backed down on anti-cut campaign and asked its chief architect, Dr. Arthur to resign his seat on the Governor's executive council. In effect, the anti-cut campaign "was far more limited than the missionaries hoped for, and less successful than other similar campaigns" (Keck and Sikkink, 1998: 72). Emboldened locals discredited leaders associated with the missions and increased the influence and membership of KCA and similar organizations (Keck and Sikkink, 1998: 71). The ensuing struggles and tensions culminated in the Kikuyu-dominated Mau Mau uprising, one of the bloodiest and most vicious movements in the history of freedom struggle in Africa and other former Western colonial "spheres of influence."[6]

Katumanga (2003) highlights secret social movements in both the Kenyatta and Moi eras when freedom of expression and assembly were greatly curtailed. Among them were *Dini ya Musambwa*, armed groups *Shifta*, underground movements like the February 18 Movement and the December 12 Movement, which published and distributed, often in the peak of the night, newsletters such as *Pambana* (struggle), *Mwakenya*, and *Mpatanishi* (reconciliation). There were also labor-related organizations like Universities Academic Staff Union (UASU) and the Central Organization of Trade Unions (COTU).

"Third Wave" Post-1990 Social Movements: Kenya and Zambia

Compared to Zambia, Kenya's NGO arena is much more crowded. A 1998 estimate puts Kenya at the very top of Africa's four countries with the highest number of NGOs (400 NGOs) (Dicklitch, 1998: 246n3), but the number of all the various types of NGOs in Kenya was estimated at 1000 in 2002[7] with the number of those registered rising to around 6000 in 2009.[8] Although NGO-NET Africa, in a project proposal for networking NGOs in Kenya,[9] did not include political NGOs in their categorization of the sector, this is mainly because for a long time NGOs did not register or describe themselves as "political," for fear of government harassment.

In Zambia, University of Zambia student riots in the 1970s, the Law Association of Zambia, and the Economic Club intellectuals in the 1980s provided the undercurrents for the 1990s civil society organizations (CSOs). Kaunda contained their power until the 1980s through measures like cooptation of trade union leaders and government controls over trade unions, but when these strategies failed Kaunda was met with a militant trade union movement (Van Donge, 1995: 197).

In the "second liberation" struggles in Zambia, the Congress of Trade Unions and its chairman, Frederick Chiluba, successfully challenged the three-decade incumbency of President Kaunda and his United Independence Party (Gyimah-Boadi, 1997: 279). In Kenya (like in Ghana and Togo), middle-class associations of lawyers, college professors, and students were highly active in the service of democratization (Gyimah-Boadi, 1997: 279).

Significant contributions to democratization have also come from Christian churches and their national organizations acting as believable and credible voices in bruising political battles. In Kenya in 1992, 15 Catholic bishops, together with 6 top officials of the National Council of Churches of Kenya (NCCK), called on President Moi and told him to his face: "Unless you change your policies, Kenya will not be KANU but a cemetery for thousands of its sons and daughters... Whether you like it or not, the truth is that the people have lost confidence in you and those close to you." Three weeks later, the bishops repeated that Moi had no legitimate claim to power (Ranger and Vaughan, 1993: 262).[10] The NCCK had been in the forefront of opposition to the authoritarianism of President Moi and his ruling party, KANU. The NCCK was an early and vocal critic of the lack of a secret ballot. Anglican bishops Manases Kuria,

Alexander Muge, and Henry Okullu earned a reputation as advocates of political change when they disagreed publicly with the conclusions of a government investigation into the causes of the 1990 "Saba Saba" (Kiswahili for "Seven Seven" or 7th July) riots in Nairobi and called for the release of two opposition politicians who had been detained for their alleged involvement in these riots (Gyimah-Boadi, 1997: 279). The Kenyan churches also played a key role in the Ufungamano consensus initiative and the Safari Park peace brokerage.

In Zambia, the churches have also acted as mediators. For instance when the Movement for Multiparty Democracy (MMD) threatened to boycott talks over constitutional matters, Law Association of Zambia (LAZ) and church leaders got them to resume dialogue with United National Independence Party (UNIP) (Van Donge, 1995: 202). Christian groups and Episcopal conferences in Zambia (like in Ghana and Nigeria) also actively fought authoritarianism and supported democratization (Gyimah-Boadi, 1997: 279).

The post-1990s CSOs in both countries have employed a number of tactics to strengthen their role in agitating for change. Like in Peru (Scurrah, 1996: 170), the tactics employed by NGOs have contributed to the undermining of national institutions. NGOs have been effective at developing links and networks involving local, regional, national, and international actors. Thus, when pressures within the country have been unsuccessful they have often been able to generate pressures and influences on foreign governments and international institutions to obtain the desired results from national governments (Scurrah, 1996: 170). Scholars (VeneKlasen, 1996: 222) have argued that donor dependence generates competition among many NGOs and makes them reluctant to build alliances, but in Kenya and Zambia collaboration—sometimes explicitly encouraged by donors—thrived. For instance the Oasis Forum in Zambia brought together different CSOs to put pressure on Chiluba to abandon his bid for a third-term presidency ahead of the 2001 general election. In Kenya, the Institute for Education in Democracy (IED) worked with the Catholic Justice and Peace Commission (CJPC) and NCCK to monitor the 1997 general election under the motto, "Together for Peaceful Elections."

Borrowing from global CSOs tactics such as reification and demonization of a common "enemy" and focus on a single issue (Patomaki, 2012), Kenyan and Zambian CSOs seemed to have succeeded where they took a largely common stand on a particular issue. For instance, Kenya's CSOs only succeeded when, together with opposition political parties, they specifically called for a repeal of Section 2A of the Constitution to allow multiparty electoral democracy.

Apart from national advocacy, political NGOs carry out civic education activities around the country—including in the rural areas for which they justify the use of donor funds on expensive four-wheel-drive vehicles. The aim as in Peru (Scurrah, 1996: 166) is usually to "enable the poor and marginalized [and less educated] people to develop the skills and resources which will enable them to become 'citizens' and participate effectively in the promotion and defence of their own interests and of the well-being of society as a whole." For instance, to realize its vision of "an informed and democratic society where all citizens participate effectively" in politics among other spheres, Kenya's IED has been at the forefront of civic and voter education. In the run-up to the 1997 general election, they produced widely distributed posters—one of them showing how to mark the ballot paper correctly. They also produced a video, *Utaratibu wa Kupiga Kura* (Swahili for *Polling Procedure*), which was aired on the eve of the poll by both the KBC and the KTN. Apart from civic and voter education, paralegal training is often conducted in both countries. In Kenya, for example, the *Muungano wa Wanavijiji* slum dwellers project was conducted by two NGOs, *Kituo cha Sheria* and *Mazingira* Institute (Ngunyi, 2003). Ahead of the 2001 elections in Zambia, 11 CSOs[11] collaborated with the Electoral Commission of Zambia (ECZ) to form a National Voter Education Committee (NVEC) funded by the Norwegian aid agency, NORAD. Of course in reaching out to the rural folk some Kenyan and Zambian NGOs have, like in Peru, adopted paternalistic, dependent or patron–client relationship, and sometimes generated conflicts and dissatisfaction with "democracy" (Scurrah, 1996: 165–6). However, Kenya's CJPC point out that they adopt the "respectful intervention model, where participants are drawn from the grassroots, trained as trainers and sent back for multiplier effects" (IED et al., 1998: 22).

Civic participation as a function of the work of civil society formations in Kenya has gradually developed from a state of political departicipation in the 1980s to active civic engagement in the 1990s (Ngunyi, 2003). An overall assessment of civic education in rural Kenya shows that levels of civic competence have been enhanced significantly. This is however only at the level of *subjective competence* where the individual believes that they are capable of influencing the actions of government. Levels of *actual competence* where the individual actually influences the actions of government in a specific area are still low. Similarly, the individual in the rural setting feels competent to influence the municipal government only. "Asked whom they believed they had capacity to influence, almost all our respondents named the local chief, his assistant and the municipal councilor. Most of them observed that they were incapable of influencing the actions of government at the district, provincial and national levels" (Ngunyi, 2003). In Zambia, CSO civic education activities—including drama shows—have resulted in greater citizens' knowledge and values (Bratton and Temba, 1999).

Another tactic is "mass action" or mass-based demands for political action or changes. Mass action in Kenya was in the form of sustained strikes and civil disobedience. The massive street demonstrations, especially in the early 1990s, were spearheaded by the National Convention Executive Council (NCEC). They often resulted in Moi's government giving in to some concessions in the political game.

Although analysts (Throup and Hornsby, 1998: 2) rightly point out the other (f)actors, that included other forms of internal pressure (for instance economic-ethnic dissent from the Kikuyu) and Western bilateral and multilateral donor conditions (especially the United States and the World Bank), urban CSOs were the focal point of funding (for donors) and activity (for the masses)—often through "mass action" that sometimes got out of control and turned violent. Their nature at that time allowed them to carry more legitimacy than openly ethnic groups or party-like political groupings and they could go further than diplomacy would allow donor representatives. However, when the CSOs had played their part and left the real political battle to real politicians in the 1992 general election, the fragmented opposition political parties, whose birth marked partial success of civic activism, derailed the liberation train—handing victory to KANU against whom a majority of electors voted. A united and focused opposition, as happened in the latter election in 2002, would have made KANU vote rigging much more difficult. "The opposition was divided, defeated and humbled, and during the 1993–4 the ruling party gradually developed a strategy which ensured that it would dominate electoral politics until the millennium" (Throup and Hornsby, 1998: 2). With regard to Zambia, Burnell (2001) highlights the weakness of the political opposition amidst attempts by CSOs to change the status quo of a dominant ruling party.

As well as the strengths over political parties, the CSOs in both Kenya and Zambia have weaknesses that make it difficult for them to play a meaningful role in the democratization process. Like Gyimah-Boadi (1997: 280) puts it, "pressure from civil society has seldom been strong enough to bring wrongdoers to book." Katumanga (2003) argues that although Kenya's NCEC (through mass action) was able to force the regime to initiate dialogue with the opposition and civil society formations, it did not succeed in engendering state commitment to the letter and spirit of accords emergent out of these engagements. Due to poor capitalization, mushrooming popular press in Nairobi are hampered by debilitating libel suits from scandalized politicians, low professionalism, and sometimes confiscation of their papers—as well as those of the major dailies—from street vendors by use of draconian laws.

CSOs in civil society must navigate between the forces at play. Neither the state nor civil society is homogenous and conflict-free. CSOs may find allies in different tiers of government depending on the matter in question, sometimes seeking assistance from parties and politicians, at other times accessing the resources of the bureaucracy. "Civil society itself is by no means a unified force . . . [it is] . . . a meeting place—sometimes a battleground—for people and organisations with widely different aims. They seek allies but not doubt find opponents as well" (Jørgensen, 1996: 40). As we have seen elsewhere, even some respected media actors often aligned themselves with the ruling elite. The Kenyan churches are as divided over political legitimacy as they are over theology—and over whether Moi's Kenya is Paradise or Purgatory. While the Catholics and Anglicans were agitating for change, the leader of the African Redeemed Gospel Church preached in front of his tribesman Moi, announcing that "in heaven it is like Kenya has been for many years. There is only one party—and God never makes a mistake" (Ranger and Vaughan, 1993: 262).[12] Moi upstaged the NCEC and other lobby groups by convincing the principal opposition parties to abandon them and join an inter-party parliamentary group (IPPG) tasked with negotiating a minimum package of reforms, which facilitated opposition participation in the 1997 general election and provided for constitutional review but gave Moi power over the Constitution of Kenya Review Commission (CKRC). One opposition politician, Kenneth Matiba who remained uneasily allied to the NCEC was known to be wary of their "more radical agenda as he was dismissive of its primarily academic, professional and middle-class leadership" (Southall, 1999: 101).

Under further pressure, the Moi government formed a 25-member interparty parliamentary committee (IPPC), chaired by the attorney-general, to suggest changes to the Constitution of Kenya Review Commission Act 1997, with NCEC still marginalized, while the churches opted to work within the official process, before conceding to pressure and take part in the Safari Park I and II meetings under the expanded IPPC. (Southall, 1999: 102–3). Ahead of the 1991 vote, the Zambia Independent Monitoring Team (ZIMT) under the leadership of former Kaunda golf partner David Phiri and supported by the British government was accused of impartiality so the churches formed the Zambian Elections Monitoring Coordinating Committee (ZEMCC) under the leadership of Rev. John Mambo of the Church of God. It worked closely with the Carter Centre and other monitors and was supported by LAZ, Women's Lobby Group, and the Press Association of Zambia (Van Donge, 1995: 207).

Another problem is that of representation. The handful of Zambia's politically significant civic associations is concentrated in Lusaka. They cannot claim to be representative of half of the country's population living in rural areas or to have strong organiational networks there (Burnell, 2001a: 207). A similar scenario is discernible in Kenya. "The NCEC is heavily Nairobi-centred, without organic linkage to mass support outside the capital and the major urban centeres" (Southall, 1998: 110).

As Schmitter (1997) points out, civil society can contribute to democratic consolidation if other institutions are also favorable and if civil society actors behave in a "civil way." In the late July 2004 "executive coup," the Kenyan government pandered to political expediency and ignored its voter mandate in a bid to calm intra-party squabbling by appointing to the cabinet opposition politicians from former President Moi's party and "demoting" anti-graft czar, John Githongo, from the Office of the President but President Kibaki only rescinded the latter decision more due to donor pressure than due to civil society agitation that dominated political sphere following the reshuffle. Commentators writing in a local daily and online, while happy about the Kibaki about-turn, expressed deep disappointment that it was a result of external rather than domestic pressure.[13]

Political heavyweights that control the police and criminal intelligence still wield power. Like other freedom fighters, the church leaders had to face the consequences of their popular actions. While Okullu died quietly in 2004 after witnessing partial achievements of his campaigns for justice and fairness, Muge was killed at the height of political tensions in a mysterious and suspicious road accident coincidentally after he openly defied a politician's public warning of dire consequences if he visited the politician's geographical sphere of political influence. The fate that befell Okullu also later caught up with another priest, American-born Father Kaiser who also died in a highly suspicious road accident after he was publicly involved in "justice fight" for victims of the early 1990s "ethnic clashes" and for a girl who had been raped by a powerful minister in Moi's cabinet but whose family was being bribed to drop Kaiser-supported rape charges by the Federation of Women Lawyers (FIDA)-Kenya.

Post-transition, retreat or dissipation of CSOs as funding run out, activists settled down to daily survival exigencies in harsh economic conditions, and the usual ethnic and other divisions take over (Schmitter, 1997). After initial agitation especially by the churches, professional interest groups, and human development NGOs around 1990, CSOs in Kenya retreated and left the battle to politicians who squandered the chance and lost to the incumbent regime in the 1992 general election. "In fact, were it not for the rise of the Democracy and Governance (DG) sector of civil society comprising of human rights groups, the democratic initiative driven from civil society would have probably died" (Ngunyi, 2003).

Although CSOs led protests in Africa, it is the class of excluded political elite with experience in past cabinets "but who had a falling out with the head of state and had been consigned to the political wilderness at some point" who emerged during the transition to take control of new governments (van de Walle, 2001: 240). Even so-called outsiders often had extensive links with the authoritarian state. "For example, in Zambia, Fred Chiluba, a long-time unionist did not have cabinet experience, but much of the rest of the MMD leadership did" (van de Walle, 1999: 240—citing Patrick Quantin). Little wonder that "Zambia's democratic reputation has been tarnished by evidence of the government's continuing authoritarian proclivities and various abuses of its power" (van de Walle, 1999: 249)[14]—due to weak reforms.

One issue that seriously limits CSO activities in both countries is their funding. Like in Peru (Scurrah, 1996: 170), most NGOs are overwhelmingly dependent upon external funding for their financial survival. This means they are subject to the often subtle pressures of the funders to promote their agendas for the country, which may or may not coincide with the priorities of the NGOs themselves or their beneficiaries (Scurrah, 1996: 170; VeneKlasen, 1996: 219). This limits their impact on the political and social priorities of their countries and the distribution of wealth and income to the poor. NGOs are heavily funded by and reliant on Western donors to the extent that, as part of what has been described as yet another "scramble" for Africa, "we can speak of the 'NGO-ization' of Kenyan society…We are not simply describing the proliferation of NGOs, but the western sponsorship of private voluntary organizations in order for them to play an increasingly pivotal role in the economic, social and political life of the country" (Hearn, 1998: 89).

A survey carried out by A. Fowler around mid-1995 indicated that the vast majority of NGOs in Kenya rely on foreign aid for more than 90 percent of their funds—resulting in the donors setting the agenda (Hearn, 1998: 98). Mutahi Ngunyi corroborates in a 1996 study:[15] "The formation of the democracy sector of civil society was the result of a partnership between the donors and local actors... between a senior and junior partner [leading to]... increasing dominance of the donor in the operations of civil society and emergence of the donor as the 'alternate' state" (Hearn, 1998: 99). Hearn points out that this raises questions of the artificiality or contrived nature of "civil society." In Ngunyi's study of eleven CSOs promoting "democracy" and human rights in Kenya, nine were donor-created or prompted (Hearn, 1998: 99). In a more recent study, Ngunyi concludes that the ability of the civil society groups to create some form of transformation is inhibited by the funding seesaw" in which the donors support an initiative today, and pull out tomorrow (Ngunyi, 2003). The fact that NGOs in Zambia orient themselves with international donors for funding present the government with a pretext to raise suspicions about their agenda, especially when they engage in criticism of the government (Burnell, 2001a: 207). Due to the weakness of their financial base, "a number of NGOs are co-opted by public money provided to them for the purpose of delivering education, healthcare and relief aid. In effect, they choose not to take part in public advocacy. They serve the government's agenda" (Burnell, 2001a: 208).

Another handicap for CSOs in both countries is the requirement that they register their details with the government, which in turn also has powers to control their finances at will. On several occasions, the Kenyan government threatened to deregister NGOs for failure to file their returns with the registrar. While these are routine procedures, governments often become malicious when it suits them. A case in point is when in 1996 the government froze the bank accounts of Zambia Independent Monitoring Team (ZIMT) and of Clean Campaign Committee (CCC), and later charged a ZIMT official with "illegal reception of foreign funds." The ZIMT official had been arrested alongside Ngande Mwanajiti of CCC for declaring that year's elections as neither free nor fair.

Conclusion

Like in Peru (Scurrah, 1996), the good-intentioned activities of NGOs in both countries have both helped as well as brought the unintended consequences of hindering the consolidation of civil society and democratic politics and political institutions.

This chapter has confirmed the ambivalence surrounding the role of CSOs in Africa, but like many things with positives and negatives it is important to point out that this category of political actors have played a key role in political transition in both Kenya and Zambia—their weaknesses notwithstanding. Without them, change would have been inconceivable. Their performance has been curtailed because of the absence of the requisite preconditions cited above. The chapter was intended to address the role of CSOs in political transformation with particular reference to Kenya and Zambia. What this chapter has not done is to connect civic–state relationships explicitly to the sphere of activity of the new media as the main focus of the book.

CHAPTER 10

Unmuzzling Old Dogs to Bark Anew Far and Wide

The media in most societies has a very important role to play in the promotion of civil society. Media organisations, whether the electronic media, the press, the Internet or other forms of communication are, in many countries around the world in general and in particular to Third World countries, powerful entities with the ability to influence the public opinion and promote issues of importance to the public.

("The Role of the Media in Promoting Democracy" programme, 14th Jan.–12th Feb. 2002, International Institute—Histadrut, Beit Berl, Kfar Saba, Israel)

Introduction

The violent raid at the Nairobi premises of the Standard Media Group in early 2006 was, like the 2007/08 post-election violence, a surprising development to Kenyans and Kenya watchers who thought the days of direct intimidation had gone. Before the dawn of the second liberation and accompanying political pluralism from the 1990s, physical and legal harassment by government officials often forced Kenyan and Zambian journalists to engage in self-censorship that enabled the state to monitor and control content for the private press, not to mention publicly owned print and broadcast media. Whereas liberal-minded citizens regularly tuned to short wave radio broadcasts on Africa by international stations like the BBC and VOA to avoid locally censored news, access to critical foreign news publications were still under government control. It was common for copies of British or US newspapers and magazines to be confiscated on arrival at the airport by security officers, especially in Nairobi.

With the arrival of donor-forced liberalization programs that included freeing the airwaves to allow FM stations as well as deregulation of the telecommunications sector in the 1990s, state stranglehold on the media loosened. Unlike in the single-party era when acquiescence was the norm with only one dominant view diffused via repressed media and every citizen expected to "follow the footsteps" of the incumbent, the internet and mobile phone era has greatly reduced state incentive to censor the media. Being what Levinson (1999: 5, 13, 14, 42) terms the "medium of media," the internet in particular has enabled the old news broadcast and print media to publish their content online to be accessed globally. This means if the government bans a newspaper and mobilizes its officials to physically remove print copies from the streets, as did the Zambian government with the *Post*, local and foreign audiences would still access the content. Similarly, confiscation of the *Times* of London or the *Washington Post* would prevent citizens from accessing the offending contents. Of course, as does China, the state can attempt to block the web sites but these can easily be mirrored, as happened in the *Post* case in Zambia. In any case, apart from Zimbabwe hardly any SSA country has seriously embarked on the futile and expensive game of internet censorship. Consequently, this chapter looks at the distribution of "old" media via new media. The chapter examines the situation of news media and democracy in Kenya and Zambia.

Mass Media and Democracy in Africa

From a disassociation paradigm (at variance with the liberal perspective), the media in Africa—like in most of the south—tended historically to serve the narrow interests of the colonial power and/or local settlers, and—since independence—those of an indigenous ruling group (Berger, 1998: 601). Paradoxically, as political freedom from colonial masters came to the African continent, so did press freedom disappear (Barton, 1979: ix). The broadcast media in particular was under the tight control of both colonial and postcolonial regimes. The rationale was that radio and TV had wider reach that makes it easy for anyone in control of these tools to exercise a considerable level of influence. Yet although the radio remains the true mass medium, "the press…is much the most important since it reaches that relative handful of people in every state who really matter—the politicians, the urban elite, the rising tide of well educated students, the businessman and, possibly the most important of all, the officer corps of Africa's armies" (Barton, 1979: 4). This argument by Barton can be applicable to any type of media—including new media—that may be considered elitist, for it is this very elitism that may result in transformative politics. Perhaps it is in this vein that Barton (1979: 7) argues that the two SSA states that are the most capitalistic, Kenya and Nigeria, are also the ones with the greatest degree of press freedom. Of course this judgment reflected the status at that time, for both countries have had nightmare periods in media history—with journalists from Nigeria resorting to "guerrilla" tactics of publishing on the move to avoid arrests or worse consequences. When did the recent rain of media repression start beating Africans?

With the 1960s independence euphoria came expectations of greater political freedom with the hope that this was an opportunity for Africans to map their own destiny. "We clapped, knowing that free press would be part of that destiny; after all nationalist media, despite all forms of colonial inhibitions, had effectively accompanied the struggle for *uhuru* (independence). This was not to be in later years."[1] Soon after independence, most African leaders were faced with some kind of ambivalence on how to handle the media. On the one hand they wanted effective mass media to convey national development and unity messages, especially the national leader's political thoughts packaged in some kind of philosophical catchword or phrase,[2] to mark a break from colonial rule. On the other hand, the pioneer African ruling elite was wary of the democratizing potential of public communications channels. John Merril argued in 1971 that in the transitional stages, truly mass media was irrelevant to African leaders and that "only elite lines of communication really mattered" (Bourgault, 1995: 47). In a similar vein more than a decade later, Graham Mytton argued that political elite do not necessarily desire an effective means of mass communication or have a clear policy on how to use it. "They may want to control the media capable of reaching large sections of the population, yet at the same time be suspicious of the power these media possess: power which is ultimately beyond their control" (Mytton, 1983: 94).

Such mixed feelings were especially manifest in the early 1970s when scholars like Daniel Lerner, Wilbur Schramm, and Everett Rogers advanced arguments on the role of the mass media in promoting positive change in developing countries. Most African leaders chose the nation-building exigency to counter the effects of not only excessive Western cultural and political influence, especially in broadcasting, but also of mass disenchantment following worsening of the economies in the 1970s and 1980s. The oral tradition feature of respected leaders meting out "kernels of wisdom liberally peppered with formularly sayings or proverbs" was exploited to justify the devotion of a lion's share of media content to didactic and moralistic speeches and pronouncements by national leaders (Borgault, 1995: 47–50). The broadcast media was particularly vulnerable to the distortion or *betrayal* of the original intent of oral tradition, yet traditional styles of chieftaincy rule was through consensus.[3] Mytton (1983: 91) shows how much broadcasting in the early 1970s in Zambia was devoted to lessons on Kenneth Kaunda's philosophy of humanism, even though research indicated these broadcasts were among the least popular programs.

News Media and Liberation Struggle in Kenya and Zambia

As in the rest of Africa, the modern news media in Kenya and Zambia were largely created by the colonial powers, primarily for their white audiences resident in these territories. Many of the large numbers of Europeans, mostly Britons, who migrated towards the end of the nineteenth century to eastern and central Africa settled in Kenya, the "white man's country,"[4] and Northern Rhodesia (Zambia). In addition to Britons, Zambia also attracted European immigrants from South Africa. Naturally "settler" media emerged in both countries as did in Kenyan newspapers owned by Asians, mostly Indians, imported to provide cheap labor to build railroad. Over the years, internal and external factors have built mainly on the colonial legacy, as well as on some aspects of pre-colonial traditions, to define the structure, operations, and content of the news media in these countries. Under the chapter heading, "From Settler Press to One-party Media: Kenya and Zambia," William Hachten (1971: 199–233) describes how the news media have evolved from newspapers and broadcasting formerly dominated by and subservient to European interests towards "Africanized" news media controlled by one-party governments.

As hinted above in this chapter, incumbents in both Kenya and Zambia preferred "tutelage" and "emergency" strategies within the endogenous communication-and-change model discussed in chapter 1 (Fagan, 1966: 115). Zambia's first President, Kenneth Kaunda expected the country's journalists to advance the cause of Humanism (Malama, 1994).[5] Yet in reality, contrary to the spirit and norms of humanism, the government and ruling party became the center of the Zambian society (Mkandawire, 1992: 16). Nearly two decades of one-party rule tended to persuade the media to accept reluctantly the basic principles of authoritarianism as a guide for social action in Zambia (Mkandawire, 1992: 40). As revealed by insider Philip Ochieng' (1992) in *I Accuse the Press*, a similar fate of self-censorship gripped the Kenyan media that were expected to support Kenyatta's *Harambee* maxim and Moi's *Nyayo* philosophy. A number of subjects were just off-limits for the media. Often, says Hilary Ng'weno, who resigned as editor-in-chief of Kenya's *Nation* Group in the mid-1960s to become later one of Africa's few owner-editors at that time, Kenyan journalists knew best how they found out how much freedom they had—"poking their necks as far as they can go without being chopped" (Barton, 1979: 9). Yet some observers are of the opinion that Kenya was comparatively better off within the African context. "Although there are careful limits to Kenya's press freedom, its biggest daily, *The Nation*, has probably more influence on the government of the country than any Fleet Street newspaper has over political life in Britain" (Barton, 1979: 7). A similar argument that has been applied to new media is that such media have greater impact in less open countries than they do on democratic societies.

A number of obstacles have over the years greatly limited the performance of news media—and by extension new media—in both countries. The first of these is political interference directly by political leaders or through harassment by state security machinery. During the Kaunda era, journalists operated in constant fear because of threats and innuendo. Kaunda often seized control of the newspapers and sacked editors and reporters who displeased him. He did his utmost to bring the country's two dailies to heel. His government owned one and controlled the other. The resulting self-censorship created a media blackout on the 1986 food riots in which more than 30 people were killed. A similar blackout faced the popular opposition rallies at the turn of the decade (Barton, 1979: 3, 9; Mkandawire, 1992: 3–4). As agitation for multipartyism mounted, Kaunda called a press conference on November 23, 1990. There, he only ordered companies and government institutions to cease advertising in the weekly *National Mirror* because, "the paper published rubbish and downright lies," but also dissolved Zambia Broadcasting Service without parliamentary approval as required (Mkandawire, 1992: 24). Between 1990 and 1991, the *National Mirror* relentlessly exposed the corruption and malpractices committed by the Kaunda government, and these articles formed part of the many forces that contributed to Kaunda and his party losing the October 1991 parliamentary and presidential election (Mkandawire, 1992: 39). In Kenya, the government often arrested and tortured "offending" journalists. For instance a photographer, Wallace Gichere was paralyzed after he was thrown from a window of *Nyayo* House, a notorious Moi-era torture headquarters. Gichere, now in a wheelchair, later sued the government, but it was not until after Moi was replaced that the Kibaki government compensated him with a pittance. The government often raided and disabled printing presses of "offending" publications.

In both countries, censorship did not cease completely with the arrival of multipartyism but it reared its ugly head in a more civilized and tactical manner—through legal and regulatory instruments. In Zambia, Kaunda's successor Chiluba attempted to adopt his predecessor's repressive tendencies, especially as his support was waning in the second term of office. In August 1997, the Zambian high court found that the government's decision to create a government-appointed Media Council of Zambia would have an impact on the freedom of journalists to assemble and associate freely with other persons. The draft bill envisaged compulsory registration of journalists and set minimum qualifications for anyone intending to practice. It was also to institute a disciplinary body for media practitioners. It would have the power to reprimand, suspend, or withdraw accreditation to offending journalists. Those without a license would be liable to a three-month jail term or a fine or both (Berger, 1998: 608). Following an outcry, the government only suspended the bill rather than scrap it. Zambian journalists, like their Swazi counterparts, responded by introducing their own voluntary independent media-driven non-statutory self-monitoring and self-regulatory body with powers to censure erring journalists. Journalists in state-owned media set up a separate one (Berger, 1998: 608). In May 2002 ahead of the general election in December that year, the Moi regime rushed through parliament a repressive "media bill" to effectively allow the government to control the media. The Statutes Law Bill (Miscellaneous Amendment Bill) required publishers to submit copies of their publications to the registrar before distribution and, ridiculously, to broadcasters to reveal their content before going on air. It also raised the cost of newspaper publishing bond from Sh10,000 (US$117) to Sh1 million (US$11,700), especially in a bid to cripple alternative "newsletter" press that often published sensitive information about the politicians that would not even appear in the mainstream press. Like other African countries, instead of creating laws guaranteeing freedom of speech and expression, Kenya has introduced new anti-terrorism laws that grant authorities even more powers to monitor communications—especially through the internet—between individuals and groups. Designed to appease the United States and the US Patriots Act, new legislation[6] makes it a criminal offence to "collect," "make" (produce and make available on a website), or "transmit" (by e-mail, voicemail, or any other telecommunication method) any record of information of a kind likely to be useful to a person committing or preparing to commit an act of terrorism (PI, 2003). Such laws can be applied very arbitrarily especially in countries like Kenya where, unlike the United States, there are no guarantees of press freedom and generally making provisions for freedom of expression in the constitution do not seem to apply to the press.

The second area of concern is proprietorial and managerial. Statistics from 1999 indicate that by market share, while Zambia press was about 74 percent state-owned, the Kenyan press was about 88 percent private-owned and about 12 percent party-owned meaning the Kenyan government does not own a newspaper. The broadcast media was nearly half-owned by the Kenyan government by share while in Zambia the government owned all broadcast media. The former ruling party KANU is the ultimate owner of *Kenya Times*, the country's fourth largest daily. However, the Kenyan Broadcasting Corporation (KBC) is state-owned (Djankov et al., 2002). As we know it, whoever pays the piper calls the tune. Although Zambia has publicly claimed the existence of a free press since 1964, the government owned nearly all media outlets to serve Kaunda's interests. "Because Zambia was a one-party state, the party so to speak, 'owned' the government and therefore the press. So media practitioners have had to toe the line on purely political issues as well as governmental concerns. Equally, the criteria of appointing editors and directors-general ceased to be professional but political" (Mkandawire, 1992: 2). In Kenya, party (KANU) ownership of the *Kenya Times* was distinct from government ownership of the KBC. Whatever ownership regime, the two governments have flexed their muscles to show they are in charge. Zambia still retains the trappings of the old political order—a predominantly government-owned media system. Despite the advent of political change in 1991, the mainstream media is still dominated by government, except for a few privately-owned newspapers that have emerged under the liberal political climate. "Diversity of opinion, a key feature of political pluralism, could not be easily attainable if the mainstream media remains an appendage of the government establishment." (Malama, 1994: v). The development of a vigorous independent media is hampered by a shortage of money. Like NGOs, the two independent newspapers, *The Post* and *The Monitor* rely on international support (Burnell, 2001a: 208). The ownership-control mentality has been applied to the new media as well, with the government not only restricting internet bandwidth offering but also sometimes demanding that ISPs produce their subscriber lists, listservs, or discussion groups. In one instance, an ISP shut down a list created to discuss the 1997 general election out of fear about what was being expressed (Mudhai, 2002; PI, 2003).

A third obstacle has to do with the media people themselves, their professional conduct and ethics. In a country deeply immersed in corruption and patron–client networks, it would be expected that politicians trying to cover up their misdemeanors or simply wanting to be projected in a positive light would not spare an instrument [perceived to be] as powerful as the media. It is not much wonder that in Kenya much has been said and written (especially in the so-called gutter press) about top editors and media managers who were on the payroll of certain corrupt and powerful personalities. (Mudhai, 1998a: 65). Top party leaders in particular did everything to ensure they "bought" or "pocketed" journalists and the publications they worked for. Not surprisingly, then official opposition leader Kenneth Matiba in the run-up to the 1997 general election sent shockwaves in newsrooms and the whole nation when he disclosed at a press conference that he bribed the *Daily Nation* investigative editor with a car. The editor sued Matiba and won the case. Yet this did not necessarily vindicate the editor given, as his colleague Kwendo Opanga put it in his September 1996 "The Week That Was" column article, corruption is "fiendishly difficult to prove for it is, after all, not a spectator sport." In this preview to the judgment, Opanga wrote: "The issue will be one of proof... It is a delicate decision. Even if, at the end of the day, he (the editor) wins (the case), a great deal of mud will have been thrown and reputations are going to be dragged through the mud" (Mudhai, 1998a: 66). Reacting to reports that top editors in the region's most successful media house were corrupt, the Nation Media Group's Chief Executive Officer, Wilfred Kiboro had this to say in an interview with the defunct *Expression Today* media journal: "Allegations against editors are not new... The question is whether there is any concrete proof from people making those allegations... If somebody comes with documentary evidence,... then we would take action but we can't run this company on the basis of rumours" (Mudhai, 1998a: 66).

Alluding to the one-time labeling of the United Kingdom's Fleet Street, then the hub of British and Commonwealth journalism, as the "Street of Shame," Opanga said in his article, "let it be very clear, we too easily stand condemned as scribes of SHAME." Indeed Opanga, then Kenya's pithiest and most virulent political columnist with a large celebrity-status following, seemed so sure his ilk were living in glass houses that if they dared hurl too many stones then they would be providing munitions for the politicians they were "doing business" with, as the Matiba court case seemed to have illustrated. In fact Opanga was sure ruling party KANU leaders in particular would not sit back and watch people they had secret dealings with throw mud at them. He wrote: "KANU will again run against the *Nation* and the most formidable weapon that the party and its paper think they could deploy against the newspapers is that there are among its reporters and editors, as there are in every sector of our national life, corrupt people."[7] Ironically, Opanga was to be the most infamous casualty among journalists posing to be critical of KANU's regime while at the same "moonlighting" (working clandestinely) with or for them. When he wrote a series of articles deeply critical of KANU and especially of President Moi in the run-up to the 1997 general election, Opanga found himself at the receiving end of propaganda from KANU-aligned press. Charges of hypocrisy, especially from the *Weekly Sun*, one of the ad hoc pamphlets or newsletters that littered Nairobi streets, and the *Kenya Times* were so prickly that Opanga found himself making history as the first journalist to call a well-attended press conference to clear his name. He ended up appearing to confirm the accusations against him, and lost his job as a result.[8] He admitted that he worked for the ruling party as part of the think-tank that designed strategies to help the ruling party win the first multiparty general election in 1992. Although his defence was that he did this as a consultant, and got paid a fee of KShs60,000 (US$1000) only in total, as opposed to the reported "bribe" of KShs50,000 (US$834) per week for more than ten weeks, there was a clear conflict of interest. Apparently Opanga was even visiting State House yet he was then the most popular and influential columnist, and his employer had promoted itself as an independent non-partisan publication. More worrying was the fact that Opanga indicated that other journalists who he would not name formed part of KANU's team of spin-doctors who included university lecturers.[9] Although Opanga later got himself rehabilitated by joining the Standard Group as one of its senior editors, his reputation, by his own words, had been dragged in the mud—even though there existed other senior private-sector journalists and media managers much guiltier of professional impropriety. Contrary to Opanga's earlier belief, the *Nation* succeeded in partially preserving its reputation while Opanga got himself soiled and sacrificed. Another senior journalist, Philip Ochieng' (the author of *I Accuse the Press*) was mentioned in 2004 as one of those who benefited from the gargantuan Goldenberg fake gold exports scandal. Observers could not help linking this to the defence in his writings of the Moi regime, especially against western donor and media attacks, towards its twilight.

Despite these bottlenecks, the Kenyan and Zambian media played a crucial role in the democratization process, especially in uncovering and condemning corruption as well as censuring the government over politically instigated violence, like tribal clashes, riots, and police brutality in Kenya, and political assassinations, like those of ambitious or dissenting ministers like Tom Mboya, J. M. Kariuki, and Robert Ouko. The emergence of new media, especially the internet has made the media's role in these realms even more significant.

Old Media Distribution via New Media

Let us start this section with a highlight of the futurist debate on whether new media such as the internet, e-mail, and mobile phones are harbingers of doom or survival of existing print and broadcast news mass media. Soon after the web emerged, pundits and technophiles began to predict the demise of newspapers. In one of the best-known pronouncements, writer Jon Katz predicted in 1994 in the pages of *Wired* magazine[10] that newspapers would vanish without trace within ten years (Nerone and Barnhurst, 2001: 468). Nearly two decades later, his prediction is of course unfulfilled. What prompted such a radical proclamation? Worried by the apocalyptic message, newspapers in the United States and the rest of the world moved quickly but reluctantly and precipitously into publishing their contents electronically from around 1994 (Nerone and Barnhurst, 2001: 468). It emerged this was a process in the "colonization" of the new media by the old. A group of media corporations even found it necessary to subscribe to the "News of the Future" project established at the Massachusetts Institute of Technology Media Lab to get regular updates on the form and technology of the digital newspaper of the future (Nerone and Barnhurst, 2001: 469).[11]

> Like previous technologies, the Internet's intrusion into newspaper operations has been both conservative and revolutionary, both progressive and retrogressive. Although often considered the anti-thesis of the press, the Internet in daily use has so far acted as a surrogate print medium. Users share Internet news in much the way that they used to clip and mail newspaper stories. (Nerone and Barnhurst, 2001: 469)

Indeed, media historians Asa Briggs and Peter Burke (2002) have asserted powerfully in their detailed work that as new media are introduced, older ones are not abandoned but coexist and interact with the new arrivals. This is exactly what the old media are doing with the new media.

There is a compelling view in the opposite direction that has been peddled—and with some telling, even if not completely convincing, illustrations. One of the most prominent of such views was widely diffused around the world following initial reporting by Associated Press journalist D. Redmont after covering an industry forum (2004). Publishers from Europe and America (the *Los Angeles Times*, the *USA Today*, and the *New York Post*) warned in early May 2004 that non-traditional communications—such as, and especially, cell phone text messages—were rapidly outflanking radio, television, and print media because of their immediacy and proximity to the public. In a two-day meeting to stimulate newspaper readership among the young, the publishers exchanged views with European media leaders on shrinking newspaper circulation and the European and American media scene. Lachlan Murdoch, then deputy chief operating officer of News Corporation, owners of the *New York Post*, said the drop in news readership "is indeed an emergency" (Redmont, 2004). The growing "thumb generation" posed the greatest new challenge to traditional media, with cell phone text messages conveying news, rumors and gossip, said Pedro J. Ramirez, editor of Spain's *El Mundo*. That challenge, it is argued, was evident after the March 11 (2004) train bombings in Madrid, Spain, that killed 191 people and injured more than 2000 others just three days before national elections. Nina Calarco, editor and publisher of southern Italy's *Gazzetta del Sud*, said information spread through cell phone messages contributed to Socialist Party candidate Jose Luis Rodriguez Zapatero's election as Spanish prime minister. "The (Jose Maria) Aznar government in Spain was unseated by a shower of telephone text messages, an alternative to the traditional print media, which was initially repeating the government line that the train bombings should be blamed on Basque terrorism instead of al Qaeda," Calarco said (Redmont, 2004). Youth participating in a round-table discussion criticized the newspaper publishers and editors for using arcane language, rehashing crime stories already seen on television and wasting space by reporting on reality TV shows (Redmont, 2004). Zapatero's Socialist Party reportedly called a massive rally in Madrid the night before the March 14 elections on short notice by having people spread the word through cell phone messages. "This is a communications circuit very difficult to control but easy to manipulate because it's as if every citizen had a printing press at home," Ramirez said. "And whoever wants to insert himself into the chain can make an exponential effect during crises. It can be ephemeral, but in Spain it had a great effect." Perhaps this "effect" was largely influenced by the already simmering and existing thinking among the majority in the populace, so that the text messages simply reinforced their inclinations and thus easily triggered their reactions—if indeed it did. Like in all media effects claims, there is no way of proving cause–effect beyond reasonable doubt.

Apart from the cell phone, the internet is even more significant for the news media and as a news medium. In a section on the changing boundaries of journalism, a book edited by Barbie Zelizer and Stuart Allan, *Journalism after September 11* highlights the internet's contribution to informing Americans and other nations about the twin bombing by terrorists of United States' power symbols in 2001. Stuart Allan (2002) in "Reweaving the Internet" praises the internet's role as an alternative source of news and as a forum for a whole range of opinions. The WWW was also a source of contacts and stories for professional journalists. However, he also criticizes internet coverage and warns that the Web also served as a source of rumors. Whether that is a good or bad thing is a matter of debate.

From his Africanist standpoint, Berger (2002) takes a media ownership-management path of analysis. He lays the ground by pointing out that in their current form, newspapers have four characteristics: privately owned, ad-dependent, delivered on paper and portable, and text-driven but integrated with visuals in a particular design. "These four factors are facing diverse development depending on where you are in the world" (Berger, 2002). The first point he makes is that although there are many state-newspapers across Africa, the only avenue for independent, opposition, or unofficial voices to make themselves heard is through the private press. In other words, newspapers' historic role in politics and democracy is a major factor in their survival—often against huge economic and repressive odds. Second, and related, is that advertising, however, remains the Achilles' heel of newspapers in the weak and/or state-controlled economies of the fourth world. For different reasons, ad- dependence also renders newspapers vulnerable in the super-competitive First World. The point is that where non-newspaper media can deliver audiences to advertisers cheaper and better than newspapers, the latter will lose out. So does this sound a death knell for the press? Perhaps not, so this leads us to his fourth point. "Digitalization has done a great deal to make newspapers more viable enterprises, but it cannot cheapen the core costs of newsprint and delivery. Unless electronic delivery to electronic paper becomes a reality, a time will come when fully digital media platforms will simply take over from the newspaper" (Berger, 2002). He points out that either of these scenarios will take much longer to unfold in the fourth world than the first world. "What digitalisation does do is make it possible to converge newspaper content onto non-newspaper platforms. Even, however, where such convergence is done on a pure-shovelware basis, the point remains that a web-published newspaper is really no longer a newspaper. There's not much point in stretching the language to pretend that it is" (Berger, 2002). Even if and when newspapers as we know them eventually die out, their text-oriented contribution to communication will live on—even if it becomes integrated with, or linked to, other elements. Stand-alone newspapers will increasingly become relics of the past. "In the interim, however, the resilience of the press ought not to be underestimated—and that's no bad thing!" So much for the debate; what does digitalism hold for the African print and broadcast media, and what are the implications for democratization and democracy?

Of particular significance in the policy arena are the deliberations of the Bamako Africa Media Forum meeting of May 2002 whose main objectives were to discuss the role of the media in the development of the information society, to outline the challenges to the media of globalization and the knowledge economy, and to create a network of journalists for promoting Africa's digital opportunities.[12] One of the four published highlights of the conference was the need for Africa to improve its presence in the information society by developing its own content. The meeting was part of the many preparatory conferences for the first round of the December 2003 World Summit on Information Society (WSIS) in Geneva, Switzerland. Among the key recommendations was the need to develop strategies for the creation of African content that finances and sustains the media in a bid to encourage "ICT media" that promotes information society. The last, but not least, recommendation was the need for investigation of new models that use electronic commerce for the delivery of content by African media. The second development is much more significant for Africa given that it focuses on the distribution of what has come to be known as the "mass medium of Africa." The "Digital Opportunities for Africa—Community Multimedia Centres" symposium was held in Dakar, Senegal, June 12–17, 2003, organized by UNESCO in collaboration with the Africa branch of AMARC (Association Mondiale des Radio Diffuseurs Communnautaires, the World Association of Community Radio Broadcasters). The aim of the pan-African symposium on Community Multimedia Centres in Africa was to find out more about how community radio stations across Africa used information and communication technologies (ICTs) to forge a strategy for a larger scale computer-mediated communication (CMC) development in the continent.[13] The meeting brought together "representatives of a selection of community radio stations that were successfully offering some form of public access to ICTs or planning to do so and also ICT-based projects such as community telecentres planning to start community radio as part of their operations" (ibid.). It also brought together "international partners including national development agencies and international governmental and non-governmental organisations in a roundtable on CMC project support in Africa" (ibid.). The gathering examined best practice models and determined partnership strategies for program development with provisions for "full community appropriation of ICTs, sustainability, networking, and technical support systems" (ibid.).

While efforts are being made to distribute African radio content, the continent's print media is firmly entrenched in the online media and helping to demolish the notion of a dearth in African content online. Upwards of 120 African newspapers and news magazines are available on the internet, many hosted by Africa's largest ISP, Nairobi-based Africa Online,[14] with offices in eight countries and ever expanding. Another outlet for African news is the Washington-based All Africa Global Media's AllAfrica.com[15] that hosts more than 100 African news publications and posts over 800 articles daily in English and French. In one month, the site served over 11 million page views (some 80 million "hits"). The reliance on it as a resource by government offices, boardrooms, educational institutions, and international organizations around the world, as well as by interested individuals has earned them good Nielsen ratings, accolades, and prize nominations, sometimes alongside media powerhouses such as BBC, MSNBC, and Google![16] There also exist two continent-wide African news agencies—Inter Press Service[17] and the Pan-African News Agency[18]—that use electronic media extensively.[19] At the subregional level, the Media Institute of South Africa Network (MISANET)[20] is one of the most comprehensive online news-resource for southern Africa.

It is not just media companies and news content that are taking advantage of the new media. It is well known that African journalists have widely turned to the internet and e-mail applications not just as a research tool but also as a "gold mine"; they contribute to foreign publications, many of which no longer need to station correspondents out there, and earn hard currencies (dollars, pounds etc.) much more than they would from their monthly salaries if employed locally. Franda (2002: 19) informs us surveys indicate that "prominent among Africa young elites using the internet and email regularly are journalists and aspiring journalists who use the internet to research and send stories, either as employees of an African news service or as freelancers." This makes journalists not to worry too much about the "spiking" of their sensitive stories—as long as they are professionally done. This way, the internet creates the opportunity for African journalists to help remedy the problem of the information rich being "in fact information poor when it comes to information about the information poor" (Berger, 1998: 609–10).

News Media and Public Sphere Expansion—Kenya and Zambia

Berger (1998: 609–10) credits the internet as "the media institution that will face the greatest test of both its accessibility to those outside of government, and its contribution to democracy." It is perhaps in this context that Berger (1998: 609) points out that the reach of the internet not only extends beyond the nation state but also creates communication between, *inter alia*, people of the North and people of the South, whereby journalists among others can discuss what to do about non-democratic states. Indeed despite various state attempts to limit media freedom in Africa, he points out that "journalists across the continent have been very active in lobbying against violations of the public sphere" (1998: 607). The fact that the recent wave of democratization in Africa has coincided with the development and spread of new information technology, notably the use of computers for communications purposes (Bourgault, 1995: 206–8), underlines the need for the traditional media to embrace these networked technologies in their service to the public. Africa's traditional print media have, as already discussed, used ICTs to enhance their contribution to the expansion of the public sphere. In fact journalists were among the first early adopters of the internet in these two countries (Kasoma, 2002; Mudhai, 2002). The *Post*, Zambia's leading independent newspaper, was one of the first in SSA to go online, in 1995. Through reciprocal arrangements with other online newspapers, such as London's the *Daily Telegraph*, the *Post* would save money and—for the most part—avoid censorship in disseminating news and commentary to its readers. With the coming of the internet, it stopped using the Zambian News Agency (ZANA), the state monopoly provider of wire service stories. The *Post* was so successful in communicating the views of the political opposition, especially abroad, that the two government-owned newspapers, *Times of Zambia* and *Daily Mail*, were forced to create their own online versions.

Although we have argued here that the old print and broadcast are dominated by the official view and therefore tend to perpetuate state hegemony, it is important to point out that the advent of the internet as well as private newspapers and FM stations in places like Zambia and Kenya has enhanced media freedom—even if this has not gone far enough. Kasoma (2002: 156) points out that although the Committee to Protect Journalists (CPJ) at one time cited Zambia as holding the record for more pending criminal defamation cases and other legal actions against journalists than any other African country, it notes that the country's independent press had remained resilient and undaunted. "There can be no doubt that the use of web sites and email by the Zambian media has helped to enhance press freedom. When the government banned one of the *Post*'s editions, it was available on the internet for some time before the government intervened and shut it down" (Kasoma, 2002: 156). In fact even though the government forced the ISP Zamnet to remove the *Post* edition 401 of February 5, 1995 from its web site where it was hosted, Zambians in the United States had already got wind of the ban of the print edition and in the intervening period (two days) had "mirrored" the online edition onto a US web site. So the government's move to shut down the original web site turned out to be futile although making it illegal for anyone to possess or read the printed copy may have worked locally. It is at this point that when the government tried (as they were to do later) to ban online hosting of the *Post* altogether, Zamnet convinced the state to publish its own newspapers online.[21]

Another way that the *Post* and other Zambian as well as Kenyan media workers have utilized new media is "to complain, within seconds of an incident of censorship or arrest, to organizations and governments throughout the world that can exert pressure on the government for denying press freedom" (Kasoma, 2002: 156). The organizations the author is referring to are journalism bodies like CPJ, Reporters sans Frontiers (Reporters Without Borders), the International Federation of Journalists, and Article 19 as well as human rights organizations like Human Rights Watch Africa and Amnesty International. All these organizations have detailed chronologies of violations of press freedom and freedom of expression in Kenya and Zambia as well as around Africa and the world.[22]

The third way is promotion of online interaction beyond the newspaper web postings. This is particularly a major feature of the recently revamped *Nation* newspaper web site. At the end of the story, the reader has the option to print, e-mail to a friend, or save. In what appears to be competition for online audiences and revenue, the *Standard* has also relaunched its web site with the options to print or forward stories. These are features that did not exist in these two countries, except in the enterprising online newspaper *Information Dispatch* of Zambia, which had some funding problems that threatened its ability to stay afloat.

The fourth way that the news media web site promote interaction is through the interpersonal online discussions and e-mail relays that often find their way into the mainstream media—sometimes without the realization of conservative newspaper editors who hardly take part in electronic networking. For example, the *Daily Nation* recently published as one of its main stories the content of a speculative e-mail that was being forwarded among some Kenyan internet users about the possible ailment of the late Vice-President Michael Wamalwa. The innuendos in the e-mail suggested that the V-P had, for a long time, been consulting his lead doctor a HIV/AIDs specialist in the United Kingdom, Dr. Margaret Johnson. The content was actually a press release on the web site of the hospital detailing Dr. Johnson's profile when she was promoted. What the *Daily Nation* editors did not realize—or conveniently chose to ignore as Tawana Kupe would suggest[23]—when they published the story headlined, "Wamalwa doctor promoted," was that the press release was more than a year old!

In more successful instances, a number of African newspapers publish protest or suggestion letters or declarations from organized groups, like the Kenya Community Abroad (KCA). One of the most concrete products of the Zambia-list listerv debates took the form of a collective letter of protest that appeared in the *Post*(Spitulnik, 2002: 187). The letter was drafted and revised on the Z-list over a period of several weeks. Entitled "Special Report: A letter to President Chiluba from Zambians living abroad" (the *Post*, no. 340, Nov. 8, 1995), it was an extremely detailed declaration of "dismay and disappointment at the state of affairs in Zambia" (Spitulnik, 2002: 187). Signed by 40 individuals, the letter carefully diagnosed the state of the nation—including interparty violence, the nose-diving economy, and political corruption—and called on then President Frederick Chiluba to "curb the culture of political intolerance" and to "create moral standards for civil servants." The letter clearly demonstrates how political discussions on the internet can be consolidated as a collective voice in a more visible mass media arena (Spitulnik, 2002: 177). Although not directly referenced, many of the themes raised in the letter subsequently recurred in the *Post* editorial columns, letters to the editor, and other

"Special Reports," and in that sense the letter joined a loud chorus of other voices in the independent press (Spitulnik, 2002: 187).

In other cases, internet users post material from mainstream newspapers as a basis for the discussions. For example, a few subscribers to Zambia-list discussion listerv regularly re-post the full texts of newspaper articles from the Web pages of the *Times of Zambia* and the *Post* (Spitulnik, 2002: 187). It is for this reason that mainstream media need to embrace more solidly the benefits accorded by the new media to expand space for dialogue that influences policy issues. This happens a lot especially among the various listservs and discussion groups for Kenyans and Zambians in the diaspora. The internet has therefore "opened up Zambia's [and of course Kenya's] media institutions to readers outside the country, giving them the opportunity to keep up with the news and to respond via email to advertisers and editors" (Kasoma, 2002: 155).

Conclusion

In 2012, Kenyans were yet to know the details and reasons for the 2006 raid at *The Standard* that was, according to the minister in charge of security, a warning: "If you rattle a snake, you will be bitten."[24] With the agitation for multiparty democracy in Africa in the 1990s came the demand for more press freedom. These "dual cries," coupled with a wave of privatization of the media and other government structures made authors like Bourgault (1995: 42–4) conclude, quite understandably, that the continent's media was "poised on the brink of change." As mainstream newspapers lost credibility, attendance of political rallies surged and privately owned newspapers like the *Weekly Post*, the *Daily Express* and the Church-owned *National Mirror* thrived (Mkandawire, 1992: 4). The role of the print media in transition to pluralism was validated by the 1992 Commonwealth Observer Group's Report[25] (p. 11):

> "Our analysis of the coverage by the leading daily newspapers showed that both the *Times of Zambia* and the *Zambia Daily Mail* made real efforts to report the campaign in a fair manner. While the other newspapers made no efforts to conceal their partisanship, the two established dailies covered the campaign in a reasonably impartial manner. Both papers used their comment columns to criticize aspects of the electoral process, the retention of the State of Emergency and the claims by both parties that violence would inevitably follow the announcement of the results. They made real attempts to identify and serve the interests of the Zambian people."

In the October 1991 election, the local media played a more prominent role than ever before in the history of Zambia (Mkandawire, 1992: 45, 16).

One may argue that the duplication of print content onto the online editions does not add much value to the news, but this is an important step in the direction of free expression in Africa. First, the media are freer than they were before. Second, a number of media web sites, like that of the *Nation*, allow users to "finish" (debate or expand on) their stories through interactive features. Even though Kasoma (2002: 155) indicates that "most newspapers and stations have an online presence that has brought news to places previously not reached," one may argue that internet access is limited—yet so is access to print and broadcast media. In fact internet and mobile phone diffusion is far greater than that of the news media in Africa. In any case, the already explained two-step flow model that has always worked in Africa can be applied to these new media as well. At the same time, it is important to point out that although digital technology and electronic distribution enhances news media effectiveness, it does not necessarily increase their effects. "Zambia's *Post* can do exposés continuously, with little apparent effect on the accountability and restraint of government" (Berger, 1998: 602). What is clear from this discussion is one of the main contentions of the thesis, that one cannot study the new media in isolation from the old; it is in the interaction between the two that much of the political impact of the new media is to be found.

In the case of Zambia, continued state control over public media has been a cause for considerable concern—especially given the dominance of the government press. In any country, particularly a developing one, there is real justification in having a government media that can be used as a genuine tool to inform and provide education for the community as well as much needed entertainment. However, public media should be under the control of an independent body whose members are not beholden to government ministers or bureaucrats. The recently formed Media Trust Fund (MTF), though mainly donor funded, has joined the Zambia Independent Media Association (ZIMA) and other organizations in filling a vacuum in this regard. In Kenya, private media managers were up in arms recently when Kenya's Information Minister, Raphael Tuju directed that broadcast media should dedicate at least 20 percent of their airtime to local content. These media operators did not give any tangible reason for their protest, other than the fact that they had not been consulted. Media houses need to display more commitment towards content creation rather than taking the shortcut of filling airtime and newsprint with stale foreign material. They should recognize the place of online or digital journalism with its unique attributes of immediacy, hypertextuality, interactivity, and multimediality and pay particular attention to accuracy. On the other hand, governments should provide enabling policies and incentives that enhance content creation. In other words, whereas the African state should not be overbearing in monitoring and controlling public communication space, it need not be rendered completely irrelevant—it needs to be strengthened, not in a coercive sense but in the sense of having the capacity to provide direction in situations where global structural matters may affect negatively healthy local democracy.

CHAPTER 11

Perceptions of Kenyan and Zambian Urban Civic Actors on their New Media Use in Political Realms

Introduction

Leslie (2002) carried out a survey of internet users in Zambia in 1996 and not only revealed the experimentation with the e-mail by the then new Radio Phoenix, which was quite radical in news reporting ahead of the 2001 elections to the point the government had it closed on a small technicality, but also other media and civil society organizations (CSOs). "A number of CSOs with emphasis on the civic education of citizens have sprung up in Zambia as part of the campaign for democracy. Although only a handful of these organisations have access to the internet, there is a growing awareness of its utility as a tool for networking" (Leslie, 2002: 116). This chapter takes a deeper look at some of the recent developments in Kenya and Zambia.

Civil Society Perception of Their Political Use of New Media

The model applied here on political use of information and communication technologies (ICTs) by social movements, to publish, collaborate, observe, and mobilize, is borrowed from the work of Surman and Reilly (2003) who point out that most CSOs have yet to learn truly strategic uses of these technologies, by moving beyond e-mail and basic web sites. Surman and Reilly's "uses" have been combined here, given that publishing tends to go with research and intelligence-gathering (observation) while mobilization, though not manifest in the African context in its online form, often results from collaboration or networking. A third aspect, that of administration, has been added. Summaries of the interviews carried out appear in Tables 11.1 and 11.2.

Observation and Publishing

As already observed, online newspapers have become one of the most visible aspects of African content on the web. In Kenya, the two main dailies, *The Daily Nation* and the *East African Standard*, competed to update their web sites with breaking news especially around election time. In its annual financial report, issued in November, the Nation Media Group said the online edition of its flagship *Daily Nation* newspaper received more than 1 million hits per day (CPJ, 2002). In September 2003, the *Nation*'s editor in charge of media convergence, said "the successes has been the over three million hits the online Nation gets."[1] Indeed the *Nation* recorded peak hits during the August 1998 Al-Qaeda bomb blasts in Nairobi and Dar es Salaam. While hosting an Africa Forum then US President Clinton suggested he sometimes read the *East African* online, *Nation*'s upmarket weekly newspaper. Little wonder President Moi, especially whenever he arrived back in Nairobi from abroad where Kenyan online newspapers would be his news source, lamented about the unpatriotic journalists who embarrassed the country by publishing negative stories on the internet for the whole world to access (Mudhai, 2002). Once, within days after arriving back from such a visit, staff on the *Nation*'s online desk claimed, in a report published by their newspaper, that they were being trailed by security agents in an unmarked car.

Perhaps the most telling sign of fear of internet news was demonstrated in the story of Zambia the *Post* newspaper edition 401, which carried a report the government claimed violated state secrets.[2] "They were planning to have a snap referendum and change the constitution which would effectively bar Dr Kaunda from contesting the Presidency. We carried a story that exposed all that," said the *Post* editor. The government banned the newspaper and confiscated copies from the streets. "It was too late; the story was already on the web site. They went to Zamnet, our ISP, and forced them to pull that edition out but it was too late as other people in the USA had already downloaded the whole edition and put in back online (on a mirror site)." The *Post* editor and his staff were arrested and charged but they won the case. The court ruled

Table 11.1 Select CSO key informant interviews in Kenya (2001, 2002, 2007 and thereafter)

Organization, Key Informant & Year NGO Formed	*New Media Status ('01/'02/'07) & Declared Communication Goals*	*Summary of Perceptions of Interviewee*
CCCC or 4Cs (Citizens Coalition for Constitutional Change); Prog Officer in charge of Advocacy; 1994.	E-mail, cell phone, web (www.4cskenyatuitakayo.org) *To give alternative proposal to the constitution*	Optimistic-skeptical: Uses e-mail to communicate with other CSOs and parties. Laments: network failure.
CJPC (Catholic Justice & Peace Commission); Projects Officer; 1988.	E-mail, cell phone, web (cjpc.partnershipforpeace.eu) *Provide info, advice & encouragement...* *No web site* (in plan)	Optimistic-skeptical: All dioceses networked. Lament: State interference.
CRECO (Constitution & Reform Education Consortium); Program Officer; 1998.	E-mail, cell phone, web (www.crecokenya.org) *Formulate national civic education programme.* *No web site* (in plan by 2002)	Optimistic: Used e-mail a lot for networking and info dissemination.
FIDA-K (International Federation of Women Lawyers – Kenya); Prog Officer; 1985.	Internet, e-mail, cell phone www.fidakenya.org *Just society free of discrimination against women*	Optimistic-skeptical: Local for networking, regional info exchanges. Laments: Problems of connectivity, especially during peak time.
IED (Institute for Education in Democracy); 1993	Internet, e-mail, cell phones. www.iedafrica.org *"To provide information & skills for positive political behaviour."*	Optimistic-skeptical: Uses cell phones for election monitoring.
LRF (Legal Resources Foundation); Project Officer Media; '93.	Internet, e-mail, cell phone www.lrf.or.ke Help Kenyans access justice	Optimistic-skeptical: More interactivity. Lament: Only a few have access.
YA (Youth Agenda); Prog Co-ordinator; Administrator; 1996	Internet, e-mail, cell phone, website (www.youthagenda.org) *Enlighten the youth on civic education.* *No web site* (in plan by 2002)	Optimistic-skeptical: Used two cell phones for office. Lament: Network problems.

Table 11.2 CSO key informant interviews in Lusaka, Zambia (2001, 2007 and thereafter)

Organization, Key Informant & Year NGO Formed	*New Media Status ('01/'02/'07) & Declared Communication Goals*	*Summary of Perceptions of Interviewee*
AFRONET (Inter-African Network for Human Rights & Development); Exec Director; 1994 (Inactive in 2012).	Internet, e-mail, cell phone. www.afronet.org.zm *"Coord & networking among HR organisations."*	Skeptical: Addressed the critical question of access and said technology cannot drive mass movements. Laments: Possible interference with their LAN.
CCJDP (Centre for Justice, Devt & Peace); Director, Renamed Caritas Zambia from 2007.	www.ccjp.org.zm (www.caritaszambia.org.zm) *A just society where pple have freedom and means.*	Skeptical: E-mails column to *Post*; State is too powerful for CSO, media forces; cell phone access limited.
CCZ (Christian Council of Zambia); Comms Officer; 1914.	Internet, e-mail, cell phone. www.ccz.org.zm	Optimistic-skeptical: Networks with churches; Uses online bulletin. Lament: limited access & cell phone expensive.
FODEP (Foundation for Democratic Process); Info & Research Mngr; 1991	Internet, e-mail, cell phone www.fodep.org.zm *Enhancing general awareness of population.*	Optimistic: Networking offices in all the nine provinces and upgrading computers.
Information Dispatch; Founder	www.dispatch.co.zm (inactive in 2012) *First online newspaper in Zambia, based in Lusaka*	Optimistic: Received highest hits at the peak of third-term debate. Lament: high costs, low speed.
LAZ (Law Association of Zambia); Chairman; 1973	Internet at secretariat, and individual law firms. www.laz.org.zm ***No web site*** in plan by 2002	Optimist-skeptical: Networks with international bodies.
LRF (Legal Resource Foundation); 1991	Internet, e-mail, cell phone www.lrf.org.zm *Enlighten people about their rights.*	Optimistic: Internet research on human rights cases in UN/EU and in the SA region.
The Monitor; Editor; 1996.	www.afronet.org.zm (Inactive in 2012, as is parent NGO)	Lament: E-mail hitches, suspects "active interference"

NGOCC (Zambia NGO Coordinating Council); Prog Officer for Comms & Advocacy; 1985 (65 afflts in 2001, and 109 in 2012)	www.ngocc.org	Optimistic: Computer centre in Lusaka, at least four workstations to enhance networking. Also two networked computers per province of nine provinces.
PANOS (Southern Africa); Regional co-ord	Internet, e-mail, cell phone www.panos.org.zm www.panos.org.uk	Optimistic: Internet can open public space for networking and antagonistic debates.
ZNWLG (Zambia Nat. Women Lobby Group) Head of Research, Info & Documentation; 1991	Internet, e-mail, cell phone www.womenslobby.org.zm *"Networking . . . a resource base for info & policies"*	Optimistic: Networks & calls meetings via e-mail. Lament: Not many people use web site for interactive discussions.
Oasis Forum; 2001; Co-ordinator.	Networking system soon.	
The Post; Editor. (Second newspaper to go online in Africa.)	Internet, e-mail, exclusively cell phone. www.post.co.zm to www.postzambia.com	Optimistic-skeptical: Stresses historical context; Uses ICTs to get round govt obstacles. Laments: virus infestation on web pages; skills shortage; cost.
SAHRINGON (Southern African Human Rights NGO Network); Zambia National Co-ordinator; 1996.	http://afronet.org.za/sahringon (Inactive in 2012, as is parent NGO's) *Collective activism against governmental organizations.* like SADC; 11 of 12 members networked by 2002.	Optimist: Relies heavily on use of internet and e-mail to network. Lament: Not all affiliate organizations within and outside Zambia are at the same level re. ICT facilities.
ZCEA (Zambia Civic Education Association); Civic Educ Prog Mngr & Leadership Devt Prog Mngr; 1993.	Internet & e-mail at secretariat; cell phones, field workers. ***No web site*** in plan by 2002. www.zamcivic.com.zm	Skeptical-optimistic: Regularly use e-mail to network with other organizations. Laments: Cost, access problems, no network in rural areas where they often work.
ZIMA (Zambia Independent Media Association)	www.zima.co.zm (Inactive in 2012) *"Media monitoring, advocacy,"*	
ZIMT (Zambia Independent Monitoring Team) President	No internet; no e-mail; no web site BUT officials had regular access via shared public areas. Inactive in 2012.	Optimistic: Ardent user of e-mail and internet.

that there was no violation of state secrets as by that time Chiluba's strategy to bar Kaunda was being executed and therefore was public knowledge. The *Post* continued to get covert and overt harassment, including phone tapping—to which the Chief Inspector of Police conceded. The editor said the newspaper's changed to exclusive use of the mobile phones, apart from making phone tapping a little difficult (but not impossible) for the government, made the *Post*'s own operations much easier and efficient. Another harassment came in the form of suspected arson by a *Post* staff suspected to be a government mole who was left behind in the office at night to update the newspaper's web site.

Yet another example is Zambia's first internet-only newspaper, *Information Dispatch* launched in 2000, a year before the general election, by a group of young journalists. The web site recorded between 10,000 and 14,000 visitors, with an average monthly figure of 300,000 visitors located in North America (especially the United States) and Europe (especially the United Kingdom) as well as Zambia and other African countries. Their web site received the highest hits whenever there was a major political debate or crisis. "During the third term debate, we were a very authentic source. Almost on a daily basis something was happening and we kept hammering and hammering until at one time we had a conflict with the state because of that," recalled *Information Dispatch* founding Managing Editor. "We had an interview with one of the Western diplomats whom I can't name. He told me categorically that 'our feeling as the diplomatic community is that the President is being hypocritical because he had promised to abide by the constitutional provision' (limiting his rule to two five-year terms). That story was picked up by the wires, and seen by officials in one of the Zambian missions abroad who faxed it back to (their superiors) Zambia," the *Dispatch* editor explained. "Agents from the government intelligence came to probe us to find out who we talked to but we chose to abide by our ethical values not to disclose the identity of our source." The government issued a press statement accusing the diplomatic community of meddling in their internal affairs. In response, the Dean of the Diplomatic Community issued its press statement to ameliorate the situation. "From then on, we have been under surveillance, but we are not intimidated. We just report accurately," said the *Dispatch* editor who later took time off to sharpen his skills with a Masters degree in new media at London's City University. The *Dispatch* editor said he felt much freer to express himself as an online journalist compared to his days as a traditional media practitioner. "Currently in Zambia, there is no law that could be applied against *Dispatch* (say to shut it down). I can operate from my home. I can host my site from free software space wherever—in the USA or the UK, on the dot.com. They can't stop me. This is bringing checks and balances to the government because they know that even if they try to censor the dailies, they can't do anything against us." Despite these pronouncements, some level of vulnerability could be discerned from the group's shoestring budget and their use of the state ISP Zamnet.

This is discernible in the experiences of the *Monitor* which viewed faults in their internet connections, that manifested themselves as technical, as acts of interference by government agents because the glitches almost always occurred when they received e-mails from two Zambian exiles critical of the government.[3] When the Monitor carried a lead story in early 2001 that President Chiluba was running for a third term and that he had drafted district administrators to voice this on his behalf, a State House media spokesperson contacted the quasi-state ISP Zamnet to get them to pull out the story. "People at the Zamnet were really scared. The ISP was really intimidated," recalled editor of the *Monitor*. It is worth noting that the state did not even try to intimidate the newspaper directly, perhaps due to the earlier experience with the *Post*. (The management of Zamnet must be commended for their diplomatic resistance of pressure to stop hosting newspapers and giving links to their web sites.) "The concern was more on why the material was being disseminated internationally. In many cases, that has always been the problem—why Zamnet, which is not a newspaper, put anti-government material on the web," said the *Monitor* editor.

It would appear the Zambian government was more worried about reports on the *Monitor* online than the hard copy on the streets. "What is posted on the internet is accessible to the wider world therefore Zambia is monitored effectively by the World Bank, the IMF and the bilateral donors. Just the fact that these lenders are aware of cases of bad governance creates pressure on the government. It makes the government uneasy," said Zambia Independent Monitoring Team (ZIMT) president who stressed that this does not necessarily mean the government is not worried about domestic opinion as well. "As the world becomes a global village and information becomes readily available, governments become a little more jittery that their conduct at home is brought to immediate international scrutiny at once and that challenges their ability to practice bad governance. It challenges them much more quicker because they are being monitored, scrutinised and examined," the ZIMT president explained further, pointing out that "the new media, the internet is not owned by anybody so they constitute a new haven—a departure from the current structure of print and electronic media."

An interesting and attractive aspect of online editions is their provision for interactive features allowing users to comment, give feedback, and vote on controversial issues. The *Nation* recently revamped their web site and included interactive features. The *Dispatch* had this feature much earlier. "We have an interactive feature—an attraction to the readership. At the end of every story, there is a provision for readers to comment. People feel free to express their views. We also get instant feedback," said *Dispatch* editor. Political and human-interest stories triggered more interest, some having up to 20 comments compared to an average of 7. However, non-media NGOs have not had much success in this area. "We have discovered that not many people visit the website. We have put discussion forum there where from time to time we update the topic but it appears people who submit to the discussion forum are not many, so we have realised that not many people visit our website. The reason could be that in Zambia, and in most of Africa, most people have no access to the Internet," said Head of Research, Information and Documentation at the Zambia National Women's Lobby Group (ZNWLG), a country-wide membership organization with 5000 members in 2001. However, the other reason could also be to do with poor advertisement.

A number of CSOs also used new media during election to issue their statements and collective positions. "We (usually) put current information on our website. For example, we monitor political party conventions where they choose top party leadership and whatever transpires there we put the statements on the website," said the ZNWLG official.

Not surprisingly, CSOs found ICTs quite useful for monitoring elections during the period under study. In the 2001 Zambia election and the 2002 Kenya election, a number of NGOs (some with staff mobile phone possession and use policy) used their field monitors to gather data at polling stations around the country and then relay information instantly to NGO head offices in the capital cities of Lusaka and Nairobi from where the information and analyses were often disseminated to media houses for immediate broadcast, say by the recently established private FM radio stations. Unlike the previous elections especially in Kenya, the greater enhanced transparency through mobile phone and internet updates on newspaper and NGO websites made it more difficult for the incumbents to rig the vote by altering figures (Mudhai, 2003)[4] although these developments could not eliminate electoral flaws as the 2007 Kenyan poll fraud showed. "In 1991 when we had our first multiparty election, this new technology was not a factor but in 1996 and 2001, it is becoming an important forceful factor in providing knowledge and information around especially the academics, scholars, researchers and the learned community," said ZIMT president. Does this not show that the ICTs are just elite tools for the privileged? The ZIMT official responded with what media scholars have referred to as the two-step flow theory. "There is a trickle-down effect that the usage of computers, the Internet and cellular phones has made Zambia a smaller space in terms of exchanging knowledge though the coverage may not be 100 per cent. In those areas where there is the Internet service and cellular phone systems, the communities are becoming more informed, there is more exchange of knowledge, there is effective communication, there is more arguments, there is more knowledge about what is happening in Chilelabombwe, in Chawama and people talk about it in Livingstone and in Mpika," the ZIMT official explained.

There are also plenty of personal experiences and anecdotes, especially with the cellular phones. "The other day I was coming (flying into the country) from Durban (South Africa) and when I arrived in Livingstone and switched on my cellular phone, I got the information that Radio Phoenix had been closed. I hadn't known about it, but I was able to get the political situation in Lusaka much more quickly compared to a few years ago," said the ZIMT leader.

ICTs have also been used in monitoring legal precedents and information. The Legal Resource Foundation (LRF) and the Law Association of Zambia (LAZ) have used the internet for their legal operations, some in challenge to the state. "The Internet has proved to be of tremendous assistance particularly in so far as getting information about what is happening around the world regarding human rights," said LRF Principal Advocate. "In fact in the recent past, we have succeeded in getting two favourable judgements against the State of Zambia at the African Commission on Human and People's Rights. We cited a number of precedents that we got from the Internet." Another example is a treason trial in which some of those accused were convicted and sentenced to death. "We did make use of cases that we got off the Internet – treason cases in apartheid South Africa," the LRF official said.

Churches within countries and in the region have also been collaborating via the internet, especially on political matters. The Christian Council of Zambia (CCZ), a parent organization of Ecumenical

Christian churches totalling 18, uses e-mail to network with not only local partners like the Zambia Episcopal Conference (Catholics) and Evangelical Fellowship of Zambia (Charismatic) but also, and especially, Christian councils in neighboring countries, Botswana, Zimbabwe, and Mozambique. "Each time we produce something, it is an agreement among ourselves as communication officers within the network to share out information," said CCZ Communication Officer, Ing'utu Mutembo. Alongside the civil society, the NGO Coordinating Council and the Law Association of Zambia, CCZ was one of the organizations that came together in early 2001 to form a strategic alliance, Oasis Forum, to lobby against attempts by Chiluba to change the constitution to allow him to vie for a third term in office.

Kenyan and Zambian Diaspora CSOs have encouraged online discussion forums (as well as chatrooms) where all manner of observations are published. The politics forum of US-based Kenyan Community Abroad (KCA) web site[5] records a lot higher number of topics and posts compared to those on "business," "computers and technology," "jobs & careers" or special debates. US-based Zambia community online[6] runs a message board and a mailing list. These complement other initiatives where participants are not necessarily Diaspora, the main criteria being that they belong to either country and are interested in developments there—wherever they are in the world. Indeed some of these forums, like Kenyans' Mambogani (www.mambogani.com) dubbed "the voice of the *wananchi* (ordinary citizens)," indicate the local time of the accessing computer as well as Nairobi time. Other, less formally constituted, political forums can be found in The Zambian (www.thezambian.com) and Mashada (www.mashada.com). Also available is web log (blog), for example The Zambian's (www.thezambian.com/blogs) and Onyango Oloo's Kenya Democracy Project (http://demokrasia-kenya.blogspot.com).[7] A former senior official of PANOS Southern Africa said Zambians living abroad have been so active in online debates about what goes on in the country that in some cases government officials have been forced to respond to some of their concerns—"which is amazing." He recalled that "some party functionaries in their own offices would write, 'we don't like what you are saying here. You don't understand what is going on in Zambia, you are only depending on what the *Post* gives you'. But it doesn't matter; the point is, debate has been generated and people are beginning to talk—which is very good." This is an explication of what Hannah Arendt and Chantal Mouffe would term "agonistic," where people do not have to agree, rather than Habermas' deliberative model, where it matters to reach some kind of consensus.

One controversial feature of online interactions among the Zambians and Kenyans abroad is the litany of loose talk and insults, but that is part of the consequences of freeing the public sphere. Due to the absence of social pressure to be civil, communications often degenerate into what Robert Putman terms "flaming out" or vicious attack campaigns (Meyer, 2002: 121). "One threat to the standards of democratic deliberations is the fact that the Internet chatrooms are notoriously full of racist statements and ungrounded, dogmatic accusations that their authors would never dare utter in a traditional public setting" (Meyer, 2002: 124). On the Zambian internet forum, ZIMT president was reported to have had constant stormy political arguments with a white Zambian whom he is said to have accused of commenting on the country disparagingly in a manner that revealed his racist point of view.[8] Whether such antagonistic dialogues threaten democracy is debatable. Here is a take on this issue by a former official of Zambia-based PANOS SA:

> I think almost all the key NGOs are online and there are a number of electronic discussion forums on which they participate actively. For example, there is an e-mail service run by David Simpson, called Go-Brain. He writes his opinions on media issues in Zambia and sends it out to all of us so that we can then comment on what he says. In fact there has been some "fights" between him and..., the ZIMT president. I think it is a good way of opening up issues as serious as racism. This simple medium of email is beginning to link people, to make them expose their fears, their worries, their celebrations, their hopes for Zambia, etc. Where else would one do this? The fax cannot do that for you, the telephone cannot, so the new media is creating spaces for people to express themselves. In my view, this is the best thing that has ever happened in Africa generally.[9]

Mobilization and Collaboration/Networking

Ahead of the elections in 2001 (Zambia) and 2002 (Kenya), CSOs in both countries networked effectively at the international level during the Jubilee 2000 NGO coalition movement that lobbied the then G-7 developed nations to cancel third world debt and denounced the Heavily Indebted Poor Countries (HIPC) initiative as a "cruel hoax" (Collins, 1999: 419).[10] Several organizations including the Green Belt Movement (GBM) led by the aggressive Wangari Maathai, churches, NGOs, and women's organizations came together in Kenya to launch the Jubilee 2000 Africa Campaign in Nairobi in 1998.

In Autumn 1999, the Jubilee 2000 Nairobi and the Kenya Jubilee 2000 Africa Campaign came together to form the Kenya Interfaith Debt Campaign under the auspices of the GBM. The new organization included women groups, youth groups, church clergy, businessmen and women as well as NGOs. "They continue to organise activities regularly including seminars and workshops as well as processions, despite occasional repression by police forces."[11] In cooperation with the Catholic Commission for Justice and Peace, Zambia (CCJP-Z), the Jesuit Centre for Theological Reflection (JCTR) coordinated Jubilee 2000-Zambia and linked it to national and international debt campaigns. On May 22, 1999 a "Freedom from Debt" event was held in six cities across Zambia and 300,000 signatures (45% from rural areas) were collected and sent to Cologne, Germany. A three-day regional conference was held in May 1999 with representatives from 14 African countries issuing the "Lusaka Declaration"; a follow-up meeting was held in August in Nairobi to move the African consensus further, rejecting HIPC and ESAF (Enhanced Structural Adjustment Facility).[12] Father Pete Henriot, a US Catholic priest actively working with the Zambian Jubilee 2000 campaign, argued that conditions imposed from the outside undercut "the responsibility of decision makers within the country to seek and effectively represent the wishes of their citizens" (Collins, 1999: 421–2).

Despite the reported harassment in Kenya, the Jubilee 2000 was an issue around which CSOs could cooperate with governments rather than in opposition to it. However, the GBM had earlier, at the peak of transition politics in 1989 and 1990, broke away from its cooperation with the government to protest attempts to build multistory complexes in Nairobi's recreation areas of Uhuru Park and Jeevanjee Gardens. "The GBM uses multiple methods to voice their opinions. This can include simple letter writing to officials as well as participating in serious protests concerning major issues."[13]

Cases of actual online (internet) or mobile phone mobilization are rare within the two countries. However, one of the most active aspects of mobilization and networking is that of lobbying the international community to put pressure on government on specific issues or crises involving NGOs. Said ZIMT president:

> I recall vividly that in 1996 working together in the Committee for Clean Campaign with Mr Ngande Mwanajiti (an official of then Lusaka-based human rights NGO network, AFRONET) and myself had made statements to the effect that the Zambian elections were not free and fair. The reaction by our government was harsh and immediate. Within

> a week, the police clamped down on us. They came to our homes in the middle of the night at 4am on a Saturday. They arrested me then they arrested Mwanajiti. We carried our cellular phones and charges. When they locked us up in the cells, we communicated with the rest of the world, with the BBC, with some colleagues in Zimbabwe and South Africa, with the Amnesty International and Africa Watch, and with NGOs within Zambia. By the time the police realised what had happened, the whole place was filled with our supporters and many journalists had filed stories about what had happened to us. There was already pressure mounting on the Zambian government. By 3pm that afternoon, the government instead of detaining us as they intended they released us on bond. This is just one example of how (we use) cellular phones as a tool of defence, and a tool of advocacy—challenging our government on bad governance and excessive use of force. The Zambian government dropped the charges and the matter never went anywhere because we were able to communicate effectively, immediately and promptly.

In Kenya, similar lobbies have been conducted on a number of issues. For example, the Kenya Human Rights Commission (KHRC) has been very aggressive in using the internet especially to lobby the international community to react to a particular issue. One area was the anti-torture campaign that was carried out in 2000 by KHRC and People Against Torture (PAT) who were in constant contact with Amnesty International. "The critical mass support was to the point where the President (Moi) was extremely alarmed and he had to make policy statements against torture, and the AG (Attorney General) had to start looking at a bill that would then eradicate torture from government institutions," recalls an official of Legal Resources Foundation Kenya (LRF-K). It is estimable that thousands of e-mails and ordinary mail letters were sent directly to President Moi, the AG Amos Wako and other senior government officials and institutions, including the police, and copied to the media. Most of the letters, sent from all over the world but mainly from Europe, were generic duplications of each other. The idea was to "swarm" Moi to take action, which he eventually did.

Diaspora Kenyans and Zambians have perfected specific forms of lobbying and networking, especially e-mail petitions. For instance, the KCA has been active on thorny issues such as dual citizenship, constitutional reforms, representation, and voting rights. From their vantage positions, Kenyans and Zambians abroad have been very actively using ICTs not only to coordinate their activities and carry out their operations, but also to lobby the government directly by sending e-petitions to the seats of power on a regular basis and sending copies to newspapers which then publish them in the letters pages for local readership. Sometimes, issues they raise are so crucial that their petitions get covered as news items in their own right. KCA motto, "connecting Kenyans abroad" and "towards accountable government and economic independence in Kenya," underscore their commitment to networking in a bid to promote democratization in their home country. One very active KCA member, Onyango Oloo, exiled in Canada e-mails politicians directly regularly and even when they do not reply he is normally satisfied to have communicated his thoughts,[14] which are known to be radical among the Kenyan online community. In essence, ICTs play a key role in maintaining links between long-distance émigrés and their rural home communities, enabling them to appropriate technologies and adapt them to their needs, sometimes in highly personalized and unexpected ways (Cline-Clone and Powell, 2004: 8; Tall, 2004).

The ICTs were particularly a bonus for women's organizations that were able to overcome gender barriers to lobby for their lot. During the run-up to Zambia's 2001 elections, women's lobby groups made considerable efforts to sensitize Zambia's female voters and persuade the parties to adopt female candidates—182 of whom contested parliamentary seats though with only 16 successes (Burnell, 2002: 1110). "We use email to send statements to various sister organisations and other organisations that monitor elections as well. We also use the email to invite women for meetings and to send messages to political parties," said a ZNWLG official. "We communicate daily with a lot of organisations with which we have similar interests. We use e-mail to get in touch with (these) other organisations," said Zambia Civic Education Association (ZCEA) Leadership Programme Development Manager. The Federation of Kenya Women Lawyers (FIDA) uses the internet to exchange notes on women's participation in politics in neighboring countries, Tanzania, Uganda, and South Africa, "especially with organisations which have been instrumental in ensuring women are well represented in political office."

Another category of CSOs taking advantage of new media is the youth. Besides such youth outfits as Zambia's *Information Dispatch*, there emerged youth-oriented CSOs like Kenya's Youth Agenda (YA). They lobbied using mobile phones, especially when their main telephone lines were disconnected around election time, to get their lot in leadership positions at various levels, including parliament. Like women, the youth feel the new media accord them better networking and lobbying possibilities compared to the conventional media, in which they are less visible. "They don't report what the youth said or deliberated but (only concentrate on) politicians' speeches," said YA's official.

Regional and issue networking were other common features among NGOs that used ICTs. "The medium has made easier, effective and more proficient our networking with various NGOs, corporate organisations and even government agencies on any issue—be it death penalty, the debt burden, the environment, the Palestinian question, immigration, xenophobia, human rights, HIV/Aids or gay rights," said ZIMT President. "We are able to interact, to exchange information and to create strategies within the 14-member nations of SADC (Southern African Development Community). We are able to communicate, meet and rally behind a particular issue using the Internet," he explained. "So the Internet has provided us with a new frontier of communication and strategising on issues of common interest, whether in Zambia, Malawi or the entire region. So networking has become more efficient." An example is the SADC Electoral Support Network of NGOs that shares information on election processes and practices, making it easier for them to engage with government agencies such as the Electoral Commission of Zambia.

One of the most successful regional purely network-based organizations is the Southern African Human Rights NGO Network (SAHRINGON), formed in 1996 and launched in February 1997 at the Regional Human Rights Network Conference in Johannesburg before being incubated at the AFRONET premises in Lusaka. It drew NGOs from Botswana, Lesotho, Malawi, Mauritius, Mozambique, Namibia, South Africa, Swaziland, Tanzania, Zambia, and Zimbabwe. The organization declares that it was established to create a platform for a collective voice to respond to the ever-increasing regional and global challenges facing human rights NGOs in Southern Africa. It boasts that its formation marked a move towards a new paradigm in collective activism in the region through collective, cross-country, and cross-cultural diversity. "As a network, we rely heavily on the use of the Internet and the email. We depend solely on the Internet to know what is happening in . . . in all countries involved. We normally come together and go through all the communication we have exchanged via email and Internet at that level," said a leader of the Zambia national coordinator of SAHRINGON. This underscores the crucial need in Africa to maintain old methods like face-to-face communication even while embracing new media. Part of the reason for this is that not all affiliate organizations (the Zambia chapter has 12 affiliates) are at the same level with regard to ICT facilities.

As part of their strategies, the CSOs initiated all forms of (donor) partnerships to enhance their effectiveness. "The Internet has provided us with good capabilities. It expands our capacity. It is a welcome useful tool," said one ZIMT official. The *Information Dispatch* operated in partnership with One World International, which has a regional office in Lusaka, and the International Institute for Communication and Development (IICD) in the Hague, Netherlands—with links to the World Bank's Infodev programme.

Administration

Virtually all the CSOs use ICTs for administrative purposes in a manner they perceive increases their efficiency. "We had no people on the ground to organise a recent workshop in Kitwe, one of the copperbelt towns, so we emailed a local Oxfam contact who went round for us so that by the time we travelled there for the workshop, everything was ready; all we did was using email and fax," said a leader of ZCEA. "We've been to get a lot of information in terms of what we can use in our work," the official corroborated. This illustrates one of the properties of new media, saving time and money—resulting in efficiency. FIDA Kenya has similar sentiments to share: "There has been a significant impact in terms of savings on time, on communication. For example, we do our hotel and ticket bookings online, and we exchange papers online," says FIDA Programme Officer for Advocacy, Anthony Mugo. A former official of PANOS Southern Africa says that the use of ICTs by journalists is reflected in the better quality of their output. "Journalists are becoming more and more inquisitive," said Banda whose information-intensive organization, a branch of PANOS London, was considering entering into a strategic alliance with ZAMNET to provide free Internet access to journalists. PANOS SA itself was at the time of the interview boosting its own information capacity by engaging database managers. "We are always sending email messages; our work would not be successful without that." For Kenya's Constitution & Reform Education Consortium (CRECO), e-mail was an ideal, cheap, timely, and efficient way of keeping in touch with its 22 affiliates involved in civic education programmes.[15]

As discussed in chapter 3, the capabilities and attributes of the new media are important for CSOs. Tracing the context to independence struggle, the *Post* editor said "anything that will enable us to communicate to not only our people but also to a maximum number of people, globally, is a medium of liberation. It is a medium of liberty, of the extension of liberties. So today more people know about what is happening in this country." This further elaborates an expansion of the public sphere for many CSOs. The expansion is not just quantitative, but also qualitative. "We are benefiting heavily from the email, in terms of columns, letters to the editor, from all over the world. Our people are able to follow debates or contribute to debates in the country. This has helped us have quality debates," explained the editor of *The Post.*

Conclusion: Enhanced-Efficiency with Limited Efficacy in Kenya and Zambia

This chapter has examined specific civic uses of ICTs in Kenya and Zambia, taking into account sociopolitical contexts. Data from interviews with CSO actors and from their literature indicate that most of these organizations started at the dawn of the so-called third wave of democracy, from around 1990. The CSOs generally perceive ICTs as enhancers of their organizational and networking efficiency, which in turn improves their potential in influencing policies, issues, and decisions on political, as well as socioeconomic, matters especially around election time. While this effectiveness is not independently verifiable, given evidence that the ruling elite often simply ignore or downplay civic agitation—as we have seen in the previous chapter, partial victories are discernible from half-hearted concessions by the incumbents.

The chapter further reinforces the central assumption that ICTs do not replace, but converge with, existing conventional networks and interactions—they provide some kind of reinforcement rather than create radical reform. The civic actors in Zambia also use other media, like land lines, faxes, letters, postal services, radio, TV, leaflets, village meetings, workshops, and conferences as well as corporeal interactions.

In both countries, governments attempt to reduce possible impacts of ICT media, however feebly, by exacting controls and opening official online platforms. Fackson Banda says the political climate in Zambia has changed, given that "politicians or perhaps the state can no longer control the flow of information, particularly if it is going over the Internet. All they can do is perhaps try to counter what is going on out there."[16] He explains that new media "forces the state machinery to open itself up to more scrutiny." What emerges here is the agonistic aspect of public sphere notion, associated with Arendt and Mouffe.

Gender-related political NGOs in particular have used new ICTs to expand political space for themselves and for women, especially among the dominant entities. However, most of the NGOs are conscious of the unique conditions and constraints that need to be taken into account. Another significant point is that the increased use of ICTs by NGOs, often to the disadvantage of some political parties, led to the launch of web sites by individual politicians and political parties in the Kenya and Zambia elections.

Infrastructural challenges like high cost and unreliable service often limit access. Interestingly NGOs and members of the public need not have their own internet access at home or in their offices to have experience. For instance ZIMT did not have in-office internet but its president was all the same very active in online discourse on Zambia.

This chapter has further illustrated the links between national and international civic networks that together combine to have some impact, however little, on the ruling regime locally.

This chapter has not quite clearly confirmed the argument by Hill and Hughes (1998, 1999) that the less democratic a country is, the more active her citizens are online; that ICTs have better prospects for democracy in faulty democracies, or what Dahl would call polyarchies, rather than in the extremes of autocracies and liberal democracies.

It is worth noting that while many of the civic actors in both countries have proved their longevity and resilience by surviving in the past decade or so, some have lost their mettle or become inactive, even de-registered. In Kenya, NCEC is no longer the potent actor it was but newer Internet-active players such as the formal Mars Group (www.marsgroupkenya.org) and the informal Bunge La Mwananchi or "The People's Parliament" (www.bungelamwananchi.org) have emerged. In Zambia, ZIMT and Afronet (as well as related organizations in their network) collapsed while the Catholic Centre for Justice, Development and Peace was renamed Caritas Zambia. Although CSOs such as LAZ and ZCEA that did not have plans for websites in 2002 embraced the space by 2012, developments have not been ICT-driven, but have been determined by societal factors—given that some of the web-active CSOs such as ZIMA receded.

PART V

Conclusion

CHAPTER 12

Civic Engagement, Digital Networks, and Political Reform in an Increasingly Open Digital Media Environment

There exists a dialectical tension on information and communication technology (ICT) impact, given that new media could be used to reinforce the status quo as well as bolster the efforts of counterhegemonic forces. McQuail (2000: 136) observed that it was "too early to conclude that politics has been given new life by new media, but there are emerging possibilities for 'electronic democracy' which do challenge" hegemonic political communication processes. Uche (1998) indicated that time was ripe for the study of the link between ICTs and democracy in Africa, more so because "empirical studies are yet to be conducted to ascertain the socio-cultural, economic and political ramifications" of ICTs. The results of this study on new media use by civil society organizations (CSOs) supports the "reinforcement" or "trend amplifier" model, and confirm that ICTs have indeed enabled the expansion of public communication space but only within the limits of what the technological, social, cultural, economic, and political environments could permit.

The majority of CSOs, especially NGO and media actors, in Kenya and Zambia as well as other African countries agreed that the communication landscape had changed significantly with the advent of new media. They used the internet or the world wide web in general, including the blogs and social networking sites, as well as e-mail and cell phones applications to gather and disseminate information, collaborate, and network with their local constituents or "clients," among themselves, and with foreign donors and partners, with much greater ease than was possible before. They could also use ICTs to lobby the central-national government and its officials and bureaucrats. In the earlier stages of the study in both Nairobi and Lusaka, the author immersed himself into typical daily routines of CSO operatives. Despite being such an attraction to petty Nairobi muggers and thugs to the extent that few wanted to risk to use it in public, the mobile phone tended to be ubiquitous and was a common method of communication among media and NGO operatives. While interviewing one NGO leader on a Friday, his mobile phone rang. It was one of the youth leaders finding out details about a meeting the NGO had organized for the following day in Buru Buru estate in the relatively more crowded "Eastlands" part of Nairobi.

Sitting in front of a computer, based at the reception of one of the NGOs, that offered a glimpse into their communication activities, the author watched all sorts of collaborative and strategic e-mails flowing in. Some e-mails would review previous operations; others would be about planning future short-term projects and many would debate the goings-on in politics, and possible courses of action for the NGO "community." To fathom what it would feel like to not to be privileged with in-office or at-home internet access, the author walked into public access internet cafes to use the facilities and also watch CSO actors as well as ordinary folk use them. In Nairobi, there were so many private internet and telephone centres competing for clients that costs had come down to KShs1 a minute with a minimum charge for 10 to 15 minutes, or KShs60 (GB£0.40 or Euros0.60, US$0.75) per hour, with generous discounts for clients staying longer; by 2010 some cybercafés were charging a third to a half this fee in Nairobi city center and in some heavily populated slums such as Nairobi's Kibera. In Lusaka, the cost was a little higher due to lower demand, lower income levels and less competition—but it kept on going down all the same. However, Lusaka was unique in the earlier stages of the study with non-corporate access centers, for example at the British Council and the UN Economic Commission for Africa, where, especially in the latter, CSO actors, particularly journalists, were offered free or nearly free access based on prior arrangements. Turning up at the World Bank premises in Lusaka for an IT-facilitated live televideo conference linking then World Bank President James Wolfensohn with NGO leaders in Lusaka, Sarajevo, London, and Brussels, it was striking that the very first question asked from Zambia, by a woman NGO leader, was about efforts to facilitate IT access for enhancement of national and regional NGO networking. Hanging around on a different day with some of the NGO officials at the Lusaka Conference Centre, it was interesting to watch one of them type a press statement using his laptop computer while discussing NGO matters with a leader of another NGO. The following day, the subject of the press statement was the lead news story in a leading local daily—and was second lead or in the inside front page of the other newspapers. Even for the researcher who had lived and worked in Africa for many years, things had significantly changed within just a few years of absence, with prospects of further changes in the horizon. A few observations need to be made.

First, local civic actors and media have developed local, regional, and international links with actors whose resources they sometimes summon to bring to bear pressure on their own governments. Violations of human rights and harassment of media workers were quickly reported via modern ICTs to international monitors of breaches in these realms, some of whom wrote directly to the president to condemn a repressive action or appeal for release of arrested journalists or NGO officials. We have seen how in one instance, two Zambian NGO officials got freed after using mobile phones to draw attention to their plight in a police cell.

Second, the new network media have rendered futile, and therefore reduced, tyrannical efforts by the Nairobi and Lusaka governments, as well as those of other countries, to clamp down on the mass media workers, owners, and their production equipment. Senior political figures have resorted to using less primitive means, such as information/media management through spin-doctors and the use of due process of the law, to control at least local media content. For instance in Kenya, former President Moi got the courts to issue a gagging order preventing the *Nation* from publishing a story on corruption scandal involving his son—although his successor President Kibaki's regime exhibited regression through a 2006 crude raid on the Standard Media Group's premises seemingly to prevent them publishing a politically sensitive story. In March 2000, Moi's henchman Nicholas Biwott was awarded KSh20 million (US$250,000) against the *People* newspaper over an energy-sector corruption story, bringing Biwott's total awards over libel to Kshs60 million (US$750,000) in two years.[1] Within 100 days of being in office, President Kibaki instituted contempt of court proceedings against the *East African Standard* and the *Kenya Times* for covering a court case for about a KShs10 million (US$125,000) debt the president had owed for a long time before he took office after the 2002 elections. In other words, even though the Presidency may no longer phone newspapers directly to successfully "kill" stories, journalists are no longer sacked, arrested, tortured, or killed for doing their work, and printing presses are no longer raided *as much as and as often as* the pre-1990s,[2] but journalists still exercise self-censorship due to new forms of curbs on their freedom. In Zambia, the *Post* editor was often arrested and arraigned in court, for instance because his newspaper quoted rival politicians calling former President Chiluba "a thief" or later President Mwanawasa a "cabbage." By the end of 1996, the *Post* faced over 90 libel and defamation cases filed against it by the government or its officials over stories on corruption and unpopular policies.[3] As a result, the editor resorted to increasing his capacity to understand the law and defend himself less expensively, by training as a lawyer at the University of Zambia.[4] The crux of the matter is that there are obstacles that still result in censorship of media content and curbing of civic activism, but governments are finding it more difficult to deal with informal networks. For as long as the mainstream media merely replicate content from their main print editions, qualitative expansion of the public sphere remains in jeopardy.

Having said that, it is important to note that journalists and NGO actors in Kenya and Zambia as well as other African countries are very resilient. They continue to report on sensitive scandals despite the risks. In fact, many are turning to ICTs to make their reporting more accurate and defensible (assuming the courts are fair—but, part of the problem is that Judiciaries in these countries are mostly not quite independent). An example is the way Kenyan journalists used the internet and e-mail to investigate various cross-border scandals.[5] In 2012, the Kenya Television Network showed footage of their investigative journalists interviewing via Skype video the infamous Artur brothers who had been linked to violence and scandals relating to corruption and abuse of power. Another point is that the mere presence of online editions of newspapers makes the leaders conscious that the world is watching, a realization that somewhat checks their excesses. Former President Moi was in the audience of an Africa meeting in 2000 where former US President Clinton said in his speech: "We can go online and read...the *East African* or dozens of other African newspapers." And the *East African*, an upmarket weekly subsidiary of the *Daily Nation* and *Sunday Nation*, reported with the headline: "I Read the *East African*—Says Clinton" (Mudhai, 2002). Moi had often complained about the way online editions of newspapers spread unpleasant news about Kenya, damaging the country's image. Soon after taking over from Moi, there were media reports that Kibaki's entourage to the United States included someone whose only job was to download stories from online editions of Kenyan newspapers and take/show them to the President and his team. This "joy rider" underscored the importance the President and his top officials attach to local media reports appearing online.

Third, it is discernible that the internet, e-mail and cell phones were useful especially for NGOs during elections in Kenya and Zambia as well as a number of other African countries given that election results were promptly posted on web sites and announced on the radio and TV. In Kenya, cell phones helped identify problems in rural polling stations and combat fraud in the 2002 elections.[6] This trend was enhanced in the controversial 2007 elections—marked by live broadcasts that were at one point banned by the government but with little effect on web and cell phone channels. Using fixed and cell phones where possible, election monitors communicated results as soon as Electoral Commission of Kenya (ECK) officials announced them—thus reducing chances of vote rig in 2002.[7] Attempts by cornered incumbents to rig in 2007 only made the situation explosive—resulting in strife that was only cooled by the international community in early 2008. It would appear the government had realized the utility of ICTs in elections, going by the blocking of internet services via state monopoly backbone in some instances.

Fourth, NGOs continue to embark on even more intensive use of ICTs in most African countries. In Nigeria, a collaborative effort by US donors and academicians brought together NGOs of 2009 and 2010 to strategize on ICT use in that country's 2011 elections. In Kenya, the National Council of NGOs put together ahead of the 2007 elections a US$180,000 proposal under NGONET.[8] One significant aspect of this proposal was its delineation of a gender component.[9] Indeed, ICTs have made it possible for previously less visible categories of elites—particularly women and the youth—to thrive as they embrace the new media much more readily. A good number of those studied for this book fall into such categories.

Fifth, CSO use of ICTs in a manner that has made them more efficient in their operations has awakened the state and top politicos to embrace similar technologies to match their CSO nemeses. In Nigeria, Goodluck Jonathan used Facebook to announce his much awaited declaration of candidacy for the 2011 election. In Zambia, the *Post*'s aggression compelled the government to launch online editions of state-owned newspapers, *Times of Zambia* and *Daily Mail.* In Kenya, new ICTs, especially computers, formed a crucial part of the government's radical reform of its justice, law, and governance structures at the total cost of Ksh2 billion (about US$25 million or GB£14 million).[10] The ruling elite that, under Moi,[11] had at some point banned government officers from using the internet and attempted to ban the use of fax machines had been converted into the discourse of Information Society. Viewed as "the most radical overhaul of the nation's governance structure in recent history," the reforms that then Justice and Constitutional Affairs assistant minister Njeru Githae described as "nothing short of a revolution" would "alter every Kenyan's way of life" through "dramatic changes into diverse areas in which the public interacts with the government"; and "when this thing is over, Kenya will be a changed country" (Mutiga, 2004). Still this did not purge the Judiciary's rotten apples as reforms that continued into 2012 showed.

It was envisaged the e-governance project would include e-voting system in future. This is perhaps what Cline-Cole and Powell (2004: 6) would see as donors urging developing countries to develop e-strategies and allocating increased shares of their aid receipts on ICT-related activities. As long as the facilities are maintained in working order, such projects—even if donor driven—would be a bonus for ordinary people not only in terms of service delivery but also in expansion of channels of communication between the rulers and the ruled.

Already, there is intra-elite communication among government officials, going by news reports indicating that former Constitution of Kenya Review Commission (CKRC) chairman Yash Pal Ghai often sent senior government colleagues official communication by e-mail while he was out of the country. The government also employed an official spokesperson and launched an official web site, with links to its organs like the State House and the National Assembly, as well as the 40 registered political parties and—wonder of wonders—the three main local daily newspapers and one weekly newspaper. A user had the facility to e-mail the State House as well as the President himself. Some countries such as Zambia may not have embarked on "wiring up" the government that much, but this trend is catching on.

This brings us back to ideas on models of communication and change. Instances of governmental information and motivation campaigns qualify as endogenous when in fact new communication facilities are created to make possible the implementation of new policies. At times such changes are truly massive in the sense that the new policy objectives of the leadership call for nothing less than the transformation of existing patterns of political communication and the creation of a new set of structures, relationships, and linkages (Fagan, 1966: 113). As Raab et al. (1996: 284) put it, such e-governance initiatives may introduce significant broad second-order e-democracy. Other than creating a "joined up" government, "the new technology will also open up the processes of administration to outside observers much more effectively than before. In so doing, administration will become more transparent, and more amenable to democratic pressures. This will lead to a virtuous circle of increasing transparency leading to greater efficiency and then to greater democracy" (Ferdinand, 2000b: 5). The mass emailing of party chief whips in South Africa as part of R2K anti-secrecy would not have happened if the officials had no email addresses to swarm in protest.

This reinforces the earlier cited point by Graham (1999: 66) on the relationship between ICT, enhancement of organizational-institutional efficiency, and democracy. Elites articulate developmental ideologies that incorporate ambitious plans for expanded media facilities designed to be used in the service of the state (Fagan, 1966: 120). Whether in the final analysis the desired systemic changes actually occur, "whether the citizens actually become more participant (*sic*), the bureaucracy more responsible, [and so on], is another question" (Fagan, 1966: 113). Countries like Malaysia embraced such endogenous change that ended up leading to a substantial expansion of the public sphere as unintended consequences (Abbott, 2001a, 2001b).

The sixth point is the fact that previously the governments of Kenya and Zambia as well as other African countries would not have taken up any such ambitious programs aimed at strengthening their institutions because there was little room for new or alien ideas. It is in this light that can be seen Kenyatta's ban on Ngugi wa Thiong'o's community theatre play, *Ngaahika Ndeeda* (Kikuyu for, *I Will Marry When I Want*) in the 1970s, for promoting dissent, and Moi's ban on the 1980s Kenyan TV family planning soap opera, *Tushauriane* (Swahili for "Let's Discuss")—ostensibly for being vulgar. Some theorists have argued that the "package" of manifestly non-political mass communication presented to audiences in the less-developed countries nevertheless has important political consequences for political change. "That is, by watching even such vulgar fare as the English-language horror, love, and adventure films widely circulated in Asia and Africa, the new citizens of these nations come to develop skills and attitudes of political relevance."[12] More simply, they learn to read the media in more sophisticated and potentially independent ways. The possible consequences of manifestly non-political artistic communication are well understood by absolutist rulers who strive to control cultural life lest the tastes and habits of independence and self-expression formed there carry over into political life (Fagan, 1966: 21). Browsing the internet, networking via social media, using e-mail or using the cell phone even if for private purposes may appear harmless to authorities but these cultural artifacts, as we have seen, have the capacity to be technologies of power—even if with some limits.

Until 2004, and perhaps more accurately up to 1998, ICTs developed in Kenya only exogenously as systemic elements and concomitants of the modernization process rather than because, endogenously, political elites decreed they should, as in Malaysia and the Super Corridor project. For a long time, all that mattered in both Kenya and Zambia as well as many other African countries were the visions of leaders, Kaunda's Humanism, Kenyatta's *Harambee*, and Moi's *Nyayoism*, which dominated all media outlets. Cabinet secrecy, intolerance of dissent, personal rule, authoritarianism, the big-man syndrome, strong-man syndrome, and "maximum" leadership have been used by various authors to characterize the leadership of Kenya and Zambia as well as other African countries, exhibited in several coup attempts or coups. Atieno-Odhiambo (1987: 189–91) saw such leadership in terms of "regimentation," "depoliticisation," and "canalisation," part of the "quest for hegemony by the state in all spheres of national life." Barkan (1992: 180) saw "manipulative and repressive" regime while Hyden saw uniform coercive political superstructure. All these lend credence to the use of state "hegemony" here, even if not necessarily in a strict Gramscian sense.

Seventh, even though Kenya and Zambia as well as a number of other African countries slipped back to a dominant party system rather than true multiparty democracy after reforms, there is little doubt that as a result of their aggressive activities, urban civic actors played a major role in some kind of weakening of the state and the authoritarian ruling elites. In Kenya,

> President Moi's authority [to govern] began to unravel and his always fairly feeble "party state" disintegrated *under pressure from radical intellectuals and politicians in Nairobi*...the "democratisaiton" process in Kenya was a relatively *peaceful affair*, providing both a classic study in *civil protest* and testimony to the *power* of the external world over the Kenyan economy and upon the *attitudes* of Kenyans. (Throup and Hornsby, 1998: 2)

The italicized [my emphases] words and phrases seem to add up to "soft power" that CSOs in particular tapped into partly through their ICT-enhanced faster global networking, especially with global CSO partners and the donor community.

> From 1990, at the peak of the government's authoritarian hold over all aspects of the country's life, it took only two years for the single-party system, with all it implied about the role of the state and the autonomy of the individual, to be *humbled* and *abandoned* [my emphases] in the last weeks of 1991. (Throup and Hornsby, 1998: 2)

The implication is that the state's sovereignty was clearly being threatened. While challenging the notion of a hegemonic postcolonial African state and the consequent perception of a counter-hegemonic functionally operative civil society, Chabal and Daloz (1999: 25–6) write:

> It could be argued that control over public media has enabled states to control information for their own hegemonic purposes. Even here, such manipulation of the information media is of little significance, for two main reasons. First, virtually all Africans have access to international radio (BBC, Radio France International, Deutsche Well, etc) and not a few can now receive satellite television. Second, informal means of communication (from gossip or rumour to the dissemination of news through non-official organizations like ethnic associations or African churches) are undoubtedly more efficient and more strongly influential than the official state-controlled media. Moreover, the resources devoted to the official media are regularly mis-employed, thus further weakening their impact. In Zambia, large sums have been spent not on improving media coverage but on air-conditioning the television headquarters.

Like many other Africanist scholars, these authors do not mention new media. Part of the answer to this omission, linked to lower ICT diffusion then, can be found in a 2002 survey by the International Republican Institute in 55 of Kenya's constituencies, which indicated that the main sources of information on politics for Kenyans were as follows: radio (68.2%), newspapers (64.7%), and TV (35.9%). Others included political meetings (15.5%), family and friends (11.4%), and religious meetings (4.9%). The mainstream media thus constituted over 70 percent of the main sources of information on political issues in Kenya (IED, 2003). The scenario has changed in most African countries since, but the concept of convergence is one to be borne in mind—in the sense that to remain relevant and sellable conventional media have embraced new media. All the same, a focus on the urban CSOs remains sensible as this category has greater access to new media according to earlier cited surveys that profile typical users.

Eighth, although we have discussed the rural–urban nexus as one that is blurred, it is important to visualize ways in which both CSOs and new media can, and often do, reach out to the rural dwellers. CSOs in Kenya and Zambia, as well as a number of other African countries, already play a major role as channels of communication with the rural folks; hence as mediators they are in a position to pass on their information and knowledge privileges or apply these plus skills in their service delivery. Zambia's Foundation for Democratic Process (FODEP) operates national, provincial, district, constituency, and ward level executive committees through which respective volunteers initiate and implement civic and voter education programs in accordance with the unique needs of their own communities. In 2001, FODEP had 6500 election monitors deployed in 5509 polling districts and 72 collation centers. They bought 81 bicycles, 1 for each of the 9 provinces and 72 districts to facilitate voter awareness and election observation. NGOCC, with 65 affiliates, reaches 75 percent of women in Zambia. The Kenyan Catholic network has about 630 parishes and around 7000 prayer houses; they deployed over 28,126 poll observers in the 1997 elections. These penetration levels are complemented by attempts to get new media to the rural areas, for instance Kenya's scheme on regional telecommunications providers. In addition, Posta Kenya uses V-SAT to link up hundreds of post offices including those in rural areas. In Zambia, an ISP publicized plans to penetrate rural areas.

> We have what they call the e-Link project and this is designed to bring broadband to rural areas…We want to provide Internet access on a single local number to bring the cost down. We're doing a pilot in Choma to prove the concept. We have done a wireless link from our broadband network using connectivity leased from a cellular phone provider.[13]

Finally, it is important to reiterate that there are limits to the democratic potential of civic actors, including CSOs-NGOs, and new media (Meadow, 1993: 442, 452–453). They do not have unlimited virtue in enhancing public participation and democratizing the practice of politics, as their abilities are limited by the cultural, economic, legal, and political environments. There are internal pressure (economic-ethnic tensions) and external weaknesses (reliance on bilateral and multilateral donors, especially the United States and the World Bank; government repression) that often result in post-transition dissipation. It is also vital to point out that CSOs and the new media are embedded in existing processes, and represent a continuity of off-line political interactions, like the national conference in Francophone Africa and Kenya's ubiquitous public political gathering or *baraza*—"an institutional window on contending forces in Kenyan social and political life" which "offer a window on processes occurring at multiple 'levels' of social agency (from locality to nation-state, from assistant chief to cabinet minister or president)" (Hageurd, 1997: 2–4,7–8). Fagan (1966: 4) reminds us that

> ultimately the communication process as it interests us must focus both on man himself and on the artefacts which man the toolmaker

> has created to extend his communicatory powers. No matter how a man's words and actions are multiplied and diffused by technology, no matter how impressive the structure of the mass media or the political organisations that he commands, it is still man the symbol producer and manipulator who stands as the one indispensable link in the communication process.

Barton (1979: 8) argued that Africans (owing to the impacts of the colonial-era struggle for independence) are the most natural politicians in the world; they are intrigued by the political process, the wheeling and dealing of politicians, the machinations of party politics. Hence, the political rumors, innuendos, and speculations taking place via new media represent continuity, rather than a radical break from Africa's past. Perhaps what may be new is the fact that new groups, like women and youth, are participating more actively in political realms, not necessarily because they had not been there before but perhaps more because the instruments of political power are more diffused and user-friendly. The soft power that is becoming more important in the information age is in part a social and economic by-product rather than solely a result of official government action (Nye Jr, 2004b: 32). Yet in the information age, governments that want to see rapid economic growth find that they can no longer maintain the barriers to information flows that historically protected officials from outside scrutiny (Nye, 2004: 91–2).

To borrow from Fagan (1966: 35), the picture revealed here is specific to the period and conditions around the time of the interviews and observations, but are pointers to more "generalizable" conclusions besides providing explanations to certain developments in the realms of ICT–CSO nexus in governance and politics.

This book has advanced the argument that urban-based political civil society actors, NGOs, and news media, in Kenya and Zambia as well as a number of African countries, perceive ICTs as presenting them with significant opportunities for achieving greater democracy at home in a global context. Representatives of these non-state actors view the internet, social media, e-mail, and the cell phone in particular as tools that have enhanced their operational efficiency and also helped them overcome obstacles often put in their way by the ruling elites whose aims are to ward off any form of challenge to their power. While recognizing that the new media enable the non-state actors to engage in cross-border communicational activities as a way of bringing about changes within states, the focus here has been on enabling or constraining local conditions and off-line factors.

Employing a recently modified public sphere concept taking into account civil society theory and social movement theory, this book takes the approach of combining interviews and media monitoring. In a departure from some of the overly deterministic literature, this study takes into account off-line contextual factors while paying particular attention to the perceptions on new media by a category of Africa's political actors who have been considered early ICT adopters and topmost users, as well as being largely accredited for recent waves of democratization.

In essence, the book advances four main arguments. First, democratization in Zambia and Kenya as well as a number of African countries does exist, and the new media have played some role in diffusing power and political activity more widely. The public sphere has opened up and broadened the elite to include groups such as women and the youth that were hitherto invisible or easily manipulated due to the dynamics of less open political arena and news values of mainstream media. Given the relatively closer relationship to the ordinary people of these new elite, this has meant possibilities of greater involvement of a wider society. For the state and politicos, the implication has been that of encroachment on a part of its authority, especially with respect to political views, by CSOs—hence the state's attempt to regain control by embracing new media as well. Up to this point, this book augments the widespread "democratization through new media" thesis. Yet, and second, it critically examines the naivety of many such arguments, and shows that such naivety is sustained mainly by a tendency to overgeneralize. Through case studies, the book demonstrates that the processes of both democratization and the deployment of the new media by civic actors—especially NGOs—are more complex and much more nuanced than the literature on the subject usually shows. Hence, third, the grounding of the study is in fieldwork carried out in some case study countries and interviews and communications with many of the key players. Finally, the study makes critical use of a modified concept of the public sphere in explaining processes of socio-political change in Kenya and Zambia as well as a number of African countries, paying attention to why the process of democratization, though real, has been partial, and why the new media have only partially fulfilled the promises commonly associated with them. It is the proposal of this book that CSOs, especially church-based organizations with their wider grassroots reach, should do more to pass on, directly through provision of hardware or indirectly through a two-step flow model, their ICT-based knowledge and skills to rural people and urban slum dwellers. In particular, they should help these categories include their own local content in the new media in order to minimize the risks, associated with globalization, of ICT-enthusiasm.

This book has looked at the use of new media by civic actors, but there are a number of related approaches and research initiatives that would be useful in future. As already hinted, a deeper analysis of e-governance, the Kenyan project cited above, is necessary using more penetrating methods than have been used so far (White, 1999). Another area worth examining is the use of ICTs by individual politicians and political parties (White, 1999; Gibson et al., 2003). The fact that in Kenya, "political parties made use of the internet for the first time in our political history, with the National Rainbow Coalition coming out strongest" (Khisa, 2003) is worth investigating. The third area that needs further investigation but which was, also, outside the scope of this book is the extent to which there exists more widespread political use of new media by ordinary folk, and if so in what forms.

Notes

Preface

1. 'Joe Donde for President www.joedonde.com [dormant]'. http://www.mashada.com/forums/politics/1109-joe-donde-president-http-www-joedonde-com-2.html (accessed April 25, 2012).
2. Event website: http://nigeria.gt4d.net (accessed May 15, 2012).
3. Event website: www.e-nigeria.org (accessed May 15, 2012).
4. Event website: www.westminster.ac.uk/research/a-z/africa-media-centre/events/events-calendar/2012/icts-new-media-and-social-change-in-africa (accessed May 15, 2012).
5. Event website: http://powerandrevolution.eventbrite.co.uk/ (accessed May 15, 2012).
6. Event website: www.crassh.cam.ac.uk/events/1323/ (accessed May 15, 2012).
7. Event website: http://summit2012.globalvoicesonline.org (accessed May 20, 2012).

1 General Introduction: Civic Challenge of Ruling Elite via New Digital Media in Africa

1. This by no means restricts the types of "waves"' (for Raymond Williams, *The Long Revolution* (London: Chatto & Windus, 1961), conceives of a cultural one, separately, as well) but is to aid this analysis as these are the key ones in the studies of politics, international relations, and media.
2. Africa's share of global FDI increased from 0.7% in 2000 to 5.3% in 2009—dipping slightly to 4.5% in 2010 (AEO, African Economic Outlook. 2012. Direct Investment Flows. www.africaneconomicoutlook.org/en/outlook/external-financial-flows/direct-investment-flows/ (accessed May 21, 2012)).
3. See US National Security Strategy, www.whitehouse.gov/.../national_security_strategy.pdf (accessed April 20, 2012).
4. Geneva pledged Swiss Francs 500,000 while Lyon pledged Euros 300,000 as Turin indicated it would also avail funds for the project aimed at funding ICT development in poor countries. (The author attended the event.)

5. The Kikuyu formed over half of Nairobi's black population, and controlled its economy. Little wonder moderate non-Kikuyu politicians and shopkeepers were the first victims of political terror in the early 1950s and in the first months of the October 1952 declaration of the State of Emergency by the colonial government (J. Lonsdale, "Explanations of the Mau Mau Revolt." In *Resistance and Ideology in Settler Societies* (Southern African Studies Vol. 4), edited by T. Lodge, (Johannesburg: Ravan Press, 1986), 168–78).

2 Private–Public Sphere: Civic Engagement, New Media, and Democracy Theory

1. See: T. Lowi, *The End of Liberalism: The Second Republic of the United States* (New York: Norton, 1979).
2. See also J. Keane, *Democracy and Civil Society* (London and New York: Verso, 1988), 1, 4; L. Diamond, "Introduction: In Search of Consolidation." In *Consolidating the Third Wave of Democracies: Themes and Perspectives*, eds L. Diamond, M. F. Plattner, Y. Chu, and H. Tien (Baltimore & London: Johns Hopkins University Press, 1997), xxx; Pinkney, R., *Democracy in the Third World* (London: Lynne Rienner, 2003), 88.
3. Karl Deutsch, "Social Mobilisation and Political Development," *American Political Science Review* 55 (1961), 439–514.
4. These include A. de Tocqueville, K. Marx, and F. Hegel, covering also the concept of "public opinion."
5. The term "public sphere" could be seen as an imperfect translation of the original *Öffentlichkeit* which does not contain the same spatial metaphor and therefore suggests a greater emphasis on the *process* rather than the institutional locus of public deliberation (L. Goode, Politics and the Public Sphere: The Social-Political Theory of Jurgen Habermas, D. Phil Thesis, (Nottingham Trent University, 1999), 6, citing Strum).
6. See also: Michael Walzer in McQuail, *McQuail's Mass Communication Theory*, 4th edn (London: Sage, 2000), 158.
7. In E. Gellner, *Conditions of Liberty: Civil Society and Its Rivals* (London: Hamish Hamilton, 1994).
8. Larry Diamond, "Rethinking Civil Society: Toward Democratic Consolidation," *Journal of Democracy* 5, no. 3 (1994) quoted by Funso Folayan, "Civil Society, Popular Culture and the Crisis of Democratic Transitions in Nigeria,"' In *African Democracy in the Era of Globalisation*, J. Hyslop (Johannesburg: Witswatserand University Press, 1999), 72–79.
9. My emphases.
10. These are Carl Schmitt and Reinhart Koselleck put together with Habermas under those taking historical approaches, as well as Michel Foucalt as a genealogical critique (Arendt's is seen as normative critique

while Luhmann's as system-theoretic critique). Cohen and Arato also show how Antonio Gramsci and Talcott Parsons, though in overly monistic and functionalist terms leading to ambivalence and apologia, improved on Hegel's original theoretical synthesis of civil society (legality; plurality and association; publicity and privacy; and mediation and interpenetration) by abandoning his statist bias and economism See J. L. Cohen and A. Arato, *Civil Society and Political Theory* (London & Cambridge, MA: MIT Press, 1992), xiv, xv, 177–341.

11. Originally published in 1996.
12. See note 25 in C. Calhoun, 2002. Information Technology and the International Public Sphere, a paper presented at International Sociological Association, Brisbane, Australia, July 11. Habermas also borrows heavily from Arendt with regard to structuring law by life world of actors, expressed in "communicative power," and "administrative power" of systemic control (S. K. White, "Reason, Modernity and Democracy," In *The Cambridge Companion to Habermas,* ed. S. K. White (Cambridge: Cambridge University Press, 1995), 12).
13. Citing from the "Citizenship and National Identity" chapter in J. Habermas, *Between Facts and Norms: Contributions to a Discourse Theory of Law and Democracy*, trans. W. Rehg (Oxford: Polity, 1996/1992), 514.
14. For Habermas, moral-practical discourse is just one form of problem-solving communication. He also refers to theoretical discourse that seeks truth in scientific investigation, aesthetic criticism that seeks beauty in artistic endeavors, and therapeutic critique that seeks understanding in self-reflection (L. Dahlberg, "Extending the Public Sphere through Cyberspace: The Case of Minnesota E-Democracy," *First Monday* 6, no. 3 (2001), March. http://firstmonday.org/htbin/cgiwrap/bin/ojs/index.php/fm/article/view/838/747, accessed April 18, 2012).
15. Attributed to Nancy Fraser.
16. He also acknowledges the *plebeian* public sphere and the regimented plebiscitary-acclamatory version.
17. Thomas McCarthy in the "Introduction" to J. Habermas, *The Structural Transformation of the Public Sphere: An Inquiry into a Category of Bourgeois Society.* Trans T. Burger with the assistance of F. Lawrence (MIT: Polity, 1989/1962), xii.
18. See also Van Dijk, *The Network Society* (London: Sage, 1999), 164–5.
19. Keane (2000: 87), quoting from Lefebvre (1974), *La production de l'espace,* 116. Jayne Rodgers applies Lefevbre's spatial theories in *Spatializing International Politics: Analysing NGO's use of the Internet* (London: Routledge, 2003).
20. Everett M. Rogers and Sheena Malhotra, "Computer as Communications: The Rise of Digital Democracy," In *Digital Democracy: Issues of Theory and Practice,* eds K. L. Hacker and J. Van Dijk (London: Sage, 2000), 11–29.

21. P. Grundy 2012. Electoral Apathy Affects All of Us. http://scan.lusu.co.uk/comment/2012/05/22/electoral-apathy-affects-all-of-us/ (accessed May 22, 2012). See also Ferdinand, 2000: 7
22. Silenced: An International Report on Censorship and Control of the Internet, by Privacy International and GreenNet Trust (2003).
23. Working research paper, The Internet in Kenya: Impacts and Development (2001), in the Telematics for Development Program of the Centre for International Development and Conflict Management, University of Maryland.
24. R. E. Rice and F. Williams, "Theories Old and New: The Study of New Media," In *The New Media,* ed. R. E. Rice (Beverley Hills, CA: Sage, 1984), 55–80. Cited in Preface, S. Jones (ed.), *Doing Internet Research: Critical Issues and Methods for Examining the Net* (London: Sage, 1999), x.
25. F. Williams, R. E. Rice, and E. M. Rogers, *Research Methods and the New Media* (New York: Free Press, 1988), 15. Cited in Preface, Jones (1999: xiii).
26. Tomlinson, J. "Reviews: G. Wang, J. Servaes, and A. Goonasekera (eds.), *The New Communications Landscape: Demystifying Media Globalisation* (London: Routledge, 2000)." *European Journal of Communication* 16 no. 2 (2001): 251–2
27. Gerhart, G. M. Review of *Democratic Experiments in Africa: Regime Transitions in Comparative Perspective* by M. Bratton and N. Van de Walle (Cambridge: Cambridge University Press, 1997)". *Foreign Affairs, September-October, 1998.*, September/October 1998.
28. Measuring internet users in Africa is difficult because accounts are predominantly shared and public. However, projections based on UN reports indicate there were 10–12 million internet users out of a population of 780 million at the end of 2003. Nearly a third of the users are in North and South Africa, leaving an average sub-Saharan access of one user for every 250–300 people. Compare this to 2002 UNDP World Development Report figures of one for 250 in South Asia, one for 166 in the Arab states, one for 43 in East Asia and one for 30 in Latin America and the Caribbean.
29. Lawrence K. Grossman, *The Electronic Republic: Reshaping Democracy in the Information Age* (New York: Viking, 1995).
30. "Government Offices to Acquire Internet Access," the *Daily Nation*, February 28, 2004.
31. See for example: Arrests Over Anti-Mugabe Emails, BBC, November 21, 2003. http://news.bbc.co.uk/2/hi/africa/3227008.stm (accessed May 22, 2012).

3 The "Wave" and "Spring" Metaphors in Networks' Struggle for Change

1. Harold D. Lasswell, "The Structure and Function of Communication in Society," In *The Communication of Ideas,* eds Lyman Bryson (New

York: Harper & Row, 1948), 37 as cited in R. R. Fagan, *Politics and Communication: An Analytic Study* (Boston: Little, Brown & Co, 1966), 4. In the general model or structure, we can say that every act of human communication involves a *source* generating a *message* (or signal) that travels through a *channel* to an *audience*. What the message means is a different matter.

2. This distinction is made in Wilbur Schramm (1955), "How Communication Works." In W. Schramm (ed.), *The Process and Effects of Mass Communication* (Urbana, IL: University of Illinois Press) (cited in Fagan, 1966: 17–18).
3. G. A. Almond and G. B. Powell, *Comparative Politics: A Development Approach* (Boston: Little, Brown & Co., 1966).
4. L. W. Pye, *Communications and Political Development* (Princeton, NJ: Princeton University Press, 1963).
5. Ibid, p. 6 (cited in Fagan, 1966: 128).
6. "Social Mobilisation and Political Development," *American Political Science Review*, LV, no. 3 (1961), 493–514.
7. James Madison, "Letter to W.T. Barry (August 4, 1822)," in *The Writings of James Madison*, vol. 9, p. 103 (cited in Keane, J., *The Media and Democracy* (Cambridge: Polity Press, 1991), p. 176.
8. In *Amérique*, 1986; *L'Autre par lui-Même*, 1987; *The Evil Demon of Images*, 1988.
9. Information Technology and Information Society: Options for the Future, London: ESRC, 1988
10. In A. Giddens, *Social Theory and Modern Sociology* (Oxford: Polity Press, 1987), 27.
11. Liberal democracy encompasses extensive protections for individual and group freedoms, inclusive pluralism in civil society as well as party politics, civilian control over military, institutions to hold officeholders accountable, and thus a strong rule of law secured through an independent, impartial judiciary (Diamond, L., "Introduction: In Search of Consolidation," In *Consolidating the Third Wave of Democracies: Themes and Perspectives*, eds L. Diamond, M. F. Plattner, Y. Chu, and H. Tien (Baltimore & London: Johns Hopkins University Press, 1997), xiv.)
12. Pinkney lists conditions as: economic development, associated with S. M. Lipset; sequences in development (R. Dahl, and L. Binder); political attitudes and behavior (G. A. Almond and S. Verba); political institutions (M. Heper and E. H. Stephens); external influences (D. M. Green); inter-elite relations (D. A. Rustow, and A. Valenzuela); social structures and interaction between social groups (B. Moore). See R. Pinkney, *Democracy in the Third World* (London: Lynne Rienner, 2003), 21–42.
13. While issues like debt relief and environmental degradation are close to the hearts of many Africans, some such as gay or lesbian identities are of greater value only in certain parts of Africa such as Uganda and Zimbabwe.

14. Launched in 1961 by British lawyer Peter Benenson to promote all the human rights enshrined in the 1948 Universal Declaration of Human Rights and other international standards.
15. For a good collection of writings on political parties and the internet, see Gibson et al., *Political Parties and the Internet: Net Gain?* (London & New York: Routledge, 2003).
16. By which no notion of freedom is really absolute, but necessarily takes the form of a normative structure, a social order.

4 Civic Engagement, the African State, and Political Reform

1. S. P. Huntington, (1965), "Political Development and Political Decay," *World Politics* 17, no. 3 (1965), 386–430.
2. See also J. H. Frimpong-Ansah, *The Vampire State: The Political Economy of Decline in Ghana* (London: James Currey, 1991) cited here.
3. Quoting M. K. Van Klinken, "Beyond the NGO-Government Divide: Network NGOs in East Africa," *Development in Practice* 8, no. 3 (1988), 349–353.
4. Quoting: Peter Lewis, "Political Transition and the Dilemma of Civil Society in Africa," *Journal of International Affairs* 27 (1992), 31–54.
5. Defined by Larry Diamond as "the process by which democracy becomes so broadly and profoundly legitimate among its citizens that it is very unlikely to break down," in "Towards Democratic Consolidation," *Journal of Democracy* 5 (1994), 4–18.
6. J. Hearn, *Foreign Aid, Democratisation, and Civil Society in Africa: A Study of South Africa, Ghana and Uganda* (Brighton: Institute of Development Studies, 2000), 19. Online at http://ntl.ids.ac.uk/eldis/hot/civsoc.htm (Pinkey, 2003: 101).
7. Weak development of political parties and the ethnic, regional, and religious divisions that often characterize African societies.
8. Citing K. Wellard and J. G. Copestake (eds.), *Non-Governmental Organisations and the State in Africa: Rethinking Roles in Sustainable Agricultural Development* (New York: Routledge, 1994), 290.

5 Power and Influence in the Digital Age: New Challenges to State Hegemony

1. The role of the Hearst press in driving the United States to war in 1898 against Spain for Cuba and the Philippines, the role of CNN in reporting the Gulf War in 1990–1991 and the US military intervention in Somalia, and the impact of media reporting (including on the internet) of the death of Princess Diana in 1997.
2. C. Beard in *The Economic Basis of Politics* (New York: A.A. Knopf, 1934), 67 on 1930s America.

3. Quoted in M. Franda, *Launching into Cyberspace: Internet Development and Politics in Five World Regions* (Boulder & London: Lynne Rienner, 2002), 236 from de Sola Pool as excerpted in Lloyd S. Etheredge (ed.), *Politics in Wired Nations: Selected Writings of Ithiel de Sola Pool* (London: Transaction, 1998), 363.
4. Katz and Aakhus, *Perpectual Contact: Mobile Communication, Private Talk, Public Performance*, (Cambridge and New York: Cambridge University Press, 2002), 315, catalogue structuration theories as including: W. Orlikowski's "duality of technology" (Giddens' duality of structure?), that technology shapes and is shaped by human action; M. S. Poole and G. DeSanctis on "adaptive structuration theory," that people appropriate advanced information systems into their work; Silverstone and Haddon propose "domestication" variant, emphasizing the integration of personal technology into everyday domestic life.
5. Manobi launches in Senegal a free-access SMS market information service. http://www.manobi.sn/sites/za/index.php?M=9&SM=20&Cle=54 (accessed April 27, 2012).
6. Vendors of mobile phone services who carry out their "mobile" business stationed under umbrellas.
7. With a population of 11 million, Filipino capital Manila is among the ten worst polluted cities in Asia–with automobile PM10 and gasoline emissions linked to 5223 deaths in 1996 (A. Tan, "Cell Phones May Be Key to Cleaner Air in Philipines," *Christian Science Monitor* Online, (July 9, 2002), http://www.csmonitor.com/2002/0719/p07s02-woap.html (12 October 2012)., qtg ADB)
8. Citizens were protesting attempts by US-educated President Gonzalo Sanchez de Lozada's $5 billion project to export the country's natural gas reserves to California and Mexico through neighboring historical enemy, Chile–which annexed Bolivia's coastline in an 1879 "War of the Pacific."
9. The payphone project by Grameen Telecom (GTC), which started in 1995 as one of Bangladesh's largest non-profit organizations, planned to install 40,000 village phones or VPs by 2004 in a bid to serve 100 million rural inhabitants in the country's 68,000 villages. By mid 2012 GTC, holding 34.2 percent share of the country's leading cell phone operator Grameenphone that is majority owned (55.8%) by Norway's Telenor, had installed 935,407 VPs in 81,000 out of 85,500 villages in the counry. See: Present Status, http://www.grameentelecom.net.bd/vp3.html; Grameenphone ownership, http://investor-relations.grameenphone.com/IRPortal/Admin/PageDetails/?id=9 (October 13, 2012).
10. "US expels Venezuelan diplomat who 'discussed cyberwar on America' ". AP/*Guardian*, (January 9, 2012), http://www.guardian.co.uk/world/2012/jan/09/us-expels-venezuelan-diplomat-cyber (October 13, 2012).

6 Platforms and Applications Diffusion: Civic Engagement and ICT Trends

1. Email interview with author (May 12, 2012).
2. Also see Mercy Corps's excellent chart on this subject in *Civic Engagement of the Youth in the Middle East and North Africa: An Analysis of Key Drivers and Outcomes* (Portland, OR: Mercy Corps, 2012), 8.

7 Identity and Issue Networks: New Media, Politics of Belonging, and Change

1. Posting title, "Africa: NGO and Electronic Communication," distributed April 29, 2002, reposted by US-based Africa Action (inc. Africa Policy Information Centre, Africa Fund & American Committee on Africa) on the Africa Policy Electronic Distribution List. http://www.africaaction.org/docs02/ict0204.htm (accessed February 2003).
2. The mass media can in themselves be CSOs.
3. Businessman Said, 28, died in police custody in Egypt in mid-2010, and Ghonim paid tribute after he himself had been incarcerated for nearly two weeks.
4. *Guardian* (UK), Egypt Activist Wael Ghonim Tells TV Station: "I'm no hero," February 8, 2011. http://www.guardian.co.uk/world/video/2011/feb/08/egypt-activist-wael-ghonim-google-video (accessed February 10, 2012).
5. Interview with author in Luton, UK (April 13, 2012).
6. Accessed via SACOMM mailing list, November 21, 2011.
7. See Avaaz "Stop the Secrecy Bill" link: http://www.avaaz.org/en/stop_the_secrecy_bill/?cl=1273599713&v=10269 (accessed May 10, 2012).
8. Avaaz, ibid. Bold text is as per original.
9. SACOMM representative at R2K, accessed via SACOMM listserv, November 22, 2011.
10. Avaaz, ibid. Bold text is as per original.
11. R2K press release, November 21, 2011.
12. R2K press release, November 21, 2012.
13. R2K press release, ibid.
14. The seven points: 1. Limit secrecy to core state bodies in the security sector such as the police, defence, and intelligence agencies; 2. Limit secrecy to strictly defined national security matters; 3. Exclude commercial information; 4. Do not exempt the intelligence agencies from public scrutiny; 5. Apply penalty for unauthorized disclosure to only those responsible for keeping secrets rather than to the society at large; 6. Do not criminalize whistleblowers and journalists, and protect those who release classified information if that information is in the public interest; 7. An independent body appointed by

Parliament, and not the Minister of State Security, should be able to review decisions about what may be made secret. See: R2K update, "The Secrecy Bill Still Fails the Freedom Test," August 29, 2011, http://www.r2k.org.za/r2k.org.za/index.php?option=com_content&view=article&id=278:the-secrecy-bill-still-fails-the-freedom-test-&catid=36:updates&Itemid=56 (accessed May 10, 2012).

15. E-mail response by R2K SA National Co-ordinator, to author's questions (May 12, 2012).
16. Ibid.
17. Ibid.
18. From web site, www.africandemocracyforum.org (accessed March 15, 2012).
19. The Malawian Kwacha figure translates to $4 or £2.50.

8 *La Luta Continua*: Transition and Disillusionment in the "Second Liberation" and the "Third Republic"

1. That is, the more democracy the less stable the state and the society.
2. The total votes to opposition presidential candidates exceeded Moi's votes.
3. It is vital to note here that there have been at least three coup attempts in Kenya from the 1970s to the mid-1990s.
4. For a further discussion of *harambee* see also P. M Mbithi and R. Rasmusson, *Self Reliance in Kenya: The Case of Harambee* (Uppsala: The Scandinavian Institute of African Studies, 1971) and B. P. Thomas, *Politics, Participation, and Poverty: Development Through Self-Help in Kenya* (Boulder & London: Westview Press, 1985).
5. Marc Howard Ross (1971), "Grassroots in the City: Political Participation and Alienation in Nairobi after Independence", unpublished manuscript, 304, cited in Bienen, *Kenya: The Politics of Participation and Control* (Princeton, NJ: Princeton University Press, 1974), 4.
6. J. M. Kariuki feared for Kenya of ten millionaires and ten million beggars (wa Gĩthĩnji, *Ten Millionaires and Ten Million Beggars: A Study of Income Distribution and Development in Kenya* (Aldershot: Ashgate, 2000)).
7. This touches on a large literature. See in particular: E. A. Brett, *Colonialism and Underdevelopment in East Africa: The Politics of Economic Change, 1919–1939* (London: Heinemann, 1973); Colin Leys, *Underdevelopment in Kenya: The Political Economy of Neocolonialism 1964–1971* (London: Heinemann, 1974); C. Leys, "Capital Accumulation, Class Formation and Dependency: The Significance of the Kenyan Case." In *Socialist Register 1978*, eds Ralph Miliband and John Saville (London: Merlin Press, 1978), 241–266; Michael Cowen, "Capital and Household Production: The Case of

Wattle in Kenya's Central Province, 1903–1964," Ph.D. dissertation, Cambridge University, 1979; Bjorn Beckman, "Imperialism and Capitalist Transformation: Critique of a Kenyan Debate," *Review of African Political Economy* 19 (1980), 48–62; Nicola Swainson, *The Development of Corporate Capitalism in Kenya, 1918–1977* (Berkeley: University of California Press, 1980); C. Leys, "Accumulation, Class Formation and Dependency: Kenya." In *Industry and Accumulation in Africa*, ed. Martin Fransman (London: Heinemann, 1982), 170–192; Raphael Kaplinsky, "Capitalist Accumulation in the Periphery: Kenya." In *Industry and Accumulation in Africa*, ed. Martin Fransman (London: Heinemann, 1982), 193–220.

8. Eric Bjornlund, Michael Bratton, and Clark Gibson, "Observing Multiparty Elections in Africa: Lessons from Zambia," *African Affairs* 91 (1992), 405–431; Larry Garber and Clark Gibson, *The October 31 1991 National Elections in Zambia* Washington: NDI, 1992).
9. "Kenya Democracy & Governance Project (615–0266) (1994–1997)," Washington DC: USAID, in Reynolds, A. *Electoral Systems and Democratisation in Southern Africa* (Oxford: Oxford University Press, 1999), 104. For details of recent projects, see: http://kenya.usaid.gov/programs/democracy-and-governance/projects (October 14, 2012).

9 Civic Actors and the Struggle for Change: Precursors to New Social Movements in Kenya and Zambia

1. The others are the 1833–1865 Anglo-American campaign to end slavery in the United States; the efforts of the international suffrage movements to secure the vote for women between 1888 and 1928; the campaign from 1874 to 1911 by Western missionaries and Chinese reformers to eradicate footbinding in China.
2. Such as land alienation for European settlers, heavy hut and poll taxes, and an oppressive labor recruiting system.
3. Citing Ann Beck (1966), "Some Observations on Jomo Kenyatta in Britain 1929–1930," *Cahiers d'Etudes Africaines* 6, no. 22: 308, 313.
4. Citing Beck (1966), 325.
5. Citing Marshall S. Clough (1990), *Fighting Two Sides: Kenyan Chiefs and Politicians, 1918–1940* (Niwot, Co: University of Colorado, 1990), 145.
6. For more on Mau Mau see Rosberg and Nottingham (1966); Kitching (1980); Lonsdale (1986). Kagwanja (2003) "Facing Mount Kenya or Facing Mecca? The Mungiki, Ethnic Violence and Politics of the Moi Succession in Kenya, 1987–2002," *African Affairs* 102, no. 407: 25–49, compares the Mau Mau with *Mungiki*, a more recent ethnic-political group also associated with the Kikuyu.
7. An estimate by an official of the country's NGO Council in a face-to-face interview (September 2002).

8. Figure provided by NGO Coordinating Board in Report on the National Validation of NGOs 2009.
9. NGO-NET, Internet for NGOs in Kenya, www.ngonet.mgn.fr /main/index-us.html (September 2004).
10. Citing Paul Gifford (1992), "Bishops For Reform," *Tablet* May 30, 1992, 672–3.
11. These included: National Organisation for Civic Education (NOCE), Zambia Civic Education Association (ZCEA), Zambia Independent Monitoring Team (ZIMT), Democratic Governance Association of Zambia (DGAZ), Zambia Reconstruction Organisation (ZAMRO), Voters Association of Zambia (VAZ), Anti-Voter Apathy Project (AVAP), Foundation for Democratic Process (FODEP), Zambia National Women Lobby Group (ZNWLG), Forum for Human Rights (FORIGHTS) and Southern African Centre for the Constructive Resolution of Disputes (SACCORD). See ECZ: www.elections.org.zm/ (September 2004).
12. Citing Gifford, as above.
13. See, for example, blogger Cidan's posting of July 7, 2004 titled "and he's back," at http://mithlond.blogspot.com/2004_07_01_mithlond _archive.html (February 2005). Githongo later resigned and fled the country to seek refuge in London amidst death threat rumors.
14. Citing Carolyne Baylies and Morris Szeftel, "The 1996 Zambian Elections: Still Awaiting Democratic Consolidatin," *Review of African Political Economy* 71 (1997): 113–28; Michael Bratton and Daniel Posner, "A First Look at Second Elections in Africa, with Illustration from Zambia." In Richard Joseph (ed.), *State, Conflict and Democracy in Africa* (Boulder, CO: Lynne Rienner, 1999), 377–408.
15. "Promoting Democracy Through Positive Conditionality," University of Leeds.

10 Unmuzzling Old Dogs to Bark Anew Far and Wide

1. Mitch Odero, "Press in Kenya: An Overview." In *Media Culture and Performance in Kenya*, eds Odero and Kamweru (Nairobi: Eastern Africa Media Institute–Kenya Chapter & Friedrich Ebert Stiftung, 2000), 11.
2. For instance J. Nyerere's African Socialism in Tanzania and Leopold S. Senghor's Negritude in Senegal.
3. George Ayittey, *Africa Betrayed* (New York: St Martin's, 1992), 37–77 (quoted in Bourgault, *Mass Media in Sub-Saharan Africa* (Bloomington and Indianapolis: Indiana University Press, 1995), 50–51.
4. In contrast, West Africa was considered the "white man's grave" (Hachten, *Muffled Drums: The News Media in Africa* (Iowa: Iowa State University Press, 1971), 199). Kenya's fertile highlands made it

more popular than the other British East Africa neighbors of Uganda and Tanzania.

5. Kaunda's personal philosophy of Humanism was adopted in 1967 by the ruling UNIP as the official philosophy of Zambia. It placed man at the center of society and above all institutions, and advocated respect for human dignity and quality of life. See K. D. Kaunda, *A Letter to My Children* (Lusaka: Government Press, 1967).
6. Part II 5 of the Suppression of Terrorism Bill (2003). The bill needs to be seen in the context of the August 1998 bombing of the US embassies in Nairobi and the neighboring Tanzanian city of Dar es Salaam, resulting in more than 250 deaths and another terrorist attack on Israeli tourists in Mombasa in 2002, and the issuance of travel advisory to US (and also British) citizens not to visit Kenya.
7. Opanga seemed to believe KANU would target the *Nation* rather than individual journalists. It did both.
8. The *Nation* reported the following day that Opanga opted to resign but he appeared to have had no choice (a jobless Opanga later said his priority was putting bread on the table) after falling into some kind of trap set by KANU and machinated within and outside the *Nation*.
9. While the few so-called KANU scholars (especially at Kenyatta University) were widely known because they did not hide their rendezvous with the then largely unpopular party, "KANU journalists" were furtive.
10. J. Katz, "On Line or Not, Newspapers Suck," *Wired* 2, no. 9 (1994): 50–58.
11. For similar ideas see Lapham (1995); Breecher (1999); Finkbeiner (2003); Gelernter (2003).
12. Among the 50 participants were representatives of the Economic Commission of Africa (Ethiopia), Media Action International (Geneva), Open Society West Africa (Senegal), Groupe Afri Concept (Benin), and AMARC Africa. See: www.geneva2003.org/bamako2002/doc_html/media-en.html (Accessed: Sept '03).
13. One World, at http://radio.oneworld.net/index.php?fuseaction=cms.fullContent&id=1280 (June 2003).
14. www.africaonline.com (July 2003).
15. www.allafrica.com (July 2003).
16. AllAfrica.com, "Who We Are," http://allafrica.com/whoweare.html (July 2003).
17. www.ips.org/africa.shtml (July 2003).
18. www.panapress.com (July 2003).
19. See also Joe S. M. Kadhi (1999), "Internet Plays Increasing Role in Africa's Press," a paper delivered at a Freedom Forum conference in Johannesburg, Sept, www.freedomforum.org; Tanya Accone (2000), "Digital Dividends for Journalism in Africa," *Nieman Reports* 54, no. 4: 67–70; O. F. Mudhai, "The Internet: Triumphs and Trials for

Kenyan Journalism," in *Beyond Boundaries: Cyberspace in Africa*, edited by M. B. Robins and R. L. Hilliard, 89–104 (Portsmouth, NH: Heinemann, 2002); Marcus Franda, *Launching into Cyberspace: Internet Development and Politics in Five World Regions* (Boulder & London: Lynne Rienner, 2002), 19.

20. www.misanet.org (July 2003).
21. Bits and pieces of this information were repeated during interviews in Zambia in 2001 with, among others, the *Post* editor.
22. Country reports can be accessed from their web sites: www.cpj.org; www.rsf.org; www.ifj.org; www.hrw.org; www.article19.org; www .amnesty.org.
23. In an open-floor contribution at Media in Africa conference at Stellenbosch University in South Africa in 2003.
24. John Michuki, to the press following the incident that appeared to have involved foreign mercenaries, the Artur borthers, who were later deported. Michuki has since died.
25. "Report of the Commonwealth Observer Group, Presidential and National Assembly Elections in Zambia 31 October 1991." (London: Commonwealth Secretaria, 1992).

11 Perceptions of Kenyan and Zambian Urban Civic Actors on their New Media Use in Political Realms

1. E-mail Interview (August 2003).
2. These were transcripts of a cabinet meeting on the MMD election campaign strategy. "They were planning to have a snap referendum and change the constitution which would bar Kaunda from contesting the presidency." (*Post* editor).
3. These were then Australia-based political activist Roger Chongwe and US-based Prof. Muna Ndera (Cornell University).
4. These together with off-line NGO agitation and political deal-making among the erstwhile divided opposition facilitated the defeat of Kenya's ruling party that had regularly rigged elections to stay in power.
5. www.kenyansabroad.org. Though based in Washington, KCA has branches in other US states like New England (Boston) and Michigan as well as in other countries, such as Canada, the UK, Germany, and France.
6. www.kachaka.com This is at one level a personal initiative of Veronica Mahongo Kachaka, based in Houston, Texas while at another level well supported by Zambians. See also: www.ukzambians.co.uk
7. Also see: http://kenya.rcbowen.com/
8. Interview with an NGO official privy to the online dialogue.
9. Interview at PANO offices in Lusaka at around 10 am Lusaka time, September 10, 2001.

10. Because 33 of the original HIPC countries were African, SSA's debt burden was a major focus of Jubilee 2000 advocacy (Collins, C. "'Break the Chains of Debt!' International Jubilee 2000 Campaign Demands Deeper Debt Relief" *Review of African Political Economy* 26, no. 81 (1999), 419).
11. Jubilee 2000 Coalitions Worldwide, at www.jubilee2000uk.org/jubilee2000/wwcol2.html (September 2004).
12. Ibid.
13. The GBM uses multiple methods to voice their opinions. This can include simple letter writing to officials as well as participating in serious protests concerning major issues.
14. Interview with Onyango-Oloo in Montreal in March 2004.
15. These included: Kenya Human Rights Commission (KHRC), Citizens Coalition for Constitutional Change (4Cs), Release Political Prisoners (RPP), Labour Caucus, Centre for Law and Research International (CLARION), Education Centre for Women in Democracy (ECWD), Youth Agenda (YA), and Pastoralists Development Community.
16. Interview in Lusaka while he was Director of Panos Southern Africa [2001].

12 Civic Engagement, Digital Networks, and Political Reform in an Increasingly Open Digital Media Environment

1. Earlier in 2000 a local bookstore was ordered to pay Biwott KShs10 million (US$125,000) merely for selling the book *Dr Ian West's Case Book* by British investigators Ian West and Chester Stern. The book implicated Biwott in the murder of former Foreign Affairs Minister, Dr. Robert Ouko. The Britons were ordered to pay Biwott Sh30 million (US$375,000) though they had refused to be drawn into the Kenyan case.
2. In January 2004, Kenya police raided newsstands and confiscated thousands of copies of "scandal sheets" (the *Independent, Kenya Confidential,* the *Citizen, News Post,* the *Weekly Wembe, Summit, Dispatch,* the *Patriot,* the *Mirror*), seized printing plates and other press equipment at the *Independent* and arrested 20 vendors. This embarrassed the Information Minister Raphael Tuju who said the police acted illegally yet it would appear they were applying an archaic, but revived, law the new government had promised to scrap.
3. US embassy Zambia report, available at www.usemb.se/human/1996/africa/zambia.html (accessed September 2004).
4. Interview with *Post* editor, Summer 2001.
5. One on purchase of military planes, another on security tender by Anglo Leasing and Finance Company, and the third child trafficking allegations against a UK-based Kenyan preacher whose accomplishments included meeting the British royal family.

6. BBC, "Africa Calling: The Mobile Revolution," Focus on Africa magazine programme, January–March 2004, 19–25, cited in Alden, C. "Let Them Eat Cyberspace: Africa, the G8 and the Digital Divide," *Millennium Journal of International Studies* 32, no. 3 (2004) 476, n. 52.
7. IED Synopsis – 2002 General Election, http://www.iedafrica.org /elections2002_synopsis.asp (accessed September 2004).
8. Internet for NGOs in Kenya: Kenya Proposal, available at http:// www.ngo-net.org/docs/html/kp-uk.htm (accessed September 2004).
9. Internet for NGOs in Africa: Gender and Research Aspects, available at http://www.ngo-net.org/docs/html/gra-uk.htm (accessed September 2004).
10. The project that started in 2003 has KPMG Peat Marwick as consultants, with financial support for the first phase from Finland, Germany, Denmark, Netherlands, Norway, and Sweden.
11. President Kibaki was for a long time Moi's vice president.
12. Herbert Hyman (1963), "Mass Media and Political Socialization: The Role of Patterns of Communication," In *Communications and Political Development*, ed. Lucian W. Pye (Princeton, NJ: Princeton University Press), cited in R. R. Fagan, *Politics and Communication: An Analytic Study* (Boston: Little, Brown & Co., 1966), 20–1.
13. Russell Southwood, State of Zambian ISP Market, interview with Thomas Lungu, Acting Chief Executive Officer, CopperNET Solutions, available at www.thezambian.com/technology/isp1.aspx (accessed September 2004).

Bibliography

Abbott, J. "Democracy @internet.asia? The Challenges to the Emancipatory Potential of the Net: Lessons from China and Malaysia." *Third World Quarterly* 22, no. 1 (2001a): 99–114.

———. The Internet and Reformasi in Malaysia: A Cacophony of Accusatory Diatribe, or an Alternative Political Medium?, presented at a Summer workshop on Transnational Activism in East Asia, Stockholm, Sweden, 2001b.

Abrahamsen, R. *Disciplining Democracy: Development Discourse and Good Governance in Africa.* London: Zed Books, 2000.

Adar, K. "The Interface between Elections and Democracy: Kenya's Search for a Sustainable Democratic System, 1960s–1990s." In *African Democracy in the Era of Globalisation*, J. Hyslop. Johannesburg: Witswatserand University Press, 344–346, 1999.

AEO, African Economic Outlook. 2012. Direct Investment Flows. www.africaneconomicoutlook.org/en/outlook/external-financial-flows/direct-investment-flows/ (accessed May 21, 2012).

Agre, E. P. "Real-Time Politics: The Internet and the Political Process." *The Information Society* 18 (2002): 311–31.

Ahmed, R. W. 2012. Armed Conflicts Cost Continent $18 Billion Annually, *Daily Trust*, April 23, 2012, via AllAfrica. http://allafrica.com/stories/201204241124.html (accessed April 27, 2012).

Ajulu, R. Kenya's Democracy Experiment: The 1997 Elections, *Review of African Political Economy* 25 (76): 275–85, 1998.

———. "Kenya: One Step Forward, Three Steps Back." *Review of African Political Economy* 28, no. 88 (2001): 197–211.

Akhter, F. "UNDP Human Development Report 2001: Shamelessly Siding with Multinational Corporations." FT Asia Intelligence *Wire/Bangkok Post*, July 21, 2001.

Albright, D. S. 2004. Voting Machine, Encyclopaedia Americana. http://ap.grolier.com/article?assetid=0406930-00&templatename=/article/article.html (accessed August 2004).

Alden, C. "Let Them Eat Cyberspace: Africa, the G8 and the Digital Divide." *Millennium Journal of International Studies* 32, no. (2004): 457–476.

Alhassen, M. 2012. Please Reconsider the Term "Arab Spring." www.huffingtonpost.com/maytha-alhassen/please-reconsider-arab-sp_b_1268971.html (accessed April 27, 2012).

Allan, S. Reweaving the Internet. In Stuart Allan and Barbie Zelizer (eds) with Victor Navasky fwd, *Journalism After September 11*, London: Routledge, 2002.

Almond, G. and S. Verba. *The Civic Culture: Political Attitudes and Democracy in Five Nations.* Princeton: Princeton University Press, 1963.

Almond, G. A. and G. B. Powell. *Comparative Politics: A Development Approach.* Boston: Little, Brown & Co, 1966.

Ansah, P. "Communication Research and Development in Africa–An Overview." In *Mass Communication Research on Problems and Policies: The Art of Asking the Right Questions*, edited by C. J. Hamelink and O. Lonné. Norwood, NJ: Ablex, 1994.

Arendt, H. *The Human Condition*, Chicago and London: University of Chicago, 1998.

Arquilla, J. and D. Ronfeldt. Preparing for Information-age Conflict, *Information, Communication & Society* 1, no. 1 (1998): 1–22 and 1, no. 2 (1998): 121–143.

Ashurst, M. "Africa's Ringing Revolution." *Newsweek* August 27, 2001, 14–18.

Atieno-Odhiambo, E. S. "Democracy and the Ideology of Order in Kenya." In *The Political Economy of Kenya*, edited by M. G. Schatzberg, 177–202. London: Praeger, 1987.

Ayittey, G. *Africa in Chaos*, New York: St Martin's Press, 1998.

Baggot, R. *Pressure Groups Today*, Manchester and New York: Manchester University Press, 1995.

Ball, D. 2000. Are African Countries Using New Media as a Means of Uplifting their Citizens or Are They Censoring Information Technology and Restricting Access as a Way of Safeguarding their Regimes? http://nml.ru.ac.za/carr/dave/main%20page.html (December 2003).

Baker, C., P. Lund, R. Nyathi, and J. Taylor. "The Myths Surrounding People with Albinism in South Africa and Zimbabwe." *Journal of African Cultural Studies* 22, no. 2 (2010): 169–181.

Banda, F. *Citizen Journalism and Democracy in Africa: An Exploratory Study*, Grahamstown, S. Africa: Highway Africa, 2011.

Banerjee, I., ed. *Rhetoric and Reality: The Internet Challenge for Democracy in Asia*, Singapore: Times Media Private Ltd, 2003.

Barber, B. *Strong Democracy: Participatory Politics in the New Age.* London: University of California Press, 1984.

———. "Three Scenarios for the Future of Technology and Strong Democracy." *Political Science Quarterly* 113, no. 4 (1998): 573–89.

Barkan, J. D. "The Rise and Fall of a Governance Realm in Kenya." In *Governance and Politics in Africa*, edited by G. Hyden and M. Bratton, 167–192. Boulder & London: Lynne Riener, 1992.

Barkan, J. D. and J. J. Okumu. *Politics and Public Policy in Kenya and Tanzania.* London and New York: Praeger, 1979.

Barker, H. and S. Burrows. *Press, Politics and the Public Sphere in Europe and North America, 1760–1820.* Cambridge: Cambridge University, 2002.

Barker, M. and J. Petley, eds. *Ill Effects: The Media/Violence Debate*, 2nd edn. London: Routledge, 2001/1997.

Barrat, E. and G. Berger. *50 Years of Journalism: African Media Since Ghana's Independence*. Johannesburg: Highway Africa, 2007.

Barton, F. *The Press of Africa: Persecution and Perseverance*. London and Basingstoke: Macmillan, 1979.

Batista, E. 2003. Bloggers Report Alt News Report from G8, *Wired*, June 4, 2003. www.wired.com/news/print/0,1294,59086,00.html (accessed April 12, 2012).

Bayart, J. *The State in Africa: The Politics of the Belly*. Essex: Longman1993.

Baym, N. K. *Personal Connections in the Digital Age*. Cambridge: Polity, 2010.

Baynes, K. "Democracy and the Rechtsstaat: Habermas's *Faktizität und Geltung*." In *The Cambridge Companion to Habermas*, edited by S. K. White, 201–232. Cambridge: Cambridge University Press, 1995.

Beard, C. *The Economic Basis of Politics*. New York: A. A. Knopf, 1934.

BBC. "Mobiles Find Right Price for Farmers." BBC News Online, December 6, 2002. http://news.bbc.co.uk/1/hi/technology/2290540.stm (12 October 2012).

Beck, U. "Risk Society Revisited: Theory, Politics and Research Programmes." In *The Risk Society and Beyond: Critical Issues for Social Theory*, edited by Barbara Adam, Ulrich Beck and Joost Van Loon, 211–229. London: Sage, 2000.

———. *Risk Society*. Cambridge: Polity, 2001.

Becket, C. *Supermedia: Saving Journalism so It Can Save the World*. Oxford: Blackwell, 2008.

Beier, J. M. "'Emailed Applications are Preferred': Ethical Practices in Mine Action and the Idea of Global Civil Society." *Third World Quarterly* 24, no. 5 (2003): 795–808.

Bell, D. *The Third Technological Revolution and Its Possible Socio-economic Consequences*. Salford: University of Salford, 1988.

———. *The Coming of Post-Industrial Society: A Venture in Social Forecasting*. New York: Basic Books, 1999/1973.

Bellis, M. 2004. The History of Voting Machines: From Paper Ballots to Computerised Voting Methods. http://inventors.about.com/library/weekly/aa111300b.htm (accessed April 15, 2012).

Benhabib, S. "Models of Public Space: Hannah Arendt, the Liberal Tradition, and Jurgen Habermas." In *Habermas and the Public Sphere*, edited by C. Calhoun, 73–98. Cambridge, MIT Press, 1992.

Berger, G. "Media & Democracy in Southern Africa." *Review of African Political Economy* 25, no. 78 (1998): 599–610.

———. "Can Newspapers Survive the Digital Revolution, the Future of News: Newspapers in the Digital Age." *Online Journalism Review* discussion forum, May 17, 2002.

———. Freedom and Techno-empowered Journalists, Acacia (Conference) Forum, April 1, 2003.

Berry, J. M. *The Interest Group Society*, 3rd edn. New York: Longman, 1997.

Biagi, S. *Media Reader: Perspectives on Mass Media Industries, Effects and Issues*, 3rd edn. London: Wadsworth, 1996.

Bienen, H. *Kenya: The Politics of Participation and Control.* Princeton, NJ: Princeton University Press, 1974.

Bimber, B. "The Internet and Political Transformation: Populism, Community, and Accelerated Pluralism." *Polity* 31, no. 1 (1998): 133–160.

———. "The Internet and Citizen Communication with Government: Does the Medium Matter?" *Political Communication* 16 (1999): 409–428.

Blumer, J. G. and S. Coleman. Realising Democracy Online: A Civic Commons in Cyberspace, Institute for Public Policy Research/Citizen Online Research Publication No. 2, March 2001.

Bourgault, L. M. *Mass Media in Sub-Saharan Africa.* Bloomington and Indianapolis: Indiana University Press, 1995.

Bratton, M. "Economic Crisis and Political Realignment in Zambia." In *Economic Change and Political Liberalisation in Sub-Saharan Africa*, edited by Jennifer A. Widner, 101–128. Baltimore: The Johns Hopkins University Press, 1994.

———. "Political Participation in a New Democracy: Institutional Considerations from Zambia." *Comparative Political Studies* 32, no. 5 (1999): 549–588.

Bratton, M. and J. Temba. "Effects of Civic Education on Political Culture: Evidence from Zambia." *World Development* 27, no. 5 (1999): 807–824.

Bratton, M. and N. van de Walle. *Democratic Experiments in Africa: Regime Transition in Comparative Perspective.* New York: Cambridge University Press, 1997.

Breecher, M. M. 1999. The Newspaper of the Future: Cyberspace Newspapers are here to Stay. www.columbia.edu/cu/21stC/issue-3.2/breecher.html (April 22, 2012).

Briggs, A. and P. Burke. *A Social History of the Media: From Guttenberg to the Internet.* Cambridge, UK: Polity, 2002.

Brooke, H. *The Revolution Will be Digitised: Dispatches from the Information War.* London: William Heinemann, 2011.

Brown, S. "Authoritarian Leaders and Multiparty Elections in Africa: How Foreign Donors Help to Keep Kenya's Daniel arap Moi in Power." *Third World Quarterly* 22, no. 5 (2001): 725–739.

Bryan, C., R. Tsagarousianou, and D. Tambini. "Electronic Democracy and Civic Network Movement in Context." In *Cyberdemocracy: Technology, Cities and Civic Networks*, edited by R. Tsagarousianou, D. Tambini, and C. Bryan, 1–17. London: Routledge, 1998.

Budge, I. *The New Challenge of Direct Democracy.* Cambridge: Polity, 1996.

Burnell, P. "Does Economic Reform Promote Democratisation? Evidence From Zambia's Third Republic." *New Political Economy* 6, no. 2 (2001a): 191–212.

———. "The Party System and Party Politics in Zambia: Continuities, Past, Present and Future." *African Affairs* 100, no. 399 (2001b): 239–263.

———. "Zambia's 2001 Elections: The Tyranny of Small Decisions, 'Non-decisions' and 'Not Decisions'." *Third World Quarterly* 23, no. 6 (2002): 1103–1120.

Calhoun, C., ed. *Habermas and the Public Sphere.* London: MIT, 1992.

———. Information Technology and the International Public Sphere, a paper presented at International Sociological Association, Brisbane, Australia, July 11, 2002.

Camilleri, J. A. and J. Falk. *The End of Sovereignty? The Politics of a Shrinking and Fragmenting World.* Aldershot: Edward Elgar Pub. Ltd, 1992.

Cammisa, A. M. *Government as Interest Group: Intergovernmental Lobbying and the Federal System*, Westport, Connecticut & London: Praeger, 1995.

Carroll, W. K. "Democratic Media Activism through the Lens of Social Movement Theory." *Media, Culture and Society* 28, no. 1 (2006): 83–104.

Carty, V. *Wired and Mobilizing: Social Movements, New Technology, and Electoral Politics.* Abingdon: Routledge, 2011.

Castells, M. *The Information Age Economy, Society and Culture Vol. 1: The Rise of the Network Society*, 2nd edn. Oxford: Blackwell, 2000a.

———. *The Information Age Economy, Society and Culture Vol.3: End of Millennium*, 2nd edn. Oxford: Blackwell, 2000b.

———. *The Internet Galaxy: Reflections on the Internet, Business, and Society.* Oxford: Oxford University Press, 2001.

Chabal, P. and J. Daloz. *Africa Works: Disorder as Political Instrument.* Oxford: James Currey, 1999.

Chakravartty, P. "Telecom, National Development and the Indian State: A Postcolonial Critique." *Media, Culture & Society* 26, no. 2 (2004): 227–249.

Chambers, S. "Discourse and Democratic Practices." In *The Cambridge Companion to Habermas*, edited by S. K. White, 233–259. Cambridge: Cambridge University Press, 1995.

Chan, S. Plurality and Fragmentation: The Kenyan Elections of 1992 and 1997, unpublished MS, 1998.

Chilambwe, P. "ICTs Workshop Gives Hope for Zambia's Rapid Economic Development." *Times of Zambia*, April 4, 2001.

Chongwe, R. "A Way Forward for National Unity." *The Monitor*, Issue No. 152, Friday April 6–Thursday April 12, 2001.

Clift, S. "Democracy Online." *On the Internet* magazine, March/April 1998. http://www.publicus.net/articles/democracyisonline.html (October 10, 2012).

———. 2004. E-Government and Democracy: Representation and Citizen Engagement in the Information Age, a research for the UN World Public Sector Report 2003, www.publicus.net/articles/cliftegovdemocracy.pdf (April 22, 2012).

Cline-Cole, R. and M. Powell. "ICTs, 'Virtual Colonisation' & Political Economy." *Review of African Political Economy* 31, no. 99 (2004): 5–9.

Cohen, J. L. and A. Arato. *Civil Society and Political Theory.* London and Cambridge, MA: MIT Press, 1992.

Cohen, J. M. "Foreign Aid and Ethnic Interests in Kenya." In *Carrots, Sticks, and Ethnic Conflict: Rethinking Development Assistance*, edited by Milton J. Esman and Ronald J. Herring, 90–112. Ann Arbor: University of Michigan Press, 2001.

Collins, C. "'Break the Chains of Debt!' International Jubilee 2000 Campaign Demands Deeper Debt Relief." *Review of African Political Economy* 26, no. 81 (1999): 419–422.

Commonwealth Observer Group, "Report of the Commonwealth Observer Group Presidential and National Assembly Elections in Zambia 31 October 1991." London: Commonwealth Secretaria, 1992.

Compaine, B. M., ed. *The Digital Divide: Facing a Crisis or Creating a Myth.* London and Cambrige, MA: MIT Press, 2001.

Cooper, G., N. Green, G. M. Murtagh, and R. Harper. "Mobile Society? Technology, Distance and Presence," in *Virtual Society? Technology, Cyberbole, Reality*, edited by S. Woolgar, 286–301. Oxford: Oxford University Press, 2002.

Cornu, J. 2002. "How People Use the Internet Today in Africa," www.unesco.org/webworld/points_of_views/180302_cornu.shtml (accessed April 15, 2012).

CPJ. 2001. Attacks on the Press 2001: Africa – Zambia, Committee to Protect Journalists, www.cpj.org/attacks01/africa01/zambia.html (accessed April 15, 2012).

———. 2002. Attacks on the Press 2002: Africa–Kenya, Committee to Project Journalists, www.cpj.org/attacks02/africa02/kenya.html (accessed April 15, 2012).

Crack, A. M. *Global Communication and Transnational Public Spheres.* New York: Palgrave Macmillan, 2008.

Cumberbatch, G. "Overview of the Effects of the Mass Media." In *A Measure of Uncertainty: The Effects of the Mass Media*, edited by Guy Cumberbatch and Dennis Howitt, 1–29. London: John Libbey, 1989.

Curran, J. *Media and Power.* London and New York: Routledge, 2002.

———. "Reinterpreting the Internet." In *Misunderstanding the Internet*, edited by J. Curran, N. Fenton, and D. Freedman, 3–33. London: Routledge, 2012.

Curran, J., A. Smith, and P. Wingate. *Impacts and Influences: Essays on Media Power in the Twentieth Century.* London: Methuen, 1987.

Dahlgren, P. *Television and the Public Sphere: Citizenship, Democracy and the Media.* London, Thousand Oaks, and Delhi: Sage, 1996.

Dahlberg, L. "Extending the Public Sphere through Cyberspace: The Case of Minnesota E-Democracy." *First Monday* 6, no. 3 (2001), March. http://firstmonday.org/htbin/cgiwrap/bin/ojs/index.php/fm/article/view/838/747 (accessed April 18, 2012).

Dalpino, C. E. *Deferring Democracy: Promoting Openness in Authoritarian Regimes*. Washington, D.C.: Brookings Institution, 2000.

Dean, J. *Publicity's Secret: How Technoculture Capitalises on Democracy*. Ithaca and London: Cornell University Press, 2002.

De Fleur, M. L. and S. J. Ball-Rokeach. *Theories of Mass Communication*, 5th edn. London: Longman, 1989/1982.

Deutsch, K. "Social Mobilisation and Political Development." *American Political Science Review* 55 (1961): 439–514.

Deuze, M. and S. Paulussen. "Research Note: Online Journalism in the Low Countries–Basic, Occupational and Professional Characteristics of Online Journalists in Flanders and the Netherlands." *European Journal of Communication* 17, no. 2 (2002): 237–245.

Diamond, L. "Rethinking Civil Society: Toward Democratic Consolidation." *Journal of Democracy* 5, no. 3 (1994): 4–17.

———. "Introduction: In Search of Consolidation." In *Consolidating the Third Wave of Democracies: Themes and Perspectives*, edited by L. Diamond, M. F. Plattner, Y. Chu, and H. Tien, xiii–xlvii. Baltimore and London: Johns Hopkins University Press, 1997.

Dicklitch, S. *The Elusive Promise of NGOs in Africa: Lessons from Uganda*. Basingstoke: Palgrave, 1998.

Djankov, S., M. Caralee, T. Nenova, and A. Shleifer. 2002. Who Owns the Media?, World Bank/Harvard University. http://econ.worldbank.org/files/2225_wps2620.pdf (accessed September 2004).

Dordick, H. S. and G. Wang. *The Information Society: A Retrospective View*. London: Sage, 1993.

Douglas, J. D. *Freedom and Tyranny: Social Problems in a Technological Society*. New York: A. A. Knofpf, 1970.

Drake, W. "Territoriality and Intangibility: Transborder Data Flows and National Sovereignty." In *Beyond National Sovereignty: International Communication in the 1990s*, edited by K. Nordenstreng and H. I. Schiller, 259–313. Norwood, NJ: Ablex, 1993.

Dunleavy, P. and B. O'Leary. *Theories of the State: Politics of Liberal Democracy*. London: Macmillan, 1987.

Earl, J. and K. Kimport. *Digitally Enabled Social Change: Activism in the Internet Age*. London: The MIT Press, 2011.

Ebo, B. L. *Cyberimperialism? Global Relations int he New Electronic Frontier*. London and Westport, CT: Praeger, 2001.

Edie, C. J. *Politics in Africa: A New Beginning?* Belmond, CA: Wadsworth, 2003.

Ehermann, H. W. *Interest Groups on Four Continents*. Pittsburgh: University of Pittsburgh Press, 1964.

Eickelman, F. D. and J. W. Anderson, eds. *New Media in the Muslim World: The Emerging Public Sphere*, 2nd edn. Bloomington and Indianapolis: Indiana University Press, 2003.

Ekine, S. *SMS Uprising: Mobile Activism in Africa*. Oxford: Pambazuka, 2010.

Elbaradei, M. Wael Ghonim: Spokesman for a Revolution, April 21, 2011. www.time.com/time/specials/packages/article/0,28804,2066367_2066369_2066437,00.html (accessed March 25, 2012).

El Ghayesh, H. "Chronicles of an Egyptian Revolution: A Protester's First-hand Account." In *African Awakening: The Emerging Revolutions*, edited by F. Manji and S. Ekine, 84–92. Oxford: Pambazuka, 2012.

Everard, J. *Virtual States: The Internet and the Boundaries of the Nation-state.* London and New York: Routledge, 2000.

Fagan, R. R. *Politics and Communication: An Analytic Study.* Boston: Little, Brown and Co, 1966.

Falch, M. Tele-centres in Ghana, *Telematics and Informatics* 21 (2004): 103–114.

Fatton, R. *Predatory Rule: State and Civil Society in Africa.* Boulder and London: Lynne Rienner Publishers, 1992.

Featherstone, M. and R. Burrows, eds. *Cyperspace/Cyberbodies/Cyberpunk: Cultures of Technological Embodiment.* London: Sage, 1996.

Ferdinand, P. ed. *The Internet, Democracy and Democratisation.* London and Portland, OR: Frank Cass, 2000.

Finkbeiner, G. 2003. The Future of the Newspaper: End of the Navel Inspection. www.wan-press.org/article264.html (accessed September 2004).

Folayan, F. "Civil Society, Popular Culture and the Crisis of Democratic Transitions in Nigeria." In *African Democracy in the Era of Globalisation*, edited by J. Hyslop, 72–79. Johannesburg: Witwatersrand University Press, 1999.

Fourkas, V. "What is 'Cyberspace'?" *Media Development* 51, no. 3 (2004): 48–49.

Franda, Marcus. *Launching into Cyberspace: Internet Development and Politics in Five World Regions.* Boulder and London: Lynne Rienner, 2002.

Fraser, N. "Rethinking the Public Sphere: A Contribution to the Critique of Actually Existing Democracy." In *Habermas and the Public Sphere*, edited by C. Calhoun, 109–142. London: MIT, 1992.

———. "Rethinking the Public Sphere." In *Between Borders: Pedagogy and the Politics of Cultural Studies*, edited by P. McLaren and H. Giroux, 74–98. New York and London: Routledge, 1994.

Freedom House / Puddington, A. Freedom in the World 2012: The Arab Uprisings and Their Global Repercussions. www.freedomhouse.org/report/freedom-world/freedom-world-2012 (accessed May 15, 2012).

Freeman, R. *Democracy in the Digital Age.* London: Demos, 1997.

Friedlander, S. "New Electronic Arab Newspapers: Techniques and Distribution." In *Civic Discourse and Digital Age Communications in the Middle East*, L. A. Gher and H. Y. Amin, 151–156. Stamford, CT: Ablex, 2000.

Frimpong-Ansah, J. H. *The Vampire State: The Political Economy of Decline in Ghana.* London: James Currey, 1991.

Fukuyama, F. "Social Capital, Civil Society and Development." *Third World Quarterly* 22, no. 1 (2001): 7–20.

Gallup / English, C. 2011. Civic Engagement Highest in Developed Countries: People Less Likely to Volunteer Time Than Donate Money, Help Stranger. January 18. www.gallup.com/poll/145589/civic-engagement-highest-developed-countries.aspx#1 (accessed May 15, 2012).

Garnham, N. "The Media and the Public Sphere." In *Habermas and the Public Sphere*, edited by C. Calhoun, 359–376. London: MIT, 1992.

Garrido, M. and A. Halavais. "Mapping Networks of Support for the Zapatista Movement: Applying Social-Networks Analysis to Study Contemporary Social Movements." In *Cyberactivism: Online Activism in Theory and Practice*, edited by Martha McCaughey and Michael D. Ayers, 165–184. New York: Routledge, 2003.

Garson, D. G. *Group Theories of Politics.* Beverley Hills and London: Sage, 1978.

Gelernter, D. 2003. The Next Generation American Newspaper, Vol. 8 Issue 40, June 23. www.weeklystandard.com/Content/Public/Articles/000/000/002/797bppbw.asp (accessed April 10, 2012).

Gellner, E. *Conditions of Liberty: Civil Society and Its Rivals.* London: Hamish Hamilton, 1994.

Gerodimos, R. Democracy and the Internet: Emerging Lessons for the 21st Century Public Sphere, a paper presented at the 54th Annual Conference of the Political Studies Association, April 6–8, 2004, University of Lincoln.

Ghonim, W. Interviewed by UK Channel Four Anchor Jon Snow at the Google Big Tent Event, May 19, 2011, London.

Giacomello, G. and F. Mendez. "State Sovereignty in the Age of the Internet." *Information & Security* 7 (2001): 15–27.

Gibson, R., P. Nixon, and S. Ward. *Political Parties and the Internet: Net Gain?* London and New York: Routledge, 2003.

Giddens, A. *Social Theory and Modern Sociology.* Oxford: Polity Press, 1987.

Gifford, P. "Bishops For Reform." *Tablet*, May 30, 1992, 672–673.

———. *Christianity, Politics and Public Life in Kenya.* London: C. Hurst and Co, 2009.

Githongo, J. "Civil Society, Democratisation, and the Media in Kenya." *Development* 40, no. 4 (1997): 41–45.

Glickman, H. "Frontiers of Liberal and Non-Liberal Democracy in Tropical Africa." *Journal of Asian and African Studies* XXIII, no. 3–4 (1988): 234–254.

Goode, L. 1999. Politics and the Public Sphere: The Social-Political Theory of Jurgen Habermas, D. Phil Thesis, Nottingham Trent University.

Gordon, N. "Arendt and Social Change in Democracies." *Critical Review of International Social and Political Philosophy* 4 no. 2 (2001): 85–11.

Graham, G. *The Internet: A Philosophical Inquiry.* London and New York: Routledge, 1999.

Grillo, R. D. *Pluralism and the Politics of Difference: State, Culture, and Ethnicity in Comparative Perspective.* Oxford: Clarendon Press, 1998.

Grossman, L. K. *The Electronic Republic: Reshaping Democracy in the Information Age*. New York: Viking, 1995.

Grossman, W. M. *From Anarchy to Power: The Net Comes of Age*. New York and London: New York University Press, 2001.

Grugel, J., ed. *Democracy without Borders: Transnationalisation and Conditionality in New Democracies*. London: Routledge, 1999.

Gunter, B. *Media Research Methods: Measuring Audiences, Reactions and Impact*. London: Sage, 2000.

Gyimah-Boadi, E. "Civil Society in Africa." In *Consolidating the Third Wave of Democracies: Themes and Perspectives*, edited by L. Diamond, M. F. Plattner, Y. Chu, and H. Tien, 278–292. Baltimore and London: Johns Hopkins University Press, 1997.

Habermas, J. *The Theory of Communicative Action Volume 1: Reason and the Rationalization of Society*, trans. T. McCarthy. London: Heinemann, 1984/1981.

———. *The Structural Transformation of the Public Sphere: An Inquiry into a Category of Bourgeois Society*, trans. T. Burger with the assistance of F. Lawrence. MIT: Polity, 1989/1962.

———. *Between Facts and Norms: Contributions to a Discourse Theory of Law and Democracy*, trans. W. Rehg. Oxford: Polity, 1996/1992.

Haberson, J. W. "Rethinking Democratic Transitions: Lessons from Eastern and Southern Africa." In *State, Conflict, and Democracy in Africa*, edited by R. Joseph, 39–55. Boulder and London: Lynne Rienner, 1999.

Hachten, W. *Muffled Drums: The News Media in Africa*. Iowa: Iowa State University Press, 1971.

Hacker, K. L. and J. Van Dijk, eds. *Digital Democracy: Issues of Theory and Practice*. London: Sage, 2000.

Hagen, M. "Digital Democracy and Political Systems." In *Digital Democracy: Issues of Theory and Practice*, edited by K. L. Hacker and J. van Dijk, 54–69. London: Sage, 2000.

Hague, B. N. and B. D. Loader, eds. *Digital Democracy: Discourse and Decision Making in the Information Age*. London: Routledge, 1999.

Hajnal, P. *Civil Society in the Information Age*. Aldershot: Ashgate, 2002.

Hallawell, S. *Beyond Access: ICT and Social Inclusion*. London: Fabian Society, 2001.

Hamelink, C. J. "Globalism and National Sovereignty." In *Beyond National Sovereignty: International Communication in the 1990s*, edited by K. Nordenstreng and H. I. Schiller, 371–393. Norwood, NJ: Ablex, 1993.

Harrison, G. *Issues in the Contemporary Politics of Sub-Saharan Africa: The Dynamics of Struggle and Resistance*. Basingstoke: Palgrave/Macmillan, 2002.

Hassan, R. *Media, Politics and the Network Society*. Maidenhead: Open University Press, 2004.

Haugerud, A. *The Culture of Politics in Modern Kenya*. Cambridge, UK: Cambridge University Press, 1997.

Hayes, J. *Democracy in the Developing World: Africa, Asia, Latin America and the Middle East.* Cambridge: Polity, 2001.

He, B. "Cosmopolitan Democracy: Beyond Nation-State Democracies." In *Politics of Civil Society: A Global Perspective on Democratisation*, edited by H. Patomaki, 13–18. Helsinki: Network Institute for Global Democratization (NIGD), 2000.

Hearn, J. "The 'NGO-isation' of Kenyan Society: USAID & the Restructuring of Health Care." *Review of African Political Economy* 25, no. 75 (1998): 89–100.

Held, D. *Democracy and the Global Order: From the Modern State to Cosmopolitan Governance.* Cambridge: Polity, 1995.

———. *Models of Democracy*, 2nd edn. Cambridge: Polity, 1996.

Herbst, J. and G. Mills *The Future of Africa: A New Order in Sight?*, *Adelphi Paper* 361, London: Oxford University Press/International Institute for Strategic Studies, 2003.

Hermdia, A. "Mobile Money Spinner for Women." BBC News Online, October 8, 2002. http://news.bbc.co.uk/1/hi/technology/2254231.stm (October 13, 2012).

Hiebert, E. R., ed. *Impact of Mass Media: Current Issues.* London: Longman, 1995/1985.

Hill, A. K. and J. E. Hughes. *Cyberpolitics: Citizen Activism in the Age of the Internet.* Oxford: Rowman and Littlefield, 1998.

———. "Is the Internet an Instrument of Global Democratisation?" *Democratization* 6, no. 2 (1999): 99–126.

Hine, C. *Virtual Ethnography.* London: Sage, 2001.

Holub, C. R. *Jurgen Habermas: Critic in the Public Sphere.* London and New York: Routledge, 1991.

Howcroft, D. "The Hyperbolic Age of Information: An Empirical Study of Internet Usage." *Information, Communication and Society* 2, no. 3 (1999): 277–299.

Huntington, S. P. *The Third Wave: Democratisation in the Late Twentieth Century.* Norman: University of Oklahoma Press, 1991.

Hydén, G. and M. Bratton, eds. *Governance and Politics in Africa.* Boulder: Lynne Rienner, 1992.

Hydén, G., M. Leslie, and F. F. Ogundimu, eds. *Media and Democracy in Africa.* New Brunswick, NJ: Transaction, 2002.

Hyslop, J., ed. *African Democracy in the Era of Globalisation.* Johannesburg: Witwatersrand University Press, 1999.

Ibelema, M. *The African Press, Civic Cynicism, and Democracy.* New York: Palgrave Macmillan, 2008.

IED, CJPC, and NCCK. 1998. Report on the 1997 General Election in Kenya 29–30 December, Institute for Education in Democracy (IED) Africa, with Catholic Justice and Peace Commission (CJPC) and National Council of Churches of Kenya (NCCK). www.iedafrica.org/documents/1997_report.pdf (accessed April 27, 2012).

IED. 2003. Enhancing the Electoral Process in Kenya: A Report on the Transition General Elections in 2002, Institute of Education in Democracy (IED), available at www.iedafrica.org/documents/elections2002_report.pdf (accessed April 27, 2012).

Ihonvbere, J. "From Movement to Government: The Movement for Multi-party Democracy and the Crisis of Democratic Consolidation in Zambia." *Canadian Journal of African Studies* 29, no. 1 (1995): 1–25.

———. *Economic Crisis, Civil Society, and Democratisation: The Case of Zambia*. Trenton, NJ: Africa World Press, 1996.

Innis, H. *The Bias of Communication*. Toronto: University of Toronto Press, 1951.

Isin, E. F., ed. *Democracy, Citizenship and the Global City*. London and New York: Routledge, 2000.

ITU. 2011. International Telecommunications Union (ITU) World Telecommunication / ICT Indicators Database. www.itu.int/ITU-D/ict/statistics/ (accessed May 15, 2012).

James, J. "The Global Information Infrastructure Revisited." *Third World Quarterly* 22, no. 5 (2001): 813–822.

Jensen, M. "Making the Connection: Africa and the Internet." *Current History* 99, no. 637 (2000): 215–221.

———. 2002. Africa Internet Status. www3.sn.apc.org/africa/afstat.htm (accessed February 2004).

Jones, S., ed. *Doing Internet Research: Critical Issues and Methods for Examining the Net*. London: Sage, 1999.

Jordan, G. "The Pluralism of Pluralism: An Anti-Theory." In *Pressure Groups*, edited by J. J. Richardson, 49–68. Oxford: Oxford University Press, 1993.

Jordan, T. *Cyberpower: The Culture and Politics of Cyberspace and the Internet*. London: Routledge, 1999.

Jørgensen, L. "What Are NGOs Doing in Civil Society." In *NGOs, Civil Society and the State: Building Democracy in Transitional Societies*, edited by A. Clayton, 36–54. Oxford: INTRAC,1996.

Kagwanja, P. M. "Facing Mount Kenya or Facing Mecca? The Mungiki, Ethnic Violence and Politics of the Moi Succession in Kenya, 1987–2002." *African Affairs* 102, no. 407 (2003): 25–49.

Kahney, L. 2003. Web Antidote for Political Apathy, *Wired*, 5 May. www.wired.com/news/politics/0,1283,58715,00.html (April 27, 2004).

Kakubo, L. 2000. Overview of the Internet in Zambia, a paper presented at The African Internet and Telecom Summit, Banjul, Gambia. www.itu.int/africainternet2000/countryreports/zmb_e.htm (accessed August 2004).

Kamarck, E. and Nye Jr, J. S. *Democracy.com?* Hollis, NH: Hollis Publishing, 1999.

Kanyinga, K. "The Social-Political Context of the Growth of Non-Governmental Organisations in Kenya." In *Social Change and Economic Reform in Africa*, edited by P. Gibbon, 53–77. Uppsala: Nordiska Afrikainstitutet, 1993.

Kaplan, I., M. K. Dorbert, B. J. Marvin, J. L. McLaughlin, D. P. Whitaker. *Area Handbook for Kenya*, 2nd edn. Washington DC: American University Foreign Area Studies, 1976.

Kapoor, I. "Deliberative Democracy or Agonistic Pluralism? The Relevance of the Habermas-Mouffe Debate for Third World Politics." *Alternatives* 27 (2002): 459–487.

Karanja, B. 2012. How Africa Tweets. Portland, March 14, 2012. www.portland-communications.com/how-africa-tweets (accessed April 2, 2012).

Kasoma, F. "Les Medias Dans Les Annees 1990." In *La Zambie Contemporarie*, edited by J. Daloz and J. D. Chileshe, Paris: Karthala-IFRA, 1996.

———. "The Internet in Zambia." In *Beyond Boundaries: Cyberspace in Africa*, edited by M. B. Robins and R. L. Hilliard, 149–61. Portsmouth, NH: Heinemann, 2002.

Katumanga, M. I. 2003. Civil Society and the Politics of Constitutional Reform in Kenya: A Case Study of the National Convention Executive Council (NCEC). www.ids.ac.uk/ids/civsoc/final/kenya/ken2.doc (accessed August 2004).

Katz, E. and F. P. Lazarsfield. *Personal Influence: The Part Played by People in the Flow of Mass Communications*. Glencoe: The Free Press, 1955.

Katz, J. E. and M. A. Aakhus. *Perpectual Contact: Mobile Communication, Private Talk, Public Performance*. Cambridge and New York: Cambridge University Press, 2002.

Kaunda, K. D. *A Letter to My Children*. Lusaka: Government Press, 1967.

Keane, J. *Democracy and Civil Society*. London and New York: Verso, 1988.

———. *The Media and Democracy*. Cambridge: Polity Press, 1991.

———. "Structural Transformations of the Public Sphere." In *Digital Democracy: Issues of Theory and Practice*, edited by K. L. Hacker and J. van Dijk, 71–89. London: Sage, 2000.

Keck, M. E. and K. Sikkink. *Activists Beyond Borders: Advocacy Networks in International Politics*. Ithaca, NY: Cornell University Press, 1998.

Kelly, T. 2000. Africa Joins the Internet, *ITU News 2000*. www.itu.int/africainternet2000/Documents/Internetage.html#ftn1 (accessed August 2004).

Keohane, R. O. and J. S. Nye. "Power and Interdependence in the Information Age: The Resilience of States." *Foreign Affairs* 77, no. 5 (1998): 81–94.

———. *Power and Interdependence*, 3rd edn. London: Longman, 2001.

Khadiagala, G. M. and M. G. Schatzberg. "The Kenyan Bourgeoisie, External Capital, and the State: An Introduction." In *The Political Economy of Kenya*, edited by M. G. Schatzberg, 1–14. London: Praeger, 1987.

Khan, S. and J. Lee, eds. *Activism and Rhetoric: Theories and Contexts for Political Engagement*. London: Routledge, 2011.

Khisa, N. "Internet boosts NARC's campaign, IT Survey." *East African Standard* (Nairobi), April 29, 2003.

KHRC and Article 19. 1997. Elections '97 Media Watch: Media Monitoring in Kenya, Nairobi: Kenya Human Rights Commission (KHRC) and International Centre Against Censorship (Article 19).

King, A. *The Coming Information Society.* London: The British Library, 1984.

Kitching, G. *Class and Economic Change in Kenya: The Making of an African Petite Bourgeoisie 1905–1970.* New Haven and London: Yale University Press, 1980.

Kizza, J. M. *Civilising the Internet: Global Concerns and Efforts Toward Regulation.* Jefferson and London: McFarland and Co, 1998.

Klapper, J. T. *The Effects of Mass Communication.* New York: Free Press, 1960.

Klein, H. K. "Tocqueville in Cyberspace: Using the Internet for Citizen Associations." *Information Society* 15, no. 4 (1999): 213–220.

Kole, E. 2003. Organising the Transfer of Electronic Network Technology to Meet the Objectives of NGOs in the South, a PhD study available at www.xs4all.nl/~ekole/research.html (accessed October 2003).

Kraut, R., M. Patterson, V. Lundmark, S. Kiesler, T. Mukopadhyay, and W. Scherlis. "Internet Paradox: A Social Technology that Reduces Social Involvement and Psychological Well-being?" *American Psychologist* 53, no. 9 (1998): 1017–1031.

Laakso, L. 2000. Difficult Democratisation in Africa and What the Global Political Economy Has to Do With It. In H. Patomaki (ed.), *Politics of Civil Society: A Global Perspective on Democratisation*, Helsinki: Network Institute for Global Democratization (NIGD), 70–9.

———. 2002. Civil Society in Kenya: Insights to the Possibilities and Constraints for Action against Political Violence, paper presented at a seminar on Democratisation and Conflict Management in Eastern Africa, Feb 28 to March 3, 2002, Centre for African Studies, Goteborg University, Ruotsi, Sweden.

Lacey, K. 1996. *Feminine Frequencies: Gender, German Radio, and the Public Sphere, 1923–1945* (Social History, Popular Culture, and Politics in Germany), Ann Arbor: University of Michigan.

Lapham, C. 1995. The Evolution of the Newspaper of the Future, *CMC Magazine*, July 1, 7. www.december.com/cmc/mag/1995/jul/lapham.html (accessed May 22, 2012).

Lasswell, H. D. and A. Kaplan. 1952. *Power and Society: A Framework for Political Inquiry*, London: Routledge.

Latour, B. 1991. Technology is Society Made Durable. In *A Sociology of Monsters: Essays on Power, Technology and Domination*, edited by J. Law, London and New York: Routledge, 103–31.

Lawson, G. 1998. *NetState: Creating Electronic Government*, London: Demos.

Lazarsfeld, P. F., B. Berelson, and H. Gaudet. 1968/1944. *The People's Choice: How the Voter Makes Up His Mind in a Presidential Campaign*, 3rd ed., London: Columbia University Press.

Leslie, M. 2002. The Internet and Democratization. In G. Hydén, M. Leslie, and F. F. Ogundimu (eds), *Media and Democracy in Africa*, New Jersey: Transaction, 107–28.

Levinson, P. 1999. *Digital McLuhan: A Guide to the Information Millennium*, London & New York: Routledge.

Lewis, J. 1991. *The Ideological Octopus: An Exploration of Television and Its Audience*, New York & London: Routledge.

Li, X. 1999. Democracy and Uncivil Societies: A Critique of Civil Society Determinisim. In *Civil Society, Democracy, and Civic Renewal*, edited by R. K. Fullindwider, Oxford: Rownman and Littlefield, 403–420.

Lievrouw, L. A. 2011. *Alternative and Activist New Media*, Cambridge: Polity.

Lindlof, T. R. 1995. *Qualitative Communication Research Methods*, London: Sage.

Lipschutz, R. D. *Global Civil Society and Global Environmental Governance: The Politics of Nature from Place to Planet*. Albany: State University of New York Press, 1996.

———. ed. *Civil Societies and Social Movements: Domestic, Transnation, Global*. Aldershot: Ashgate, 2006.

Loader, B. D. 1997. *The Governance of Cyberspace: Politics, Technology and Global Restructuring*, Routledge: London.

Loader, B. D. and Mercea, D., eds. 2012. *Social Media and Democracy: Innovations in Participatory Politics*, London: Routledge.

Lonsdale, J. "Explanations of the Mau Mau Revolt." In *Resistance and Ideology in Settler Societies* (Southern African Studies Vol. 4), edited by T. Lodge, 168–178. Johannesburg: Ravan Press, 1986.

Loveday, P. "Group Theory and Its Critics." In *Groups in Theory and Practice* (Sydney Studies in Politics), edited by P. Loveday and I. Campbell, 3–44. Sydney: F. W. Cheshire, 1962.

Lowery, S. A. and M. L. DeFleur. *Milestones in Mass Communication Research: Media Effects*, 3rd ed. London: Longman, 1995/83.

Lowi, T. *The End of Liberalism: The Second Republic of the United States*. New York: Norton, 1979.

Lumumba-Kasongo, T. *The Rise of Multipartyism and Democracy in the Context of Global Change: The Case of Africa*. Westport, CT: Praeger, 1998.

Lyon, D. *The Information Society: Issues and Illusions*. Cambridge: Polity, 1988.

Main, L. "The Global Information Infrastructure: Empowerment or Imperialism?" *Third World Quarterly* 22, no. 1 (2001): 83–97.

Malama, G. Press and Democracy: A Case Study of Media Reforms in Zambia, MA Thesis. Cardiff: University of Wales, 1994.

Mann, C. and F. Stewart. *Internet Communication and Qualitative Research: A Handbook for Researching Online*. London: Sage, 2000.

Manji, F. and S. Ekine, eds. *African Awakening: The Emerging Revolutions*. Oxford: Pambazuka, 2012.

Margolis, M. and D. Resnick. *Politics as Usual: The Cyberspace 'Revolution'*. London: Sage, 2000.

Marres, N. "Net-Work Is Format Work: Issue Networks and the Sites of Civil Society Politics," in *Reformatting Politics: Information Technology and Global Civil Society*, edited by J. Dean, J. W. Anderson and G. Lovink, 3–17. London: Routledge, 2006.

Martin, W. J. *The Global Information Society*. Aldershot: AslibGower, 1995.

Mathews, J. T. "Power Shift: The Rise of Global Civil Society." *Foreign Affairs* 76, no. 1 (1997): 50–67.

May, C. *The Information Society: A Skeptical View*. Cambridge: Polity, 2002.

May, T. *Social Research: Issues, Methods and Process*, 2nd edn. Buckingham, Open University, 2001.

Mbithi, P. M. and R. Rasmusson. *Self Reliance in Kenya: The Case of Harambee*. Uppsala: The Scandinavian Institute of African Studies, 1971.

McLean, I. *Democracy and New Technology*. Cambridge: Polity/Blackwell, 1989.

McNair, B. *Journalism and Democracy: An Evaluation of the Political Public Sphere*. London: Routledge, 2000.

McPhail, T. L. *Global Communication: Theories, Stakeholders, and Trends*. London: Allyn & Bacon, 2002.

McQuail, D. *McQuail's Mass Communication Theory*, 4th ed. London: Sage, 2000.

McQuail, D. and J. G. Blumler. "Communication Scholarship as Discipline." In *Beyond Media Uses and Effects*, edited by U. Carlsson, 17–30. Göterbo: Nordicom, 1997.

Meadow, R. G. "New Technologies in Political Campaigns." In *Beyond National Sovereignty: International Communication in the 1990s*, edited by K. Nordenstreng and H. I. Schiller, 442–458. Norwood, NJ: Ablex, 1993.

Medearis, J. *Joseph Schumpeter's Two Theories of Democracy*. Cambridge: Harvard University Press, 2001.

Meena, R. "Democratisation Process in Eastern Africa: Kenya, Tanzania and Uganda, a paper presented at Cosmopolis: Democratising Global Economy & Culture conf." Helsinki, June 2000. www.valt.helsinki.fi/vol/cosmopolis/papers/meena.html (accessed April 12, 2012).

Meikle, G. *Future Active: Media Activism and the Internet*. London: Routledge, 2000.

Meldrum, A. "Mugabe Introduces New Curbs on the Internet." *The Guardian*, June 3, (2004): 17.

Mercer, C. "Engineering Civil Society: ICT in Tanzania." *Review of African Political Economy* 31, no. 99 (2004): 49–64.

Mercy Corps. *Civic Engagement of the Youth in the Middle East and North Africa: An Analysis of Key Drivers and Outcomes*. Portland, OR: Mercy Corps, 2012.

Meyer, T. with Lew Hinchman, *Media Democracy: How the Media Colonize Politics*. Cambridge: Polity, 2002.

Miller, D. and D. Slater. *The Internet: An Ethnographic Approach.* Oxford: Berg, 2000.

Mills, M. "Conceptualising the Fourth World: Four Approaches to Poverty and Communication." *Media Development* 1 (2000): 3–7.

Mkandawire, J. B. Role of the Media in Zambia's Transition to a Democracy, MA Thesis. Cardiff: University of Wales, 1992.

Mouffe, C. *The Democratic Paradox.* London and New York: Verso, 2000.

Mowlana, H. *Global Information and World Communication: New Frontiers in Internatinal Relations*, 2nd ed. London: Sage, 1997.

Mphaisha, J. J. C. "Retreat from Democracy in Post One-Party State Zambia." *Journal of Commonwealth and Comparative Politics* 34, no. 2 (1996): 65–84.

Mudhai, O. F. 1998a. "The *Kitu Kidogo* Phenomenon that is Ruining Kenya." In *Caught in the Act: Corruption and the Media*, Brussels: International Federation of Journalists (IFJ) Media for Democracy in Africa (MFA) project conference report, 60–66, 1998a.

———. "The Need to Centrestage Culture: The Media and Cultural Identity in Kenya." In *Orientations of Drama, Theatre and Culture: Cultural Identity and Community Development*, edited by O. Mumma, E. Mwangi and C. Odhiambo, 116–134. Nairobi: KDEA, 1998b.

———. "The Internet: Triumphs and Trials for Kenyan Journalism." In *Beyond Boundaries: Cyberspace in Africa*, edited by M. B. Robins and R. L. Hilliard, 89–104. Portsmouth, NH: Heinemann, 2002.

———. Methodological Issues in the Study of Digital Media and Perceptions of Civil Society in Urban Kenya and Zambia, US Social Science Research Council IT Civil Society Network background paper, 2003.

———. ICTs and Civil Society as Challengers to the Ruling Elite in Africa, a paper presented at the International Studies Association (ISA) conference, Montreal, 2004a.

———. Possible Impacts of NGO-divide on ICT4D Agenda, SSRC memo, 2004b.

———. "Researching the Impact of ICTs as Change Catalysts in Africa." *Ecquid Novi* 25, no. 2 (2004c): 313–335.

———. Challenges to the Hegemonic African State: Media and Civil Society in Kenya and Zambia [Unpublished thesis]. Nottingham: Nottingham Trent University, 2005.

———. "Exploring the Potential for More Strategic Civil Society Use of Mobile Phones." In *Reformatting Politics: Information Technology and Global Civil Society*, edited by J. Dean, J. E. Anderson, and G. Lovink, 107–120. London: Routledge, 2006.

———. " 'Africa at 50' and the Digital Future: Implications for Journalisms." In *The Internet and Journalism Today: Face the Future – Tools for the Modern Media Age*, edirted by J. Mair and R. L. Keeble, 256–262. Bury St Edmunds: Arima, 2011a.

———. "Africa and the 'Arab Spring': Analysis of Selected *Nation* (Nairobi) Commentaries." In *Mirage in the Dessert? Reporting the 'Arab Spring'*, edited by J. Mair and R. L. Keeble, 324–330. Bury St Edmunds: Arima, 2011b.

Mueller, M. *Ruling the Root: Internet Governance and the Taming of Cyberspace*. London and Cambridge, MA: MIT Press, 2002.

Mukungu, K. Prospects for Greater Press Freedom in Zambia, MA Thesis. Cardiff: University of Wales, 1993.

Mulford, D. C. *Zambia: The Politics of Independence 1957–1964*. London: Oxford University Press, 1967.

Mutiga, M. "Radical Reforms Planned for Justice System." *Sunday Standard* (Nairobi), August 29, 2004.

Mutume, G. *Africa-Development: More than Just Internet Connections Required*. Addis Ababa: ECA Communication Team, 2000.

Mutunga, W. *Constitution-Making from the Middle: Civil Society and Transition Politics in Kenya 1992–1997*. Nairobi: SAREAT (Series on Alternative Research in East Africa), 1999.

Mwesige, P. G. "Cyber Elites: A Survey of Internet Café Users in Uganda." *Telematics & Informatics* 21 (2003): 83–101.

Myer, J. D. Communication Technology and Social Movements: Contributions of Computer Networks to Activism, *Social Science Computer Review* 12, no. 2 (1994): 250–260.

Myerson, G. Heiddeger, *Habermas and the Mobile Phone*. Duxford: Icon, 2001.

Mytton, G. *Mass Communication in Africa*. London: Edward Arnold, 1983.

Ndegwa, S. N. *NGOs as Pluralising Agents in Civil Society in Kenya*. Nairobi: University of Nairobi Institute for Development Studies, 1993.

———. *The Two Faces of Civil Society: NGOs and Politics in Africa*. West Hartford, CT: Kumarian Press, 1996.

Ndlela, N. "Reflections on the Global Public Sphere: Challenges to Internationalizing Media Studies." *Global Media and Communication* 3, no. 3 (2007): 324: 9.

Negroponte, N. *Being Digital*. New York: Knopf, 1996.

Neocosmos, M. "Rethinking State and Civil Society in Africa in the Era of Globalisation." In *Politics of Civil Society: A Global Perspective on Democratisation*, edited by H. Patomaki, 80–100. Helsinki: Network Institute for Global Democratization (NIGD), 2000.

Nerone, J. and Barnhurst, G. K. 2001. "Beyond Modernism: Digital Design, Americanization and the Future of Newspaper Form." *New Media & Society* 3, no. 4 (2001): 467–482.

Ngunyi, M. Transition Without Transformation: Civil Society and the Transition Seesaw in Kenya, Series on Alternative Research in East Africa (SAREAT), 2003. www.eldis.org/assets/Docs/11429.html (April 17, 2012).

Nicholas, D., P. Williams and H. Martin. *The Media and the Internet: The Changing Information Environment – the Impact of the Internet on Information Seeking Behaviour in the Media*. London: Aslib/British Library Board, 1998.

Nicholls, D. *Three Varieties of Pluralism*. London & Basingstoke, 1974.

Niombo, S. NGOs and ICTs Use in the Republic of Congo, US SSRC ITIC, 2003a.

———. Online Mobilisation and Publishing for African Civil Society: Stakes and Impact on Audience, US SSRC ITIC, 2003b.

Njoroge, N. "Promoting E-commerce in Kenya." 2002. www.stanford.edu/class/e297c/war_peace/africa_struggles_with_slavery_colonialism_and_hiv_aids/njoroge.html (accessed August 2003).

NMG About Nation Media Group, Nation Media Group. 2004a www.nationmedia.com/about_us.html (accessed April 25, 2012).

———. A brand new *Daily Nation* coming online, 2004b. Nation Media Group, February 12, 2004.

Nordenstreng, K. and H. I. Schiller, eds. *Beyond National Sovereignty: International Communication in the 1990s*. Norwood, New Jersey: Ablex, 1993.

Nordenstreng, K. "Sovereignty and Beyond," in *Beyond National Sovereignty: International Communication in the 1990s*, edited by K. Nordenstreng and H. I. Schiller, 461–463. Norwood, NJ: Ablex, 1993.

Norris, P. *A Virtuous Circle: Political Communication in Postindustrial Societies*. Cambridge: Cambridge University Press, 2000.

———. *The Digital Divide: Civic Engagement, Information Poverty and, the Internet Worldwide*. New York: Cambridge University Press, 2001.

———. Deepening Democracy via E-Governance: Draft Chapter for the UN World Public Sector Report, posted or updated online February 16, 2004 at 8.36pm, http://ksghome.harvard.edu/~.pnorris.shorenstein.ksg/Acrobat/World%20Public%20Sector%20Report.pdf (accessed April 18, 2012).

Nowak, K. "Effects No More?" In *Beyond Media Uses and Effects*, edited by U. Carlsson, 31–40. Göterbo: Nordicom, 31–40, 1997.

Nwokeafor, C. U. and K. Langmia. *Media and Technology in Emerging African Democracies*. Lanham, MD: University Press of America, 2010.

Nyangira, N. "Ethnicity, Class and Politics in Kenya." In *The Political Economy of Kenya*, edited by M. G. Schatzberg, 15–32. London: Praeger, 15–32, 1987.

Nye Jr., J. S. *Power in the Global Information Age: From Realism to Globalisation*. London and New York: Routledge, 2004a.

———. *Soft Power: The Means to Success in World Politics*. New York: Public Affairs, 2004b.

Nyong'o, P. A. "Democratisation Process in Africa." *Review of African Political Economy* 19, no. 54 (1992): 97–102.

Nzomo, M. "External Influence on the Political Economy of Kenya: The Case of MNCs." In *Politics and Administration in East Africa*, edited by W. O. Oyugi, 429–467. Nairobi: East African Educational Publisher, 1994.

Ochieng', P. *I Accuse the Press: An Insider's View of the Media and Politics in Africa*. Nairobi: Initiative & ACTS Press, 1992.

Odero, M. and E. Kamweru, eds. *Media Culture and Performance in Kenya.* Nairobi: Eastern Africa Media Institute – Kenya Chapter & Friedrich Ebert Stiftung, 2000.

Odhiambo, E. S. A. Ethnic Cleansing and Civil Society in Kenya 1969–1992, *Journal of Contemporary African Studies* 22, no. 1 (2004): 29–42.

Odhiambo, L. O. The Media Environment in Kenya Since 1990, *African Studies* 61, no. 2 (2002): 295–318.

Olesen, T., ed. *Power and Transnational Activism.* London: Routledge, 2011.

Olukoshi, A. O. and L. Laakso. *Challenges to the Nation-State in Africa.* Sweden: Nordiska Afrikainstitutet, Uppsala, 1996.

Osaghae, E., ed. *Between the State and Civil Society in Africa*, Oxford: CODESRIA, 1994.

Ott, D. "Power to the People: The Role of Electronic Media in Promoting Democracy in Africa." *First Monday* 3, no. 4 (1998). http://firstmonday.org/htbin/cgiwrap/bin/ojs/index.php/fm/article/view/588/509 (May 15, 2012).

Ott, D. and Rosser, M. "The Electronic Republic? The Role of the Internet in Promoting Democracy in Africa." In *The Internet, Democracy and Democratisation*, edited by P. Ferdinand, 137–155. London: Frank Cass, 2000.

Ott, D. and Smith, L. "Tipping the Scales? The Influence of the Internet on State-Society Relations in Africa." *Mot Pluriels* no. 18, August 2001.

Outhwaite, W. *The Habermas Reader.* Cambridge: Polity Press, 1996.

Oyelaran-Oyeyinka, B. and C. N. Adenya. "Internet Access in Africa: Empirical Evidence from Kenya and Nigeria." *Telematics & Informatics* 21 (2003): 67–81.

Pankhurst, D. "Striving for 'Real' Democracy in Africa: the Roles of International Donors and Civil Society in Zimbabwe." In *Democracy and International Relations: Critical Theories/Problematic Practices*, edited by H. Smith. 151–170. London: Macmillan Press, 2000.

Papacharissi, Z. A. *A Private Sphere: Democracy in a Digital Age.* Cambridge: Polity, 2010.

Parada, C. [with G. Garriot and J. Green]. *The Essential Internet: Basics for International NGOs.* Washington, DC: InterAction, 1997.

Patomaki, H., ed. *Politics of Civil Society: A Global Perspective on Democratisation.* Helsinki: Network Institute for Global Democratization (NIGD), 2000.

Patomaki, H., T. Teivainen, and M. Rönkkö. *Global Democracy Initiatives: The Art of Possible.* Helsinki: NIGD, 2002.

Patomaki, H. "Towards Global Political Parties," *Ethics and Global Politics* 4 no.2, 2011. http://www.ethicsandglobalpolitics.net/index.php/egp/article/view/7334/8826 (October 14, 2012).

Phiri, A. K. Prosecution of Journalists in Zambia, MA Thesis. Cardiff: University of Wales, 1994.

PI. An International Report on Censorship and Report on Censorship and Control of the Internet, Privacy International/GreenNet Educational Trust, 2003.

Pinkney, R. *Democracy in the Third World*. London: Lynne Rienner, 2003.

Plath, H. E. "Re: Potential for Strategic Use of Cell Phones" (reaction to messages from F. O. Mudhai). *itcivilsociety* (closed listserv), November 10, 2003.

Polikanov, D. and I. Abramova. Africa and ICT: A Chance for Breakthrough?, *Information, Communication and Society* 6, no. 1 (2003): 42–56.

Pool, I. S. *Technologies of Freedom*. Cambridge, MA: Belknap, 1983.

Poster, M. *The Second Media Age*. Cambridge: Polity, 1995.

Potts, D. and Mutambirwa, C. "The Government Must Not Dictate: Rural-urban Migrants' Perceptions of Zimbabwe's Land Resettlement Programme." *Review of African Political Economy* 24, no. 74 (1997): 549–566.

Price, M. E. *Television, the Public Sphere, and National Identity*. Oxford: Clarendon/Oxford University, 1995.

Price, V. and J. N. Cappella. "Online Deliberation and its Influence: The Electronic Dialogue Project in Campaign 2000." *IT & Society* 1, no. 1 (2002): 303–29.

Pye, L. W. *Communications and Political Development*. Princeton, NJ: Princeton University Press, 1963.

Raab, C., C. Bellamy, J. Taylor, W. H. Dutton, and M. Peltu. "The Information Polity: Electronic Democracy, Privacy, and Surveillance." In *Information and Communication Technologies: Visions and Realities*, W. H. Dutton, 283–299. Oxford: Oxford University, 1996.

Rakner, L. *Political and Economic Liberalisation in Zambia, 1991–2001*. Stockholm: Nordic Africa Institute, 2003.

Ranger, T. and O. Vaughan. "Postscript: Legitimacy, Civil Society and the Return of Europe." In *Legitimacy and the State in Twentieth-Century Africa*, edited by R. Terence and O. Vaughan, 258–262. Basingstoke: Palgrave, 258–262, 1993.

Redmont, D. Newspapers See Danger in Text Messaging, AP wire, May 7, 2004, Bagnaia, Italy: Associated Press, 2004.

Reynolds, A. *Electoral Systems and Democratisation in Southern Africa*. Oxford: Oxford University Press, 1999.

Rheingold, H. *Smart Mobs: The Next Social Revolution*. Cambridge, MA: Basic Books, 2002.

Richardson, J. J., ed. *Pressure Groups*. Oxford: Oxford University Press, 1993.

Roberts, J. M. and N. Crossley. Introduction. In *After Habermas: New Perspectives on the Public Sphere*, edited by N. Crossley and J. M. Roberts, 1–27. Oxford: Blackwell, 2004.

Rodgers, J. Gendered Political Spaces in International Relations: The Case of NGO Use of ICTs, PhD Thesis, Leeds: Institute of Politics and International Studies, University of Leeds, 2000.

———. ed. *Spatializing International Politics: Analysing NGO's Use of the Internet*. London: Routledge, 2003.

Rogers, E. M. *Diffusion of Innovations*, 4th ed. New York: Free Press, 1995.

Rogers, E. M. and S. Malhotra. Computer as Communications: The Rise of Digital Democracy. In *Digital Democracy: Issues of Theory and Practice*, edited by K. L. Hacker and J. Van Dijk, 11–29. London: Sage, 2000.

Ronfeldt, D. Overview of Social Evolution (Past, Present and Future) in TIMN Terms, 2009 http://twotheories.blogspot.co.uk/2009/02/overview-of-social-evolution-past.html (accessed April 21, 2012).

———. Praise for "Monitory Democracy": A Concept Attuned to TIMN (Part 1 of 2), 2012a. http://twotheories.blogspot.co.uk/2012/03/praise-for-monitory-democracy-concept.html (accessed April 21, 2012).

———. Praise for "Monitory Democracy": A Concept Attuned to TIMN (Part 2 of 2), 2012b. http://twotheories.blogspot.co.uk/ (accessed April 21, 2012).

Rosberg, C. G. and J. Nottingham. *The Myth of 'Mau Mau': Nationalism in Kenya*. London and New York: Pall Mall & F.A. Praeger, 1966.

Ross, K. K. "'Worrisome Trends': The Voice of the Churches in Malawi's Third Term Debate." *African Affairs* 103, no. 410 (2004): 91–107.

RSN. Reporters Without Borders, 2004 www.rsf.fr/rubrique.php3?id_rubrique=20 (accessed April 2004).

Rugwabiza, V. "Africa Trade More with Africa to Secure Future Growth." speech at the University of Witwatersrand in Johannesburg, South Africa on April 12, 2012. www.wto.org/english/news_e/news12_e/ddg_12apr12_e.htm (accessed May 22, 2012).

Samii, B. The Iranian Media in 2003, Radio Free Europe/Radio Liberty Iran Report 6(50), 2003, 29 December. www.rferl.org/reports/iran-report/2003/12/50–291203.asp (accessed April 17, 2012).

Sassen, S. *Losing Control? Sovereignty in an Age of Globalisation*. New York and Chichester: Columbia University Press, 1996.

———. *Globalisation and Its Discontents: Essays on the New Mobility of People and Money*. New York: New Press, 1998.

Sassi, S. "The Controversies of the Internet and the Revitalization of Local Political Life." In *Digital Democracy: Issues of Theory and Practice*, edited by K. L. Hacker and J. Van Dijk, 91–104. London: Sage, (2000).

Scheeres, J. "Net Dissidents Jailed in China," *Wired*, February 24, 2004. www.wired.com/news/politics/0,1283,62391,00.html (accessed April 21, 2012).

Schement, J. R. 2001. "Of Gaps by Which Democracy We Measure." In *The Digital Divide: Facing a Crisis or Creating a Myth*, edited by B. M. Compaine, 303–308. London and Cambrige, MA: MIT Press, (2001).

Schiller, D. *Digital Capitalism: Networking the Global Market System*. Cambridge, MA & London: MIT, 1999.

Schmitter, P. C. "Civil Society East and West." In *Consolidating the Third Wave of Democracies: Themes and Perspectives*, edited by L. Diamond, M. F. Plattner, Y. Chu, and H. Tien, 239–62. Baltimore and London: Johns Hopkins University Press, 1997.

Schneider, M. S. "Creating a Democratic Public Sphere through Political Discussion: A Case Study of Abortion Conversation on the Internet." *Social Science Computer Review* 14, no. 4 (1996): 373–393.

Schneider, S. M. and K. A. Foot. "The Web as an Object of Study." *New Media and Society* 6, no. 1 (2004): 114–122.

Schramm, W., ed. *Mass Communications*, 2nd ed. Chicago: University of Illinois Press, 1960.

Schuler, D. What is the Public Sphere?, *CPSR Newsletter* 18, no. 3 (2000).

Schumpeter, J. *Capitalism, Socialism and Democracy*, 5th ed. London: Allen & Unwin, 1976/1942.

Scurrah, M. J. "NGOs, Civil Society and Democracy in Peru." In *NGOs, Civil Society and the State: Building Democracy in Transitional Societies*, edited by A. Clayton, 157–171. Oxford: INTRAC, 1996.

Seiter, E., H. Borchers, G. Kreutzner, and E. Warth. *Remote Control: Television, Audiences, and Cultural Power.* London: Routledge, 1991/89.

Siebert, F. S., T. Peterson, and W. Schramm. *Four Theories of the Press.* Urbana, Chicago: University of Illinois, 1963/56.

Signorielli, N. and G. Gerbner. *Violence and Terror in the Mass Media: An Annotated Bibliography.* New York: Greenwood Press, 1988.

Signorielli, N. and M. Morgan. *Cultivation Analysis: New Directions in Media Effects Research.* London: Sage, 1990.

Simon, L. D. "Democracy and the Net: A Virtuous Circle?" In *Democracy and the Internet: Allies or Adversaries?*, edited by L. D. Simon, J. Corrales, and D. R. Wolfensberger, 1–29. Washington DC: Woodrow Wilson Centre Press/John Hopkins, 2002.

Sklar, R. L. "Democracy in Africa." *African Studies Review* 26, no. 3/4 (1983): 11–24.

Slaughter, A. "The Real New World Order." *Foreign Affairs* 76, no. 5 (1997): 183–198.

Slevin, J. *The Internet and Society.* Cambridge: Polity Press/Blackwell, 2000.

Smith, A. "Mass Communications." In *Democracy at the Polls: A Comparative Study of Competitive National Elections*, edited by D. Butler, H. R. Penniman, and A. Ranney, 173–195. Washington and London: American Enterprise Institute for Public Policy Research, 1981.

Smith, J. and H. Johnston. *Globalization and Resistance: Transnational Dimensions of Social Movements.* Oxford: Rowman & Littlefield, 2002.

Soll, C. and N. Ali. UNDP Topic 2: Civic Engagement for Development, Preview Brief to National High School Model United Nations (New York, March 2013), 2012. http://imuna.org/nhsmun/committee/united-nations-development-programme-2012 (accessed May 20, 2012).

Solocombe, M. *Max Hits: Building and Promoting Successful Websites.* Hove: RotoVision, 2002.

Southall, R. "Moi's Flawed Mandate: The Crisis Continues in Kenya." *Review of African Political Economy* 25, no. 75 (1998): 101–152.

Southall., R. "Re-reforming the State? Kleptocracy & the Political Transition in Kenya." *Review of African Political Economy* 26, no. 79 (1999): 93–108.

Spitulnik, D. "Alternative Small Media and Communicative Spaces." In *Media and Democracy in Africa*, edited by G. Hydén, M. Leslie, and F. F. Ogundimu, 177–205. New Jersey: Transaction, 2002.

Splichal, S., A. Calabrese, and C. Sparks. *Information Society and Civil Society: Contemporary Perspectives on the Changing World Order.* West Lafayette: Purdue University Press, 1994.

Stevenson, N. "The Future of Public Media Cultures: Cosmopolitan Democracy and Ambivalence." *Information, Communication & Society* 3, no. 2 (2000): 192–214.

Street, J. *Mass Media, Politics and Democracy.* Basingstoke: Palgrave, 2001.

Sudweeks, F. and J. S. Simoff. "Complementary Explorative Data Analysis: The Reconciliation of Quantitative and Qualitative Principles." *Doing Internet Research: Critical Issues and Methods for Examining the Net*, edited by In S. Jones, 29–55. London: Sage, 1999.

Sunstein, C. *Republic.com.* Princeton: Princeton University Press, 2001.

Surman, M. and Reilly, K. Appropriating the Internet for Social Change: Towards the Strategic Use of Networked Technologies by Transnational Civil Society Organisations, background report prepared for US Social Science Research Council Information Technology & International Co-operation, IT and Civil Society Network, 2003.

Tai, Z. *The Internet in China: Cyberspace and Civil Society.* London: Routledge, 2006.

Tall, S. M. "Senegalese Émigrés: New Information & Communication Technologies." *Review of African Political Economy* 31, no. 99 (2004): 31–49.

Tambini, D. "New Media and Democracy: The Civic Networking Movement." *New Media & Society* 1, no. 3 (1999): 305–329.

Tan, A. "Cell Phones May Be Key to Cleaner Air in Philipines." *Christian Science Monitor* Online, July 9, 2002. http://www.csmonitor.com/2002/0719/p07s02-woap.html (12 October 2012).

Tang, S. P. and Ang, P. H. "The Diffusion of Information Technology in Singapore Schools: A Process Framework." *New Media & Society* 4, no. 4 (2002): 457–478.

Taylor, P. *Munitions of the Mind: A History of Propaganda from the Ancient World to the Present Day.* Manchester: Manchester University Press, 1995.

Thomas, B. P. *Politics, Participation, and Poverty: Development Through Self-Help in Kenya.* Boulder and London: Westview Press, 1985.

Thompson, M. "Discourse, 'Development' & the 'Digital Divide': ICT & the World Bank." *Review of African Political Economy* 31, no. 99 (2004): 103–123.

Thomson, A. 'Hacktivist' Expats Plan Cyber Sit-in, *New Zealand Herald*, April 29, 2004.

Throup, D. and C. Hornsby. *Multi-Party Politics in Kenya: The Kenyatta & Moi States & the Triumph of the System in the 1992 Election*. Oxford: James Currey, 1998.

Tiemann, C. Teen Confesses to Creating Sasser Worm, AP, May 8, 2004, Hanover, Germany: Associated Press, 2004.

Toffler, A. *Future Shock*. London: Pan Books, 1973/1970.

———. *The Third Wave*. London: Collins, 1980.

Toffler, A. and H. Toffler. *Creating a New Civilization: The Politics of the Third Wave* [foreword by Newt Gingrich], Atlanta: Turner Publishing, 1995.

Tourane, A. *The Post-industrial Society – Tomorrow's Social Hisotry: Classes, Conflicts and Culture In the Programmed Society*. Trans. Leonard F. X. Mayhew. London: Wildwood House,1974/1969.

Traugott, W. M. Elections: U.S. Election Procedures, 2004. http://usinfo.state.gov/products/pubs/election04/procedure.htm (accessed August 2004).

Tsagarousianou, R. "Electronic Democracy and the Public Sphere: Opportunities and Challenges." In *Cyberdemocracy: Technology, Cities and Civic Networks*, edited by R. Tsagarousiano, D. Tambini, and C. Bryan, 167–178. London: Routledge, 1998.

Tsagarousianou, R., D. Tambini, and C. Bryan, eds. *Cyberdemocracy: Technology, Cities and Civic Networks*. London: Routledge, 1998.

Tsui, L. Internet Opening Up China: Fact or Fiction?, a paper submitted at the Media in Transition: Globalisation and Convergence Conference, MIT, Boston, 10–12 May, 2012.

Uche, U. U. Democratic Process in Africa and the New Information Technologies: Theoretical and Methodological Approaches for Communication Research in Africa of the Emergent Dialogue on Democratization of the Media, paper presented at the African Council for Communication Education 5th Biennial Conference, Jos, Nigeria, 1998.

Ulrich, K. H. "Expanding the Trade Debate: The Role of Information in WTO and Civil Society and Interaction," in *Civil Society in the Information Age*, edited by P. I. Hajnal, 175–199. Aldershot: Ashgate, 2002.

UN. World Public Sector Report 2003: E-Government at the Crossroads, UN Department of Economic & Social Affairs, New York: United Nations, Nov. 03, 2003. http://unpan1.un.org/intradoc/groups/public/documents/un/unpan012733.pdf (April 25, 2012).

———. *World Economic Situation and Prospects 2012*. New York: United Nations, 2011.

UNDP. *Human Development Report 1993: People's Participation*. New York: Oxford University Press, 1993.

———. *Human Development Report 2001: Making New Technologies Work for Human Development*. New York: Oxford University Press, 2001.

UNDP. *Human Development Report 2002: Deepening Democracy in a Fragmented World.* New York: UNDP with Oxford University Press, 2002.

———. *Human Development Report 2011: Sustainability and Equity: A Better Future for All.* New York: Palgrave Macmillan, 2011.

Van Audenhove, L., J. C. Burgelman, G. Nulens, and B. Cammaerts. "Information Society Policy in the Developing World: A Critical Assessment." *Third World Quarterly* 20, no. 2 (1999): 387–404.

Van Audenhove, L., B. Cammaerts, V. Frissen, L. Engels, and A. Ponsioen. Transnational Civil Society in the Networked Society: On the Relationship Between ICTs and the Rise of a Transnational Civil Society, 2004.

Van de Donk, W., B. D. Loader, P. G. Nixon, and D. Ruchte. *Cyberprotest: New Media, Citizens, and Social Movements.* London: Routledge, 2004.

Van de Walle, N. *African Economies and the Politics of Permanent Crisis, 1979–1999.* Cambridge: Cambridge University Press, 2001.

Van Dijk, J. *The Network Society.* London: Sage, 1999.

Van Donge, J. K. "Zambia: Kaunda and Chiluba, Enduring Patterns of Political Culture." In *Democracy and Political Change in Sub-Saharan Africa*, edited by J. A. Wiseman, 193–219. London: Routledge, 1995.

Van Klinken, M. K. "Beyond the NGO-Government Divide: Network NGOs in East Africa." *Development in Practice* 8, no. 3 (1988): 349–353.

VeneKlasen, L. "The Challenge of Democracy-Building: Practical Lessons on NGO Advocacy and Political Change." In *NGOs, Civil Society and the State: Building Democracy in Transitional Societies*, edited by A. Clayton, 219–240. Oxford: INTRAC, 1996.

Virilio, P. *The Information Bomb.* London: Verso, 2000.

Virmani, K. K. *Zambia: The Dawn of Freedom.* Delhi: Kalinga Publications, 1989.

Wade, R. H. "Bridging the Digital Divide: New Route to Development or New Form of Dependency?" *Global Governance* 8 (2002): 443–466.

Wa Gĩthĩnji, M. *Ten Millionaires and Ten Million Beggars: A Study of Income Distribution and Development in Kenya.* Aldershot: Ashgate, 2000.

Waltz, M. *Alternative and Activist Media.* Edinburgh: Edinburgh University Press, 2005.

WAN. Shaping the Future of Newspapers: Distribution Revolution, 2002a. www.wan-press.org/article248.html (accessed May 21, 2012).

———. Shaping the Future of Newspapers: Internet Strategies for Newspapers Revisited, 2002b www.wan-press.org/article221.html (accessed May 21, 2012).

———. Shaping the Future of Newspapers, World Association of Newspapers, special report.

Ward, S. and R. Gibson. "On-line and on Message? Candidate Websites in the 2001 General Election." *British Journal of Politics and International Relations* 5, no. 2 (2003): 188–205.

Warleigh, A. "'Europeanising' Civil Society." *Journal of Common Market Studies* 39, no. 4: 619–639.

Warkentin, C. *Reshaping World Politics: NGOs, the Internet and Global Civil Society*. Lanham, MD: Rowman & Littlefield, 2001.

Warren, M. E. "The Self in Discursive Democracy." In *The Cambridge Companion to Habermas*, edited by S. K. White, 167–200. Cambridge: Cambridge University Press, 1995.

Wasserman, H. The Internet, Civil Society and a Pan African Public Sphere: Renaissance or Delusion?, a paper presented at the CODESRIA 30th Anniversary conf, Dakar, 2003.

Webster, F. *Theories of the Information Society*. London & New York: Routledge, 1995.

Wheeler, M. Democracy and the Information Superhighway, *Democratization* 5, no. 2 (1998): 217–237.

White, D. "How Africa Joined the New Wireless World." *Financial Times*, Nov 17 (2003):12.

White, J., ed. *Politico's Guide to Politics on the Internet*. London: Politico's Publishing, 1999.

White, S. K. "Reason, Modernity and Democracy." In *The Cambridge Companion to Habermas*, edited by S. K. White, 3–16. Cambridge: Cambridge University Press, 1995.

Whitley, A. E. Habermas and the Non-humans: Towards a Critical Theory for the New Collective, Centre for Social Theory and Technology seminar, February, Keele University, 1999.

Widner, J. A. *The Rise of a Party-State in Kenya: From Harambee to Nyayo*. Berkley: University of California Press, 1992.

Wilhelm, A. G. *Democracy in the Digital Age: Challenges to Political Life in Cyberspace*. New York & London: Routledge, 2000.

Wilkins, K. and J. Waters. "Current Discourse on New Technologies in Development Communication." *Media Development* 1 (2000): 57–60.

Williams, R. *The Long Revolution*. London: Chatto & Windus, 1961.

Wootton, Graham. *Interest-Groups*. Englewood Cliffs, NJ: Prentice-Hall, 1970.

WSIS Bamako. Report on the Pre-WSIS Media Forum, Bamako, May 26, 2002.

Xinhuanet. Cult Activists Jailed for Libelling Government, *Xinhua* Online, February 19, 2004. http://news.xinhuanet.com/english/2004–02/19/content_1322676.htm (accessed May 22, 2012).

Ya'u, Y. Z. "The New Imperialism & Africa in the Global Electronic Village." *Review of African Political Economy* 31, no. 99 (2004): 11–29.

Young, C. "The End of the Postcolonial State in Africa? Reflections on Changing African Political Dynamics." *African Affairs* 103, no. 410 (2004): 23–49.

Zhu, J. H. J. and H. Zhou. "Information Accessibility, User Sophistication, and Source Credibility: The Impact of the Internet on Value Orientations in Mainland China." *Journal of Computer-Mediated Communication* 7, no. 2 (2002).

Ziegler, D. and M. K. Asante. *Thunder and Silence: The News Media in Africa*. Trenton, NJ: World Press Inc, 1992.

Zuckerman, E. "Citizen Media and the Kenyan Electoral Crisis." In *Citizen Journalism: Global Perspectives*, edited by S. Allan and E. Thorsen, 187–96. New York: Peter Lang, 2009.

Selected Websites

Centre for Democracy and Technology (CDT), Washington, DC, www.cdt.org

Centre for Voting and Democracy (CVD), Maryland, nr Washington DC, www.fairvote.org

Howard Rheingold's Brainstorm, www.rheingold.com

Institute for Global Communications (IGC), San Francisco, CA, www.igc.org/html/aboutigc.html

Minnesota E-Democracy, www.e-democracy.org

Index

Note: Reference is to table where "t" is indicated after page number, and to figure where "f" is indicated after page – e.g., 110f